Y0-BVO-597

ACHIEVEMENT AND TASK MOTIVATION

Arizona State Univ.
West Campus Library

Achievement and Task Motivation

A15060 075399

edited by

J.H.L. van den Bercken
E.E.J. De Bruyn
Th.C.M. Bergen

BF
503
.A23
1986
WEst

SWETS NORTH AMERICA INC. / BERWYN
SWETS & ZEITLINGER B.V. / LISSE
1986

ASU WEST LIBRARY

Library of Congress Cataloging-In-Publication Data

Achievement and task motivation.

Bibliography: p.
1. Achievement motivation.   2. Competition
(Psychology) I. Bercken, J. J. L. van den.
II. Bruyn, Eric E. J. de. III. Bergen, Theo C. M.
BF503.A23 1986   153.8   86-22981
ISBN 90-265-0739-9 (Netherlands)

CIP-GEGEVENS KONINKLIJKE BIBLIOTHEEK, DEN HAAG

Achievement

Achievement and task motivation / ed. by J.H.L. van den
Bercken, E.E.J. De Bruyn, Th.C.M. Bergen. - Lisse : Swets
& Zeitlinger ; Berwyn : Swets North America
Met lit. opg.
ISBN 90-265-0739-9
SISO 415.3 UDC 159.944
Trefw.: prestatiemotivatie.

Cover design H. Veltman
Printed by Offsetdrukkerij Kanters B.V., Alblasserdam
© Copyright 1986 Swets & Zeitlinger, Lisse

Alle rechten voorbehouden. Niets uit deze uitgave mag worden verveelvoudigd,
opgeslagen in een geautomatiseerd gegevensbestand, of openbaar gemaakt, in enige vorm
of op enige wijze, hetzij elektronisch, mechanisch, door fotokopieën, opnamen, of op enige
andere manier, zonder voorafgaande schriftelijke toestemming van de uitgever.

*All rights reserved. No part of this publication may be reproduced, stored in a retrieval
system, or transmitted, in any form or by any means, electronic, mechanical, photocopying,
recording, or otherwise, without the prior written permission of the publisher.*

ISBN 90 265 0739 9

TABLE OF CONTENTS

Research on human motivation has been flourishing in Europe for several decades, at various places: Bochum, Louvain, Oslo, to name a few. In recent years motivation research in Europe appears to become both more intensified and more extended, as indicated by the growing number of publications and the growing number of students involved. As a consequence a growing need for personal contact among the researchers became apparent. In response to that need , we organized a symposium on achievement and task motivation. The primary goal of that meeting, held at Nijmegen in june 1985, was to promote contact and cooperation between individual researchers, and to provide an opportunity for exchanging ideas and research findings. It was the general impression of the participants that this goal had been realized. In order to ensure cumulative achievement, however, there should be some tangible result of the meeting. So the papers presented at the symposium were reviewed and revised and as a result the present book offers a sample of current research on motivation in Europe.

The papers are grouped under four headings. Heckhausen's invited lecture constitutes the first part. While offering some kind of a guided tour through the recent history of motivation research, the author identifies some persistent problems and proposes some remedies. The remaining papers are classified according to the width of their scope. The papers in part two are mainly dealing with various aspects of task motivation by itself: theory (Houtmans, Brunstein), measurement (Kuhl & Stahl, Van den Bercken), and development (Ulvund). Part three contains papers on the same aspects of motivation in the context of education: theory (Nenniger, Brugman & Beem), measurement (Neuwahl & Van den Bogaart), development (Trudewind et al.), and application (Bergen & Alberts). In part four, finally, the papers are mainly focusing on educational outcomes, particularly academic achievement, as determined by motivation (and other factors): a theoretical orientation is apparent in the paper of De Volder et al., while measurement problems are the main concern in the papers of Boekaerts and Mooij.

As a whole, the papers illustrate the present lack of a generally accepted theoretical framework in the field. The paradigm of expectation-value models, as developed by Atkinson and Heckhausen, is exemplified by the papers of Houtmans, Kuhl and Stahl, Van den Bercken, Trudewind et al., and Bergen and Alberts. The somewhat less well articulated tradition that goes under the generic name of intrinsic motivation theory, constitutes the context of the

1

papers of Ulvund, Brugman and Beem, De Volder et al., and Mooij. Brunstein's research builds on the ideas of attribution and learned helplessness theory. Finally, there are some eclectic papers that do not appear to be explicitly committed to a specific theoretical tradition: Nenniger, Neuwahl and Van den Bogaart, and Boekaerts.

Heckhausens state-of-the-art lecture provides an opportunity to see whether its conclusions apply to ongoing research as sampled in this book. The era of the fifties was, according to Heckhausen, mainly concerned with motive measurement. After 25 years, however, we are still facing some fundamental problems. Some of these indeed show up in this book. The problem of operant versus respondent measurement is treated in the paper of Kuhl and Stahl, the problem of domain-specificity in the papers of Neuwahl and Van den Bogaart, Boekaerts, and Mooij. Although Heckhausen's formulation of the problems created by the interactionistic approach of the seventies, particularly by the risk-taking model, may be slightly biased by the coping strategy he proposes - distinguishing motivation and volition - the purport of his diagnosis is certainly correct. Several papers are essentially dealing with problems of interactionism. Van den Bercken addresses the problem of motivation versus performance and the closely related problem of situation-specificity or the state-trait distinction. The latter problem is the main topic of the paper of Boekaerts. The paper of Neuwahl and Van den Bogaart witnesses the fact that achievement motive and self-concept of ability are intrinsically related. The era of the seventies is viewed by Heckhausen as the decade of the causal attribution urge. No paper in this book appears to be conceived exclusively or explicitly in the framework of attribution theory as forged by Weiner and his associates. The papers of Brunstein and of Neuwahl and Van den Bogaart, however, do reflect some of the main ideas of attribution theory.

Heckhausen's characterization of the era of the eighties is particularly fascinating in that it combines historical and predictive evaluations. According to Heckhausen, a way out of the conceptual and methodological dilemmas hampering progress in motivation research since the fifties, may be found in some lessons, or rather suggestions, from a still more distant past: the distinction between motivation and volition, as implied in Ach's psychology of will. Disentangling domains of reference, however, is one thing, modelling actual behavior in each domain is another. It is our guess that only a careful specification of the structure of tasks, and a diligent analysis of the organization of observed task behavior, will give motivation research the firm empirical basis that still is lacking. A clear and unambiguous definition of the

2

kind of data appropriate to motivation theory remains one of the tasks for the near future. In any case, Heckhausen's diagnosis of persistent problems in motivation research actually constitutes a set of yardsticks by which progress in the field can be measured. The next symposium on task motivation and achievement will show whether they prove to be valid.

Acknowledgements
Thanks are due to Miss Gemma Indemans and Mrs Ciska Peters who patiently transformed the various drafts into the final shape of this book.

J.H.L. van den Bercken
E.E.J. De Bruyn
Th.C.M. Bergen

LIST OF CONTRIBUTORS

R.V.J. Alberts, Dutch National Institute for educational measurement
Nieuwe Oeverstraat 65, 6801 MG Arnhem, The Netherlands

A.L. Beem, University of Leyden
Stationsplein 10-12, 2312 AK Leiden, The Netherlands

J.H.L. van den Bercken, University of Nijmegen
Erasmusplein 1, 6500 HD Nijmegen, The Netherlands

Th.C.M. Bergen, University of Nijmegen
Erasmusplein 1, 6500 HD Nijmegen, The Netherlands

M. Boekaerts, University of Nijmegen
Montessorilaan 3, 6525 HR Nijmegen, The Netherlands

P.H.M. van den Bogaart, University of Leyden
Hooigracht 15, 2312 KM Leiden, The Netherlands

D. Brugman, University of Leyden
Stationsplein 12, 2312 AK Leiden, The Netherlands

Th. Brünger, Ruhr Universität Bochum
Universitätstrasse 150, 4630 Bochum, West Germany

J.C. Brunstein, Justus-Liebig-Universität Giessen
Otto Behagel Strasse 10, 6300 Giessen, West Germany

W. de Grave, University of Limburg
Tongersestraat 53, 6211 LM Maastricht, The Netherlands

H. Heckhausen, Max-Planck-Institut für psychologische Forschung
Leopoldstrasse 24, D-8000 Munich, West Germany

M.J.M. Houtmans, University of Nijmegen
Erasmusplein 1, 6500 HD Nijmegen, The Netherlands

K. Krieger, Ruhr Universität Bochum
Universitätstrasse 150, 4630 Bochum, West Germany

J. Kuhl, Max-Planck-Institut für psychologische Forschung
Leopoldstrasse 24, D-8000 Munich 40, West Germany

T. Mooij, Institute for Applied Sociology
Graafseweg 274, 6532 ZV Nijmegen, The Netherlands

J. Moust, University of Limburg
Tongersestraat 53, 6211 LM Maastricht, The Netherlands

P. Nenniger, University of Freiburg
Lehrstuhl für Erziehungswissenschaft 1, D-7800 Freiburg i.Br, West Germany

N.M.E. Neuwahl, University of Leyden
Hooigracht 15, 2312 KM Leiden, The Netherlands

H. Schmidt, University of Limburg
Tongersestraat 53, 6211 LM Maastricht, The Netherlands

J. Stahl, Max-Planck-Institut für psychologische Forschung
Leopoldstrasse 24, D-8000 Munich 40, West Germany

Cl. Trudewind, Ruhr Universität Bochum
Universitätsstrasse 150, 4630 Bochum, West Germany

S.E. Ulvund, University of Oslo
Box 1092, Blindern, 0317 Oslo 3, Norway

M. de Volder, University of Limburg
Tongersestraat 53, 6211 LM Maastricht, The Netherlands

PART I

RESEARCH ON HUMAN MOTIVATION: AN OVERVIEW

WHY SOME TIME OUT MIGHT BENEFIT ACHIEVEMENT MOTIVATION RE-SEARCH

Heinz Heckhausen[1]

Max-Planck-Institut für Psychologische Forschung Munich

INTRODUCTION

I consider this meeting of European researchers as an attempt to join forces vis-á-vis the dominant impact of American psychology. If this is true you may wonder at my title because it recommends a pause, instead of a boost, in sheer amount of research activity - and this may seem odd in the face of endeavors to keep up with our American colleagues. In order to convince you that my advice is sound, let me describe the main issues of achievement motivation research in historical order; I will then point out where research has run into trouble and where old, unresolved problems may be worth a new try after a time out for thought.

Achievement motivation research has been alive and well for three decades. Having taken part in this enterprise since the mid-fifties you may regard me as a veteran of that enterprise. Two years ago, when I was offered the opportunity to move from Bochum to a pure research institute at Munich I began to doubt whether our usual research should be continued. We had to wait for experimental facilities to be set up and thus enjoyed an involuntary moratorium on research. During this time we intended to think through those last problems that appeared to us really basic and worthwhile.

Jokingly we spoke of the "remainder problems" that we wanted to solve quickly in order to wrap up the field forever. During the last years, even we had realized that achievement motivation research suffered from a depletion of ideas and approaches. I will disclose later on what, for us, these remainder problems are. For the moment, let me only say that we are presently tackling some such problems, we find them exciting and we have post-

---

[1] The author gratefully acknowledges the assistance of Merry Bullock in improving the english text.

poned the moment of quiting the field. And, yes, we have become aware of getting again into the throes of achievement motivation research.

RESEARCH HISTORY IN A QUICK RETROSPECT

Now let me sketch briefly what has happened in the history of achievement motivation research. For the sake of simplicity I will divide the research history into four decades, from the fifties to the eighties. After describing these decades I will turn to the problems they have given us.

The *fifties* brought a breakthrough in measurement of the achievement motive with McClelland's thought-sampling device, the TAT (McClelland, Atkinson, Clark & Lowell 1953). In those days the achievement motive was considered to be a compact and stable attribute of the individual. Everybody was knitting nomological networks of the TAT motive scores. We have never again seen such a richness in the diversity of things correlated with motivation as in the roaring fifties, from perceptual thresholds to preferred metaphors (Atkinson 1958; Heckhausen 1963). The fifties can be summed up as the *era of motive measurement.*

The *sixties* were dominated by the risk-taking model. This contribution by Atkinson (1957; Atkinson & Feather 1966) protected the need achievement construct from the fate of being a short-lived affair as has happened to so many proposed personality traits. The risk-taking model put the achievement motive into an equation with task difficulty, creating a person-situation interaction long before the interactionism debate became popular in the seventies (Nygård 1981). The mathematical structure of Atkinson's model, intricate but not too complex, has attracted many researchers outside the field, even from the peripheral areas of psychology. Atkinson's paper, published in 1957, became one of the most cited articles in psychology. We can call the sixties the *era of motive interaction.*

In the *seventies* achievement motivation research was overtaken by attribution theory. The causal factors to which subjects attributed their successes or failures upon post-experimental soliciting were believed not only to be intervening cognitions but to act as the prime movers of expectancy, affect and action. Under the conceptualizing leadership of Bernie Weiner, causal attribution became the focus of much achievement motivation research (Weiner, Frieze, Kukla, Rest & Rosenbaum 1971). Weiner's fourfold table of causal factors, with its two dimensions of locus and stability were taken as mediators of incentive and of expectancy effects. Another contribution was the discovery that underlying the two achievement motives were differences in attribution bias (Weiner & Kukla 1970; Heckhausen 1975). With their assumed impact on motives expectancies, and incentives, causal attributions were discovered as the hidden determinants of each of the three elements of the risk-taking model. Attribution theory generated so much enthusiasm that I sometimes got the impression that, in the view of its proponents, achievement-related acts were undertaken only because they provided opportunities for satisfying an urge to explain one's action outcomes. Achievement motivation had been redefined as a need to indulge in one's "capacity for perceiving success as caused by internal factors, particularly effort" (Weiner et al. 1971, p. 18). Therefore, we may call the seventies the *era of the causal attribution urge.*

The *eighties* confront us with a totally changed scene. After hovering over cognition the pendulum is swinging back to action. The periods of motive measurement, the risk-taking model and causal attribution no longer make us feel enthusiastic. Each era looks like a ghost town after a gold rush. Many claims were staked out but were abandoned after some superficial digging. Researchers, gold diggers as they are, keep looking for land where prospective digging promises easy and quick pay-offs. Only a few persist in the abandoned settlements, others have retreated to the more established towns where they gamble in outmoded saloons with highly specific decks of cards such a test anxiety. But suddenly there is a new vision of a land of promise.

What has emerged over the past few years is the resumption of arguments stemming from two old and incompatible traditions whose present-day proponents do not yet recognize, or even know, the working of the other side. However, I predict an open clash in the near future. I have already taken sides and will, as a partisan, try hard to make my prediction come true. The traditions revolve around will psychology and expectancy-value theory. The older of the two traditions stems from turn-of-the-century, Central European will psychology, and is associated with the names of Narziss Ach and Albert Michotte (or, to speak of places, with Würzburg and Louvain). The younger tradition, which I will describe first, goes back, ironically, to a scientific grandson of Narziss Ach, to Hans-Werner Wendt, a student of Heinrich Düker who was a student of Ach. Attracted by McClelland, Wendt went to Wesleyan where he, in a 1955 study, hypothesized and found that achievement motive scores best predict performance when "performance is mainly left to S's own initiative" (1955, p. 449). That is, when extrinsic incentives for which the task goal is expected to be instrumental such as money or affiliation are available, the impact of differences in achievement motive strength are washed out.

Atkinson soon jumped on this lead, recognized in it Tolman's principle of performance and formulated a theory of achievement motivation that even preceded his risk-taking model (Atkinson & Reitman 1956). A shorthand label for this theory is "multi-incentive summation of action tendency". In detail, it consisted of three propositions linking motivation to performance: (1) motivation strength is the sum of all incentives, intrinsic or extrinsic, that are available upon goal-attainment; (2) motivation strength is equivalent to the strength of action tendency. This implies that motivation is directly translated into effort intensity - let me say beforehand that this implicit assumption will become a major clashing point between the two traditions; and (3) the strength of action tendency, i.e., effort, directly determines the performance output.

All further advances in this tradition have concentrated on this last and simple proposition. For example, US research had consistently excluded females from its subject pool, because of confusing results. But findings from mice and women taught a lesson. The Yerkes-Dodson law formulated on mice was rediscovered in men and Matine Horner (1972) created some enthusiasm with her unreplicable fear-of-success effects in women (see Heckhausen 1980a). In the mid-seventies Atkinson resurrected and reanalyzed six early Ann Harbor dissertations and stated the overmotivation thesis (Atkinson & Raynor 1974) according to which multi-incentive arousal impairs efficiency on complex tasks - evidence only weakly supportive of the overmotivation thesis. A triple interaction - between task requirements, individual motives, and incentives of the situation - became integrated into a theoretical framework, to which Willy Lens from Louvain has contributed (Atkinson, Lens & Malley 1976). Nowadays, the idea of multi-incentive summation in achievement, affilitation and leadership situations is most actively pursued in the research of Richard Sorrentino at Western Ontario, a student of Joel Raynor and therefore a scientific grandson of Jack Atkinson (Sorrentino 1974; Sorrentino & Field, in press). Falko Rheinberg, a student of mine now at Heidelberg, does not merely sum up or subtract incentives. Instead, he looks for necessary of sufficient combinations between incentives in order to best postdict amount of preparatory work for an exam or the yearly number of accidents of younger motorcyclists (Rheinberg 1983; Rheinberg, Dirksen & Nagels, in press).

Let us now turn to the older tradition of European will psychology. Ach (1910; 1935) had nothing to say about motivation proper but said much about action tendencies, i.e., about volition, how it starts with the act of will, how it prompts and leads action. Later in this century, when Boring first ran into the now familiar abbreviation of *"nAch"* for need achievement, he asked himself what it could have to do with N(arziss) Ach. We owe an enlightened answer to that question to Julius Kuhl who recently reviewed the old literature. You are familiar with Kuhl's (1983) distinction between selection motivation and realization motivation and with the two modes of processing information or two personality types, action versus state orientation. In a joint paper, we have recast the whole of motivation simply as a process of elaborating incentives and expectancies in order to select among options for later action. What follows, when a chosen option has to be put into action, is not simply a continuation of motivation tendencies into action tendencies but a process of another, of a beyond-Rubicon, i.e., a you-cannot-return nature, for which we prefer to term "volitional". In other words, we have been led to problems of volition: How it starts, an intriguing question that has never been pursued since Michotte and Prüm's illumination study in 1910; and how it steers action, the problem that occupied Ach and has so promisingly been taken up by Kuhl. Admittedly, it is still too early to label the present decade; tentatively, however, I do not hesitate to call it the *era of volitional action*.

After this short review let me stop and return to each of the successive decades to point out those problems that appear to me, after substantial reflection, profitable enough to deserve new attempts at resolution. For each decade I list just five problems that wait for your fresh efforts, too.

Let me add that I will not deal here with important segments of achievement motivation research that have branched off from the basic ideas which characterize each decade. This research mainly consists of applied and developmental work. Applied work has concentrated on procedures to change individuals' motives to enable them to obtain more scholastic or economic success (deCharms 1976; Heckhausen & Krug 1982; McClelland & Winter 1969; Rheinberg 1980). Developmental research has followed the history of the field. It was initially dominated by the individual-difference approach of the fifties, especially by searching for socialization antecedents of individual differences. Recent developmental studies have been inspired by risk-taking and attribution research. This led to a broader view of looking for general patterns in the development of achieving behavior (Heckhausen 1982; Nicholls 1984; Nicholls & Miller 1984; Schneider 1984). Development of volitional action in early childhood is already being studied (e.g., Geppert & Küster 1983) and may perhaps not only accompany, but even encourage the emergence of the theme of the eighties - volitional action.

The impact of the motive measurement fifties was a loss of interest in further measurement development after the initial endeavors to develop the TAT as a motive measure had attained an early level of empirical respectability (cf. Atkinson 1958; Heckhausen 1963). Thereafter, the measuring device was only used as a tool to provide motive scores for the assignment of subjects to experimental conditions. Indeed, many researchers considered the TAT procedure to be too time-consuming and preferred, instead, one of an increasing number of questionnaires that had been constructed as quick surrogates for the TAT.

To be brief, after 25 years we face the following five problems in measuring the achievement motive.

1. Theories of the original motive construct have decomposed it into a set of individual-difference parameters, such as personal standards, attribution patterns, self-concepts of ability, future time orientation (Gjesme 1975), etc. However, we are still satisfied with one-score summary indices of a given motive. That is, measurement has not kept pace with theoretical progress.

2. The theoretical assumption that the "projective" or "apperceptive" nature of the TAT procedure is more valid, than the "respondent" nature of self-report measures has remained somewhat mysterious. The lack of any exploration into the apperceptive processes has meanwhile become embarrassing in light of modern models of memory that the activation spread along semantic networks (e.g. Anderson 1983) or studies that investigate the impact of emotion on information processing by means of the apperceptive method (Bower 1981).

3. McClelland (1951; 1980; 1981) keeps reiterating that "operant" and "respondent" measures are different and that only operant measures such as the TAT yield valid motive scores, whereas respondent questionnaire scores are valid indices of attitudes, values or aspirations; in his terms: of schemas and traits, but never of motives. There is much suggestive evidence for this "dichotomic validity theorem" as we may call it. Some of the best support comes from a new study by Zumkley (in press) that tests the predictive power of the strength of the aggression motive, with regard to the perceptual threshold of aggressive words. The aggression motive was measured either by Kornadt's (1982) TAT measure or by Hampel & Selig's (1975) questionnaire. Only the TAT measure yielded significant predictions. However, is the TAT

necessarily the only way to get at operant thought? Can a questionnaire be constructed so that it releases and taps operant thought? I will come back to this question.

4. A longstanding problem is the domain specificity of an individual's achievement strivings. What we still measure is intensity, not extensity of a motive (deCharms 1968; Heckhausen 1968). Schmalt's (1976) grid technique, originally designed to come to grips with domain specificity, lost momentum halfway to the goal and was no longer pursued.

5. The fear-of-failure motive has turned out to have a double- or even multi-faceted nature - to say the least. One facet is coping and approach-oriented, the other fearful and avoiding, as has been, for example, revealed by Schmalt's semiprojective grid-technique. Even more disquieting is the habit of American researchers to use the Test Anxiety Questionnaire (Mandler & Sarason 1952), or one of its equivalents, as the fear-of-failure component in the resultant motive equation of hope-of-success minus fear-of-failure. Because test anxiety is indicative of self-perceived lower or inadequate ability, the fear-of-failure component in most American research is contaminated with perceived low ability, as Nicholls (1984) has rightly pointed out. This contamination might by itself devalue a large part of the risk-taking literature.

Now what to do? Our time out for thinking about motive measurement problems had led us to reconsider some of them. Initially we did not do this for its own sake, but in the course of running another study (with Frank Halisch) that scrutinizes the fundamental tenet of the risk-taking model, that the motive-dependent slope of incentive gradients of success and failure are a function of subjective task difficulty. Of course, such a venture depends on valid motive measurement. In addition to the TAT and the usual questionnaires, we decided to construct a questionnaire that we call a "scenario technique" in order to address three of the five problems mentioned before. We wanted, first, a set of motive parameters that reflects our present theorizing about the motive construct; second, a reflection of domain specificity, for example work versus leisure time activities; and third, a respondent measure allowing us to test the dichotomic validity theorem.

Since our results are still being analyzed I can, for the time being, make only three points based on the correlational matrix and the factor loadings of 14 to 21 variables from one TAT and five self-report measures. First, there is virtually no overlap between the TAT and the self-report scores while all self-report variables overlap substantially in expected patterns. This speaks to the dichotomic validity theorem. Second, self-report measures that tap a success versus a failure motive, as do the Gjesme-Nygård Scale (Rand 1978) and the Hermans Scale (Hermans 1970), yield substantial negative correlations between the two variables, revealing some simple antagonism. Third, all self-report scores for a success or failure motive have a substantial component of perceived ability (as measured by a scale of Wulf-Uwe Meyer, 1972/85) confirming the suspicion of a contamination I already referred to. In addition, all self-report scores for a failure motive load highly on a variable tapping fear of social consequences in case of failure - perhaps this is what scale constructors had in mind when they looked for fear-of-failure items. Finally, being in Nijmegen I am glad to say that the Hermans Scale contains one promising variable, i.e., the performance-facilitating test anxiety, because it does not correlate with any other self-report variable and, furthermore, because it has a common factor loading with two TAT categories of the fear-of-failure scoring key, namely "need to avoid failure" and "uncertainty of a failure outcome". I cannot yet report on our scenario technique. Therefore I stop here and turn to the next decade.

INTERACTIONISM - THE ERA OF THE SIXTIES

The risk-taking model, the predominant motivation theory of the sixties, has begotten mixed results. It has been well confirmed for success-motivated individuals but has fared less well for their failure-motivated counterparts. As I see it, the field still abounds with problems and flaws. Unfortunately, Atkinson did not guide the burgeoning research by setting increasing standards and criticizing sloppy work, with the exception of questionable motive measurement. Instead, he invested his effort into another enterprise, namely the conception of inertial forces of latent tendencies, the forerunner of the *Dynamics of Action* (Atkinson & Cartwright 1964; Atkinson & Birch 1970). Unwittingly, he has thus passed from motivational to volitional problems. The *Dynamics of Action* have still not become popular, partly because they are too "dynamic" and entail too much computer work. However, that may change in the era of volitional action that may characterize the decade to come.

I want to list five problems the era of interactionism has created.

1. The fundamental tenet of the risk-taking model, that the motive strength determines the slope of the difficulty-related gradient of success, or failure,

incentives, is still up in the air. Only two of five attempts have been even partly supportive, and these only for the incentive gradient of success (Litwin 1966; Cooper 1983; but not Feather 1967; Karabenick 1972; Schneider 1973, with the exception of one among several experiments). This failure does not come as a surprise if one considers the tremendous problems one has to master if one wants to get at the roots of the motivation process. I will list some of them among the following problems.

2. In the original version of the 1957 paper Atkinson contended that subjects with a predominant fear-of-failure motive avoid tasks of intermediate difficulty but try hardest if they are constrained to perform such a task. Note, that he relied here on good common sense by making an implicit distinction between motivation (i.e., avoiding an option of intermediate difficulty) and volition (i.e., putting out maximal effort if a task of intermediate difficulty cannot be avoided). Later on he streamlined his view because, as he confessed, he had "failed to understand what (the) theory is trying to say" (1983, p. 100). According to Atkinson the theory said that "motivation to avoid failure should always be conceived as inhibitory in character" (1983, p. 209). By this premature stretching of a decision-making model, that is, his risk-taking formula, to a performance model, he lost sight of his initial distinction between choosing and doing. This distinction meanwhile has been supported by many studies, such as Locke's (1968) finding that raising the difficulty level of goals increases performance, or the many results bearing on the double-faced nature of fear of failure. Still, in present research within the overmotivation paradigm, I suspect that the belief in the inhibitory nature of fear of failure impairs progress.

It is strange that for so long nobody has become aware that persistence and performance are not motivational problems like choice but are volitional ones. Only Locke treated it that way but he, too, did not see the distinction but believed, instead, to have discovered a contradiction to the risk-taking model. But what about Feather's (1963) work on persistence that so marvellously fits the risk-taking model? My answer is that in his experimental paradigm persistence has been framed into the format of a choice between two alternative activities, turning it into a motivational question.

3. The pivotal construct with which all research based on the risk-taking model stands or falls is subjective probability of success. The operationalization of success probability has been a real mess and has rendered most risk-taking studies incomparable (cp. Heckhausen 1977). No research standards have been developed with regard either to reference norms used, such as feedback from individual practice or social comparison norms (Rheinberg

1980), or with regard to familiarity with the task at hand, where subjects place themselves on a subjective learning curve, and so on.

4. The risk-taking model consists of three elements: first, motive-weighted incentives of anticipated success or failure: second, the subjective probabilities of those events and, third, a means to integrate the first two elements, multiplication. It is unlikely that all these elements are processed at the same time. More probable is a microgenesis: perhaps a gradual elaboration of incentives comes first, then the related probabilities and then some integration of both. We do not know the exact nature of the elements nor their order, nor whether complete elaboration is the rule or if shortcuts or rules of thumb are used. I do no know of any research intruding into the genuine realm of motivation. Is that not amazing?!

5. As I already mentioned, fear-of-failure subjects, preselected by the TAT Need Achievement score and Test Anxiety Questionnaire (TAQ) scores, feel less competent compared to hope-of-success subjects. This use of the TAQ to assess fear of failure has led to a contamination between the achievement motives and the self-concept of ability. On this contamination Nicholls (1984) has recently based a reformulation of the theory of achievement motivation.

Looking back on these five problems makes one hesitate to continue work in such research paradigm. However, after some time out Frank Halisch and I have begun to reconsider the risk-taking model. We have decided to try hard to avoid the pitfalls listed so far, in order to prove the fundamental tenet of the model, the motive-dependent slope of the incentive gradients across the range of subjective probabilities. We had to surmount a psychophysical scaling problem in getting our subjects to assign incentive values to different levels of task difficulty or subjective probability. Unfortunately, the analysis could not yet be completed. At he moment we can only say that the data support the expected motive effects on incentive gradients.

I turn now to the next decade.

CAUSAL ATTRIBUTION URGE - THE ERA OF THE SEVENTIES

Elsewhere (Heckhausen 1980a,b) I have discussed the results of the causal attributional analysis of achievement motivation as well as the unresolved problems that this approach has left us. Throughout the decade of the seventies the attributionists continuously increased their level of aspiration regarding the reformulation of achievement motivation theory by progressively stretching the explanatory power of attributional propositions as compared to the traditional risk-taking model.

At first the attributionists aspired simply to elaborate the risk-taking variables. The two achievement motives can, to some degree, be redefined by a difference in attributional bias. Moreover, processing information about consistency, consensus and distinctiveness of prior outcomes, as proposed by Kelley's (1967) cube of covariance, into cognitions provides mediational links between input and the formation of expectancies, as well as other factors such as incentives related to the anticipated outcome, readjusted expectancies, and affect after the actual outcome.

So far, the attributionists stood on a relatively solid, although only casually explored ground. Data from many studies confirm a mediational role for attributions at single steps in the action process, although hardly in a pervasive sequence of information processing steps (cf. Covington & Omelich, 1979a). Moreover, compared to mediating attributions, motive variables were shown to have additional or even greater influence on expectancy, affect and performance (Heckhausen 1978; Patten & White 1977; Schmalt 1978; Schneider 1977).

A more ambitious attempt to explain achievement motivation as attribution consisted first, in supplementing the "hedonic" aspect of incentive motivation with the "cognitively" nominated principle of information seeking. Such a proposition was introduced in the seminal 1971 article by Weiner and his associates. Here, Atkinson's motive definition "capacity of experiencing pride in accomplishment" (1964, p. 247) was contrasted with "capacity for perceiving success as caused by internal factors, particularly effort" (Weiner et al. 1971, p. 18). Initially both meanings of incentive were used, albeit in a mixed and somewhat arbitrary way. However, attributionists soon attempted to replace the hedonic meaning of incentive with the cognitivistic counterpart, self-diagnostic information seeking. As it turned out, the issue of definition remained moot because predictions from each position are, in fact, the same (see Heckhausen, Schmalt & Schneider, in press).

A last, and more radical rise in aspiration level consisted in the attributionists' denial of any motive effects at all including motive-linked attributional bias. Rather, they argued that each individual strives for maximal information about his or her competence (Buckert, Meyer & Schmalt 1979; Meyer, Folkes & Weiner 1976; but see the critique of Sohn 1984). Such a contention is, however, at variance with the bulk of empirical evidence. Meanwhile the boom in attributional studies has subsided. It has become clear that the explanatory power of causal attributions was grossly overestimated. Broad answers to the big initial questions have bred a lot of small but intricate issues which are difficult to clarify. Here is my list of five unresolved problems.

1. Attribution theorists have been so convinced that people are indefatigable "why-askers" that they have neglected to ascertain the frequency of attributional cognitions. There is no doubt that causal cognitions occur with full awareness when an outcome runs counter to what has been expected - particularly if a failure is encountered - because causal cognitions are in these cases instrumental for dealing with surprise, embarrassment and revised decision-making. This has recently been confirmed in a review of "spontaneous causal thinking" (Weiner 1985). But, more decisive for the theory, is whether causal cognitions in fact occur in the many experiments, or simulational experiments, of the attributionists. In typical studies subjects experience, or imagine, success and failure and are afterwards asked about causality. Most of attribution research has relied on such reactive data. Such a procedure raises the suspicion that subjects may have used a strategy Nisbett and Wilson (1977) have labelled "telling more than we know". That is, subjects may not have recalled their own causal thinking, but may have resorted to plausible common-sense theory; for example, saying that increased effort expenditure generally fosters success may be a common-sense cliché, not a recalled cognition.

2. This brings us to the question of the psychological status of "causal cognitions". Must they be conscious to be effective, or can they be subconscious or even irretrievably unconscious and at the same time effective? In other words, are causal cognitions like other information processes that cannot be directly observed, although one may become aware of some of their effects (see also Brody 1980)? I do not know of any attribution theorists who have raised such questions, let alone proposed strategies for answering them, although the implications of the answers are important. The pervasive nature of causal thinking in the phenomenological sense, I believe, is to a large extent a fiction entertained by attribution theorists.

3. The antecedents of the attribution of a given action outcome to certain causal factors have usually been neglected. Most attributionists in the achievement domain have simply treated inferred causal cognitions as independent factors in order to account for additional variance in some dependent variables, such as expectancy shift, resulting affect, task choice or performance. Such designs do not allow a test of the programmatic assumption

that causal cognitions mediate between information offered by the task situation and motivational effects. By task information I refer to the three dimensions of covariance with success and failure: distinctiveness, consistency, and consensus, as Kelley (1967) has outlined them in his cube.

Investigators have rarely varied these three dimensions as antecedent conditions (e.g., by Frieze & Weiner 1971), and when they did, hardly sufficiently so. I would like to add that, in achievement situations, consensus information is more readily and more fully used than it is in non-achievement actions (cp., McArthur 1972; Nisbett & Borgida 1975). This suggests that not only consistency and distinctiveness, but also social comparison is a routinized kind of information processing in the achievement domain. In general, we know little about the extent to which antecedent covariation information in the achievement area is used and distorted, or whether there are motive-linked biases in the pick-up and processing of information. It is from other research domains that we have learned about the "shortcomings of the intuitive psychologist" (Ross 1977), such as the "fundamental attribution error", "false consensus", "egocentric attribution" or "illusion of control" (Langer 1975).

An example of the effect of neglecting antecedent covariance information is a premature derivation from Weiner's early definition of the achievement motive as "the capacity for perceiving success as caused by internal factors, particularly effort" (Weiner et al. 1971, p. 18). According to this definition, tasks with an intermediate subjective probability of success should be preferred because the attained outcome can be most easily attributed to internal causes that, in turn, maximize self-evaluative affect (Weiner, Heckhausen, Meyer & Cook 1972). However, an internal attribution presupposes covariance information, especially consensus, or social comparison information, because this provides a normative concept of one's ability (cp. Nicholls 1984). However success of failure at the same objective level of moderate difficulty need not invoke ability as a causal factor when subjects have consistency information (from repeated practice trials), and distinctiveness information provided by various difficulty levels of the same task. Imagine a psychomotor task with difficulty levels arranged in an ascending order and imagine that you know your own performance. Under such conditions, success and failure at levels of intermediate difficulty are attributed to increasing task difficulty, an external cause, and not to one's ability (Schneider & Posse 1978).

4. The theorem of attribution theorists (see Weiner 1980) that expectancy and expectancy shifts are mediated by the perceived stability of the causes for past performance on the same task seems intuitively compelling on first, but not on second thoughts and has received only little support. An unex-

pected outcome ascribed to stable causes - let us say a failure attributed to one's own low ability - gives more reason to revise an original expectancy than the same outcome ascribed to unstable causes such as bad luck. This is because, in the latter case, the unexpected failure appears to be an unreliable event and can therefore be dismissed. One may ask, however, why the outcome was unexpected in the first place. The answer is simple: the explanation for the past performance was already based on stable causes. This being so, one might just as well maintain one's original expectancy based on stable causes and explain the last performance as an exception caused by unstable factors. This alternative to the attributional theorem appears equally compelling. Namely, the ascription to stable causes makes one's expectancies more resistant to revision.

We have thus a cycle of sequential and mutual determination. The more certain, based on consistency information, outcomes at a task appear to be, the more the causes of future performance are perceived as being determined by stable factors such as ability and task difficulty. If, in retrospect, the past performance deviates considerably from what has been expected, unstable causes may be the best explanation because they allow one to retain the prior expectancy that one has based on stable causes. Of course, repeated failure may force the revision of the stabilized expectancy. And so on. This line of reasoning implies that the stage in the information of an expectancy makes an important difference. Getting familiar with a new task is, as a rule, accompanied by a reallocation of the attributed causes and their weights. The two stable causes, task difficulty and ability, whose relation forms Fritz Heider's (1958) concept of "can", become gradually more decisive at the expense of the variable causes. The "can-concept" becomes more and more stable. If social comparison norms are available, one can infer one's own degree of ability from the level of task difficulty one is momentarily able to master. However, one adjusts the weights for ability and task difficulty, the "can"-concept stabilizes when performance reaches an asymptote. After this point, outcomes have to deviate repeatedly and markedly from what has been expected in order to induce, first, a reallocation of causes for past performance, and second, the maintenance of the reallocated causal pattern for future performance. Only then will there be an expectancy shift for the task.

In sum, it is not causal attribution, but consistency and consensus information that are the decisive determinants of expectancy. However, causal attribution, particularly the "can"-concept, with its relative causal weights for task difficulty and ability, develops along with the formation of expectancies. It then provides a rational base for predicting future outcomes, or for explaining unexpected outcomes, of for revising the underlying "can"-concept.

Of particular importance is that unexpected outcomes can be dismissed as unreliable by ascribing them to unstable causes.

Now to the available evidence. Quite a few studies simply found that expectancy increases with repeated success, and decreases with repeated failure. An initial higher rate of attributions to stable causes was not followed by a higher rate of expectancy shifts. Instead, attributions to stable causes interacted with the level of expectancy in the very first and in part the second trial. What made a difference was whether the initial outcome was a success or a failure. In subjects who made attributions to stable causes to start with, initial success led to high expectancies, initial failure to low expectancies (Fontaine 1974; McMahan 1973; Valle & Frieze 1976; Weiner, Nierenberg & Goldstein 1976). In the Weiner et al study, the group that made attributions to unstable causes had the highest rate of expectancy shifts in a series of successes, contrary to the contention of the attributionists.

These data can be explained when one proposes that subjects were in different stages in the formation of an expectancy. In the Weiner et al. study, attributions to unstable causes were coupled with lower expectancies. If these subjects felt they were in an early stage of practice, initial success should have led to a higher upward shift of expectancy than success at a later stage when one is more familiar with one's performance capacity. In a similar way, results of the other studies can be explained if subjects were further along in expectancy formation, i.e., if they were stabilizing the "can"-concept. In an often cited study by Meyer (1973), subjects were first familiarized with a digit-symbol substitution task and were then confronted with a fixed number of such problems, a task that is "neither easy nor difficult" - as was painstakingly made clear to the individual subject. Note that this procedure contributes to a highly stabilized "can"-concept. Then in a series of five trials subjects were made to fail. After each trial the perceived weights of the four Weiner causes of past performance as well as the subjective probability of success for the next trial were assessed. Meyer divided his subjects into two groups, those above and those below the median for ascription of performance to stable causes (ability plus task difficulty). Under the special conditions of the Meyer paradigm, the group above the median in ascription to stable causes showed a steep expectancy decrement across the failure series whereas the group low in ascription to stable causes showed only a slight drop. However, the group that tended to attribute their series of failures to stable causes consisted mainly of fear-of-failure subjects (14 of 20), while the group that preferred unstable causes for explaining the failures was mainly hope-of-success subjects (13 of 19). That is, the Meyer data on expectancy shift are a nice example for the motive-linked attribution bias, particularly in the face of failure (see Heckhausen 1980a).

The best example of the sequential cycle of expectancy shifts is a recent study by Brown (1984). Brown had his subjects succeed or fail in a concept formation task. Before this task he made his subjects either confident or pessimistic about success by inducing elated or depressed moods. Subjects with higher pretask expectancy of success tended to ascribe posttask success to stable causes, and posttask failure to unstable causes. However, there was an interaction between pretask expectancy and the direction of change. Confident subjects had a much higher expectancy of success than pessimistic subjects prior to task performance. Compared to these, they attributed posttask success more to stable causes. Accordingly, they maintained their high expectancies after success, and lowered their initial expectancies after failure. In contrast, pessimistic subjects maintained their initial low expectancies irrespective of a success or failure outcome. Neither outcome had an effect on their causal attributions. Thus, pessimistic subjects or those in a depressed mood appear to be more cautious in forming a "can-concept" than confident subjects. Whether they remain perhaps "sadder but wiser" (Alloy & Abramson 1979), even in the face of a long series of successes or failures (as Meyer, 1973, designed his experiment), has yet to be ascertained.

Future research should study subjects as they get familiar with a new task, and trace the gradual formation of expectancies for future outcomes separately from the development of attributions for past outcomes. Motive differences should also be controlled because they are additional factors producing interactional effects through attribution bias.

5. It is still a puzzle which one of the two internal causes, effort or ability, generates more affect in self-evaluation. There is no question that internal attribution is a necessary prerequisite for self-evaluative affect. It is also clear that when evaluated by others, praise has a maximal effect when a positive outcome is based on high effort, and blame a maximal effect when a negative outcome is due to low effort (Weiner & Kukla 1970; Rest, Nierenberg, Weiner & Heckhausen 1973). Originally, Weiner (1972; 1974) extended conclusions from other-evaluation data to self-evaluation. He suggested that effort attributions are more affect-generating than ability attributions in self-evaluation as well.

Several subsequent studies by other authors lent support to an opposite view with regard to self-evaluation. Success ascribed to high ability and low effort produced more positive affect than when ascribed to low ability and high effort. Conversely, failure ascribed to low ability and high effort was more depressing than attribution to lack of effort and unquestioned ability (Covington & Omelich 1979b,c; Heckhausen 1978; Meyer 1973; Nicholls 1975,

1976; Sohn 1977). Compared to ability, effort attributions have the inverse affective consequences that one would expect from the compensatory causal schema (Kelley 1972). Ascription of success to high expenditure of effort diminished positive feelings and, after failure, enhanced negative feelings because in both cases it can be inferred that ability has to be relatively low (Covington & Omelich 1979b; Nicholls 1975).

However, the pattern of results is rather complex and cannot yet be schematized into any simple structure. An important aspect is the kind of affect asked about. Pride and shame, the self-evaluative emotions (or incentives) in Atkinson's (1964) definition of the achievement motive, are coupled with high and low effort attributions, respectively (Brown & Weiner 1984; Nicholls 1976). In a recent study by Brown and Weiner (1984) further clarifications were achieved. For instance, public shame and humiliation are associated with low ability, whereas shame in the sense of guilt is linked with lack of effort.

When preparing this talk I was struck by the idea that much of the confusion about self-evaluative affect might be clarified if we were to bear in mind our new distinction between motivation and volition. Effort as an affect-raising cause refers to volition, i.e., to problems related to the realization of one's intentions through action, output of effort and persistence, coping with obstacles, failures and the temptations of more pleasurable activities; in short effort is related to all aspects of behavior over which we have voluntary control and for which we are therefore responsible. In contrast, ability as an affect-producing cause concerns a facet of the motivation process, namely the elaboration of an action-outcome expectancy as it is determined by one's ability in tasks of skill, knowledge and problem-solving. Ability, particularly as a concept of one's own intellectual capacity, should come into focus when the prospects of competition with peers are salient.

Listing tentative antecedents for a volitional versus a motivational focus, I suspect that a volitional focus is invoked by the following conditions: (1) a retrospective concern with one's activity; (2) activities which do not call into question important abilities such as intellectual capacity, especially in comparison to others; (3) attainment of, or failure to attain, a longterm goal; (4) evaluation based on integration of consistency, and not of consensus, information, (i.e., a normative ability concept has not been activated); (5) awareness of being responsible for one's activity and independent from relevant others. In contrast, a motivational focus is aroused by the following conditions: 1) a prospective concern with future activities for which one's ability has instrumental value; 2) activities that place high demands on a central self-relevant concept of ability; 3) having attained or not attained, in a contingent action path, a first subgoal that appears to be predictive for further performance; 4) evaluation based primarily on consensus (social comparison) information, particularly when competing with others; 5) awareness of being dependent on others and under their surveillance.

We first designed a simulation experiment to contrast the effects of a volitional versus a motivational focus. We asked university students to imagine doing a half-year study project of their own. They had to scale how strongly they would experience various positive or negative emotions upon eventual success or failure with their project. The positive emotions were "satisfied", "happy" and "proud", the negative emotions "dissatisfied", "unhappy", "ashamed" and "painful". The cover story contained three successive parts. Each part was phrased to generate either a volitional or a motivational focus, as defined above: Specifically, the first part was phrased to induce a retrospective or prospective concern, the second part was phrased to suggest consistency or consensus information and the third part to suggest that work intensity was more decisive than ability for successful completion of the project or vice versa. Subjects rated their imagined emotions after reading the entire cover story.

The results lend support to our distinction between a volitional and a motivational focus in postperformance self-evaluation, because the two foci led to emotions at different extremes in the intensity range of positive or negative emotions. A consistent motivational focus (i.e., all story parts induced a motivational focus) evoked the highest, and a consistent volitional focus, the lowest levels of emotional intensity. In all other mixed-focus combinations, the intensities of the emotional reactions ranged between the upper and lower extremes. Throughout, ability attribution generated more affect than did effort attribution, with the exception of the emotion "painful" which tended to be strongest when failure was ascribed to (lack of) effort. In addition to intensity differences due to ability (instead of effort) attributions, the scaled emotions were intensified by (1) a prospective concern, (2) consensus (social comparison) information and (3) success feedback, as compared to (1) a retrospective view, (2) consistency (ipsative) information and (3) failure feedback. These preliminary findings have yet to be replicated.

Other suggestive, though partial, evidence for one facet of our focus distinction, namely holding a retrospective versus a prospective concern can be seen in one of the vignettes of the simulation experiment by Brown and Weiner (1984). Their subjects preferred, when imagining a moderate life outcome in old age, to have tried hard with little natural ability over not having tried hard with much natural ability. In contrast, when choosing between analogous options for the first year of college, the same subjects preferred to have attained a particular grade by high ability and little effort instead of low ability and much effort.

So these are the five problems from the attribution decade. As with achievement motivation, we were at first tempted to stay on the sidelines of a field as confused and overestimated as attribution. However, after our time out for thought, we have begun to look again into two issues. One of them is the last one mentioned: the causal mediation of self-evaluative affect under motivational or volitional focus. The other problem concerns the assumed preference of task difficulty over ability as a cause for one's performance when covariation information includes only consistency, not consensus.

VOLITIONAL ACTION - WILL THE EIGHTIES BECOME ITS ERA?

One should always be cautious in predicting the future, particularly the course of future research. We are already in the middle of the eighties and it is still a surprising message for every insider that research in this decade might revolve around ideas about volitional action.

The first thing I can say is that such ideas already abound, although they are not labelled according to their volitional focus; for instance in Locke's work or much more explicitly in Atkinson and Birch's (1970) *Dynamics of Action.* All the waxing and waning forces that, according to the Dynamics-of Action model, struggle for temporary access to the action system are truly volitional in nature. Note, that the resultant forces that gain to action certainly can be traced back to their respective motivational tendencies, but they are independent from them in their momentary strength. This independence thus accomplishes a main tenet of any theory of volitional action or "will". However, it is often overlooked that, as a volitional model, the Dynamics-of-Action model is no rival to motivational models such as the risk-taking model. Quite the contrary. The Dynamics-of-Action model presupposes a motivational model that elaborates incentives and expectancies in order to fuel the necessary variables that then will fall into the vicissitudes of their volitional careers. However, the difference between motivation and volition has, in this model, remained unnoticed. The problems of how processes and forces of motivaton turn into those of volition, and what kind of metamorphosis is associated with such a transition, have been overlooked. This is not surprising, because the model includes a host of forces that, although certainly dynamic, appear more as blind urges from the unconscious than as volitions aimed at purposively planned actions.

25

I have already outlined our Rubicon-type partition between motivation and volition. Let me repeat the distinctive features and add some more:
- Motivational processes prevail whenever it is uncertain which one among two or more goals or actions is the more preferable (or the less to-be-avoided).
- Motivational processes include two parts: first the elaboration of incentives and expectancies associated with goals, action outcomes and their consequences, and second attempts to integrate these incentives and expectancies.
- Under certain conditions motivational processes come to a natural end by providing only one option among possible goals and courses of action.
- At that point in time a transition into a volitional state might occur, although the conditions for this are not yet clear. Sometimes this transition is consciously marked by the formation of a decision or an intent. Perhaps more often, some other point-of-no-return process launches the individual from a motivational period of elaboration into a volitional period of focussing on when and how to act, eventually, to accomplish what one is determined to do. One knows only the result: that one now is committed to act in a certain way and at a certain time or opportunity in order to attain a certain goal.
- The state of volition in reference to a certain goal includes the phases of action that bring one closer to goal attainment.
- Information processing in motivational states is oriented to an unpartial appraisal of reality whereas in volitional states, it is selective and biased in such a way that promotes the execution of intended acts and the attainment of the goal to which one is committed.
- Preliminary or final outcomes on the route to the intended goal generate short, postactional phases of consummation of attainment-related incentives as well as retrospective self-evaluations. Each of these has a double-centered concern. One concern refers to the antecedent motivational processes, for instance to the comprehensiveness and reality-orientation in the elaboration of values and expectancies. The other concern is directed toward volitional aspects of the performed action, for instance to effort and persistence, or to the procedures applied. The emphasis on motivational or volitional concerns in self-evaluative retrospection may vary and depends on several conditions. Each concern is based on different reference norms for the evaluation of outcomes, causal factors in attribution, and incentive functions. In addition they generate different emotions. (Remember that I have raised the same issue from quite another direction asking which perceived causes for an achieved outcome generate most self-evaluative affect). Each state - motivational, volitional or postactional - has its own basic functions as well as its metaprocesses or directives that safeguard the execution of these functions.

So much for how we look with new interest at old problems. Our current and planned research has been inspired accordingly. Let me sketch briefly five areas that we think are worth extended effort. We are already conducting diverse experiments in three of these areas in a joint venture with Peter Gollwitzer, Jürgen Beckmann, and doctoral students, Dorette Lochner, Heike Ratajczak and Monika Schütt.

1. I have already mentioned our prediction that there are different modes of information processing in motivational versus volitional states, (i.e., on each side of the Rubicon). A central initial problem in testing our prediction was to be sure we could keep subjects in a motivational state and prevent them from passing the "commitment threshold" into a volitional state. In a study with Peter Gollwitzer we did this by instructing subjects to deliberate over a choice, but not to come to a decision until they were told to (Heckhausen & Gollwitzer, in press). Our data came from interrupting subjects and asking them to report their thoughts from the previous 90 seconds. The 90 seconds internal was either just prior to a decision (motivational state) or just after a decision (volitional state). A content analysis of the reported thoughts yielded evidence for basic processes and metaprocesses quite in line with our assumptions. In the predecision motivational state, as compared to the post-decision state of volition, subjects deliberated the incentives of options under question, and their action-outcome expectancies, and also reported control thoughts in the form of metamotivational directives. These included taking a critical stand against one's first preference as being possibly biased, or as indicating bottom-line tendency.

In contrast, thoughts that prevailed in the postdecision volitional state concerned procedural steps for future action. Control subjects who were not allowed a decision at all, but were assigned to one of the options and interrupted before of after assignment, showed neither motivational nor volitional thoughts. They focussed on outward aspects of the experimental situation in the thoughts, and recalled biographical episodes that were irrelevant to the present task.

Furthermore, we predicted and found that short-term memory span is wider in a motivational than in a volitional state, a result consistent with our view that motivational state processing is oriented toward wide gathering of information. Cognitive psychology offers many sophisticated methods to further elucidate different modes of information processing, particularly with regard to memory or attention.

2. Particularly intriguing to us is the question of how people proceed from a motivational into a volitional state without having consciously made a decision

or formed some perhaps vague intention. We put subjects in a motivational state by asking them to imagine unresolved problems of their own with which they would be confronted during the next two weeks. In one condition the subjects then imagined the volitional state of beginning an action that might lead to an outcome they were still unresolved to attain (see Anderson 1983). Such a mental exercise brought more people across the Rubicon from motivation to volition than designing action plans or musing about the expectancies and incentives for a promising goal state. Another leap across the Rubicon that might avoid the waters of decision-making, has still to be explored, namely the elicitation of an emotional mood that properly fits into the volitional action under question. We are looking for still other "dry" passages that do not require formation of explicit intent for the transition from motivational to volitional action.

3. I have already discussed the multi-incentive summation idea for predicting performance outcomes. This product of the expectancy-value tradition lets the strength of action tendency be equal with the strength of the resultant motivation tendency. This equivalence is a contradiction of an assumption of the older tradition of will psychology, now rediscovered and favored, that strength of an action tendency - or for short: volition strength - certainly stems from motivation strength but modulates its actual strength according to the momentary requirements of goal attainment. In essence, this is the old Ach-Hillgruber *Law of Difficulty* (Ach 1935; Hillgruber 1912), the effect of which was rediscovered by Locke (1968).

To follow up on this idea, we wanted to demonstrate that volition strength can become independent from motivation strength, when it stands in the service of an efficient action. Our subjects were overmotivated athletes. We asked how their efficiency changes as a function of their ability to regulate volition strength. In collaboration with Hanno Strang, a sport psychologist from Kiel, we conducted experiments with top rowers (Heckhausen, Strang, Schirmer & Janssen, in press) and basket-ball players (Heckhausen & Strang, in prep.). In one condition, immediately before a training session, rowers were flooded with failures at an intellectual task taken from Seligman's helplessness paradigm. This increases motivation as we know from Kuhl's work (1981). In another condition basket-ball players were instructed to expend maximal effort while running a course with deep dribbling and basket throw. This condition should also induce overmotivation.

Fortunately, we had a sensitive and objective index of volition strength, namely lactate values indicating the degree to which the athlete's exertion has exhausted an immediate oxygen supply and has led to an anaerobic metabolism. We found good evidence for what we had expected. Many, but by no means all, athletes in the overmotivation conditions were able to decrease volition strength (i.e., they had decreased lactate values). This most often led to an increased efficiency, manifested in improved performance. Interestingly, the individual differences in the ability to regulate one's volition strength inthe service of present task requirements could be predicted by questionnaires tapping metavolitional knowledge and strategies, such as Kuhl's scale on action versus state orientation (see Kuhl 1981; 1982).

4. One interesting derivation from our Rubicon concept concerns what I have already mentioned about the centeredness of self-evaluation in postactional retrospection. Imagine you have chosen to do a very hard task and you fail. According to the motivational rationale of the risk-taking model, this should not bother you. That is, you will not feel much shame because the negative incentive of failure is lower, the harder the task. Up to now we were sure that this inverse incentive function summed up all we know about failure incentives. But that conclusion may be premature, if self-evaluation is volition-centered, after an act; or, even if self-evaluation arises from anticipation of such a volitional perspective when one is still in the motivation phase.

When centered on volition, the inverse failure incentive function should become a direct relation between task difficulty and negative affect, given that effort and persistence were appropriately squared with task difficulty. In short, self-evaluative failure affect should increase with the amount of effort and time that have been invested in vain. If this suggestion turns out to be true, we should expect that failures at very hard, as well as at very easy tasks give rise to self-evaluative affects that oscillate between reproach and excuse depending on whether one has a volitional or a motivational perspective. One wonders if there are, perhaps, masters at self-serving perspective shifting. These masters would have excuses for failing at any task difficulty; they would center on motivation when they fail at hard tasks, and on volition when they fail at easy tasks. Certainly, educational applications could easily be derived from this formulation. Let me add that a reversal of the incentive function does not hold in the case of success. Here, incentive of success increases with higher levels of task difficulty which, in turn, require increasingly greater amounts of effort.

5. A fifth area of possible, but as yet only contemplated, research concerns the postulation of motivation versus volition-type metaprocesses, i.e. metamotivations and metavolitions, and the question of whether differential effects can be induced an explained by them. Although the postulation of metaprocesses that act upon or steer more basic processes has been stimulated by the fruitful role of metacognition in developmental memory research

(see Brown 1978), metaprocesses are not new to motivation research. For instance Harriet and Walter Mischel have shown that children have some strategic knowledge which allows them to delay eating appetizing marshmallows (Mischel & Mischel 1983). For achievement motivation, metaprocesses arise in Kukla's (1972) and Meyer's (1973) models of effort calculation or in self-serving attribution patterns for self-evaluation (Heckhausen 1980a).

Ordinarily, metaprocesses in motivation or volition are unconscious but, in principle, they are accessible and one may become aware of them. The functional character of a metaprocess, i.e., that it is superordinate to and directive of more basic processes, has been made explicit by Kuhl (1983) in his theory of action control (Kuhl & Beckmann 1985). There, he revives a tradition begun by Narziss Ach (1910) that has been ignored. Presently we postulate lower and higher level metaprocesses, which belong to either the motivation or the volition phase (Heckhausen 1984). Primary metamotivations such as the "bottom-line tendency" (Fazittendenz), serve the immediate function of motivation by speeding up or integrating the elaborated value and expectancy aspects. Higher order metaprocesses may lead to individual difference parameters, that hitherto have been defined as motive differences. Moreover, they can be conceived of as special strategies for when greater difficulties must be overcome. This might occur, for instance, if two options were equally inviting and the "bottom-line" metamotivation was of no use. In completing the motivational process. A higher-order metamotivation might be useful, for example, in extending the frame of the problem (i.e., introducing additional goals with new incentives).

Another feature in our conception of metaprocesses is that they all are highly specific as to phase and level. For instance, shielding against competing action alternatives is assumed to be a basic volitional process during action and to be very functional. But during the motivation phase the same process of shielding-off would be a dysfunctionaly higher-order metamotivation because it would curtail realistic assessment, the proper aim of motivation. Of course, although dysfunctional it might in the long run be less dysfunctional than remaining unable to make any decision at all. Thus, higher order metaprocesses may also serve an emergency or makeshift function.

It is not yet clear how Kuhl's distinction between state versus action orientation fits into our theoretical frame-work. State orientation appears to involve a predominance of metamotivational over metavolitional processes whereas action orientation represents the opposite. If that is true, then state-oriented individuals should be superior in complex motivation problems that demand a careful elaboration of values and expectancies. In contrast, when an intended goal has to be realized, action-oriented individuals should be superior. However, Kuhl's (1983) data suggest that state-orientation is a generally dysfunctional state of excessive and perseverative informationprocessing, coupled with self-doubt and ruminations about past failures. This picture looks very much like the fear-of-failure personality. It may be that state orientation (or fear-of-failure, to come full circle) involves a deficiency in keeping different phases along an action path separate, particularly the phases on our two sides of the Rubicon, motivation and volition.

Here, I stop. You have seen that we do not suffer from a lack of new and interesting issues. When it comes to empirical evidence let me say that our data encourage us to elaborate further our Rubicon look on motivation and volition. The Rubicon look also resurrects many an old problem that we thought had been laid to rest, if not solved. Thus, we do new things and redo old things. Both have the same aim of a deeper understanding of what we have so mindlessly called "motivation".

After all this, I hope I have convinced at least some of you that it was and is beneficial to impose a time out to reconsider what the more important questions and problems are in achievement motivation research. As with all time outs, we have returned to the field, refreshed and ready to play.

REFERENCES

Ach, N. (1910). *Über den Willensakt und das Temperament.* Leipzig: Quelle und Meyer.

Ach, N. (1935). Analyse des Willens. In E. Abderhalden (Ed.), *Handbuch der biologischen Arbeitsmethoden. Band VI.* Berlin: Urban & Schwarzenberg.

Alloy, L.B., & Abramson, L.Y. (1979). Judgment of contingency in depressed and non-depressed students: Sadder but wiser? *Journal of Experimental Psychology: General, 108,* 441-485.

Anderson, C.A. (1983). Imagination and expectation: The effect of imagining behavioral scripts on personal intentions. *Journal of Personality and Social Psychology, 45,* 293-305.

Anderson, J.R. (1983). *The architecture of cognition.* Cambridge, Mass.: Harvard University Press.

Atkinson, J.W. (1957). Motivational determinants of risk-taking behavior. *Psychological Review, 64,* 359-372.

Atkinson, J.W. (1964). *An introduction to motivation.* Princeton, N.J.: Van Nostrand.

Atkinson, J.W. (1969a). Change of activity: A new focus for the theory of motivation. In T. Mischel (Ed.), *Human action* (pp. 105-133). New York: Academic Press.

Atkinson, J.W. (1969b). Comments on papers by Crandall and Veroff. In C.P. Smith (Ed.), *Achievement-related motives in children* (pp. 200-206). New York: Rusell Sage.

Atkinson, J.W. (1983). *Personality, motivation, and action.* New York: Praeger.

Atkinson, J.W., & Birch, D. (1970). *A dynamic theory of action.* New York: Wiley.

Atkinson, J.W., & Cartwright, D. (1964). Some neglected variables in comtemporary conceptions of decision and performance. *Psychological Reports, 14,* 575-590.

Atkinson, J.W., & Feather, N.T. (Ed.) (1966). *A theory of achievement motivation.* New York: Wiley.

Atkinson, J.W., & Reitman, W.R. (1956). Performance as a function of motive strength and expectancy of goal attainment. *Journal of Abnormal and Social Psychology, 53,* 361-366.

Atkinson, J.W. (Ed.) (1958). *Motives in fantasy, action, and society.* Princeton, N.J.: Van Nostrand.

Atkinson, J.W. & Raynor, J.A. (Eds.) (1974). *Motivation and achievement.* Washington, D.C.: Winston.

Atkinson, J.W., Lens, W., & O'Malley, P.M. (1976). Motivation and ability: Interactive psychological determinants of intellective performance, educational achievement, and each other. In W.H. Sewell, R.M. Hauser & D.L. Featherman (Eds.), *Schooling and achievement in American society* (pp. 29-60). New York: Academic Press.

Bower, G.H. (1981). Mood and memory. *American Psychologist, 36,* 129-148.

Brody, N. (1980). Social motivation. *Annual Review of Psychology, 31,* 143-168.

Brown, A. (1978). Knowing when, where, and how to remember: A problem of metacognition. In R. Glaser (Ed.), *Advances in instructional psychology* (pp. 77-165). Hillsdale, N.J.: Erlbaum.

Brown, J. (1984). Effects of induced mood on causal attributions for success and failure. *Motivation and Emotion, 8,* 343-353.

Brown, J., & Weiner, B. (1984). Affective consequences of ability versus effort ascriptions: Controversies, resolutions, and quandaries. *Journal of Educational Psychology, 76,* 146-158.

Buckert, U., Meyer, W.-U., & Schmalt, H.-D. (1979). Effects of difficulty and diagnosticity on choice among tasks in relation to achievement motivation and perceived ability. *Journal of Personality and Social Psychology, 37,* 1172-1178.

Cooper, W.H. (1983). An achievement motivation nomological network. *Journal of Personality and Social Psychology, 44,* 841-861.

Covington, M.V., & Omelich, C.L. (1979a). Are causal attributions causal? A path analysis of the cognitive model of achievement motivation. *Journal of Personality and Social Psychology, 37,* 1487-1504.

Covington, M.C., & Omelich, C.L. (1979b). Effort: The double-edged sword in school achievement. *Journal of Educational Psychology, 71,* 169-182.

Covington, M.V., & Omelich, C.L. (1979c). It's best to be able and virtuous too: Student and teacher evaluative responses to succesful effort. *Journal of Educational Psychology, 71,* 688-700.

deCharms, R. (1968). *Personal causation.* New York: Academic Press.

deCharms, R. (1976). *Enhancing motivation: Change in the classroom.* New York: Irvington.

Feather, N.T. (1963). Persistence at a difficult task with alternative task of intermediate difficulty. *Journal of Abnormal and Social Psychology, 66,* 604-609.

Feather, N.T. (1967). Valence of outcome and expectation of success in relation to task difficulty and perceived locus of control. *Journal of Personality and Social Psychology, 7,* 372-386.

Fontaine, G. (1974). Social comparison and some determinants of expected personal control and expected performance in a novel task situation. *Journal of Personality and Social Psychology, 29,* 487-496.

Frieze, I.H., & Weiner, B. (1971). Cue utilization and attributional judgments for success and failure. *Journal of Personality, 39,* 591-606.

Geppert, U., & Küster, U. (1983). The emergence of "wanting to do it oneself": A precursor of achievement motivation. *International Journal of Behavioral Development, 6,* 355-368.

Gjesme, T. (1975). Slope of gradients for performance as a function of achievement motive, goal distance in time, and future time orientation. *Journal of Psychology, 91,* 143-160.

Hampel, R., & Selig, H. (1975). *Fragebogen zur Erfassung von Aggressivitatsfaktoren (FAF).* Göttingen: Hogrefe.

Heckhausen, H. (1963). *Hoffnung und Furcht in der Leistungsmotivation.* Meisenheim: Hain.

Heckhausen, H. (1968). Achievement motive research: Current problems and some contributions toward a general theory of motivation. In W.J. Arnold (Ed.), *Nebraska Symposium on Motivation* (pp. 103-174). Lincoln: University of Nebraska Press.

Heckhausen, H. (1975). Fear of failure as a self-reinforcing motive system. In G. Sarason & C. Spielberg (Eds.), *Stress and anxiety (Vol. II)* (pp. 117-128). Washington, D.C.: Hemisphere.

Heckhausen, H. (1977). Achievement motivation and its constructs: A cognitive model. *Motivation and Emotion, 1,* 283-329.

Heckhausen, H. (1978). Selbstbewertung nach erwartungswidrigem Leistungsverlauf: Einfluss von Motiv, Kausalattribution und Zielsetzung. *Zeitschrift für Entwicklungspsychologie und Pädagogische Psychologie, 10,* 191-216.

Heckhausen, H. (1980a). *Motivation und Handeln.* Berlin: Springer.

Heckhausen, H. (1980b). *Attributional analysis of achievement motivation: Some unresolved problems.* Paper presented at the "Conference on Attributional Approaches to Human Motivation" at the Center for Interdisciplinary Research of the University of Bielefeld (FRG), 27-28 June.

Heckhausen, H. (1982). Development of achievement motivation. In W.W. Hartup (Ed.), *Review of child development research. (Vol. 6)* (pp. 600-668). Chicago: The University of Chicago Press.

Heckhausen, H. (1984). *Motivationspsychologische Metaprozesse in den verschiedenen Handlungsphasen.* Max-Planck-Institut für psychologische Forschung. München: Unpublished manuscript, 13.

Heckhausen, H., & Gollwitzer, P. (in press). Information processing before and after the formation of an intent. In F. Klix & H. Hagendorf (Eds.), *In memoriam Herrmann Ebbinghaus: Symposium on structure and function of human memory.* Amsterdam: Elsevier/North Holland.

Heckhausen, H., & Krug, S. (1982). Motive modification. In A.J. Stewart (Ed.), *Motivation and society* (pp. 274-318). San Francisco: Jossey-Bass.

Heckhausen, H., & Strang, H. (in prep.). *The translation of record motivation into volitional strength as reflected in basket-ball efficiency.*

Heckhausen, H., Schmalt, H.-D., & Schneider, K. (in press). *Achievement motivation in perspective.* New York: Academic Press.

Heckhausen, H., Strang, H., Schirmer, K.R., & Janssen, J.-P. (in prep.). Die Wirkung einer vorangehenden Leistungserfahrung auf die Energie-Mobilisierung und deren Effizienz im Hochleistungsrudern. In H. Lenk (Ed.), *Rudern im Spiegel der Wissenschaft.*

Heider, F. (1958). *The psychology of interpersonal relations.* New York: Wiley.

Hermans, H.J.M. (1970). A questionnaire measure of achievement motivation. *Journal of Applied Psychology, 54,* 353-363.

Hillgruber, A. (1912). Fortlaufende Arbeit und Willensbetätigung. *Untersuchungen zur Psychologie und Philosophie, 1,* Heft 6.

34

Horner, M.S. (1972). Toward an understanding of achievement-related conflicts in women. *Journal of Social Issues, 28,* No.1, 157-175.

Karabenick, S.A. (1972). Valence of success and failure as a function of achievement motives and locus of control. *Journal of Personality and Social Psychology, 21,* 101-110.

Kelley, H. (1967). Attribution theory in social psychology. In D. Levine (Ed.), *Nebraska Symposion on Motivation* (pp. 192-238). Lincoln: University of Nebraska Press.

Kelley, H.H. (1972). *Causal schemata and the attribution process.* New York: General Learning Press.

Kornadt, H.-J. (1982). *Aggressionsmotiv und Aggressionshemmung.* Bern: Huber.

Krug, S., & Hanel, J. (1976). Motivänderung: Erprobung eines theoriegeleiteten Trainingsprogramms. *Zeitschrift für Entwicklungspsychologie und Pädagogische Psychologie, 8,274-287.*

Kuhl, J. (1981). Motivational and functional helplessness: The moderating effect of state versus action orientation. *Journal of Personality and Social Psychology, 40,* 155-170.

Kuhl, J. (1982). Action versus state orientation as a mediator between motivation and action. In W. Hacker, W. Volpert & M. von Cranach (Eds.), *Cognitive and motivational aspects of action.* Amsterdam: North-Holland-Publishing.

Kuhl, J. (1983). *Motivation, Konflikt und Handlungskontrolle.* Berlin: Springer.

Kuhl, J., & Beckmann, J. (1985). *Action control: From cognition to behavior.* Berlin: Springer.

Kukla, A. (1972). Foundations of an attributional theory of performance. *Psychological Review, 79,* 454-470.

Langer, E.J. (1975). The illusion of control. *Journal of Personality and Social Psychology, 32,* 311-328.

Litwin, G.H. (1966). Achievement motivation, expectancy of success, and risk-taking behavior. In J.W. Atkinson & N.T. Feather (Eds.), *A theory of achievement behavior* (pp. 103-115). New York: Wiley.

Locke, E.A. (1968). Toward a theory of task motivation and incentives. *Organizational Behavior and Human Performance, 3,* 157-189.

Mandler, G., & Sarason, S.B. (1952). A study of anxiety and learning. *Journal of Abnormal and Social Psychology, 47,* 166-173.

McArthur, L.A. (1972). The how and what of why: Some determinants and consequences of causal attribution. *Journal of Personality and Social Psychology, 22,* 171-193.

McClelland, D.C. (1951). *Personality*. New York: Holt, Rinehart and Winston.

McClelland, D.C. (1980). Motive dispositions. In L. Wheeler (Ed.), *Review of personality and social psychology. Vol.1.* (pp. 10-41). Beverly Hills: Sage.

McClelland, D.C. (1981). Is personality consistent? In A. Rabin (Ed.), *Further explorations in personality* (pp. 87-113). New York: Wiley.

McClelland, D.C., & Winter, D.G. (1969). *Motivating economic achievement*. New York: Free Press.

McClelland, D.C., Atkinson, J.W., Clark, R.A., & Lowell, E.L. (1953). *The achievement motive*. New York: Appleton-Century-Crofts.

McMahan, I.D. (1973). Relationship between causal attributions and expectancy of success. *Journal of Personality and Social Psychology, 28*, 108-114.

Meyer, W.-U. (1972). *Überlegungen zur Konstruktion eines Fragebogens zur Erfassung von Selbstkonzepten der Begabung.* Unpublished Manuscript, Psychol. Institut, Ruhr-Universität, Bochum, (Revised manuscript, Psychol. Institut, Universität Bielefeld, 1985).

Meyer, W.-U. (1973). *Leistungsmotiv und Ursachenerklärung von Erfolg und Misserfolg.* Stuttgart: Klett.

Meyer, W.-U, Folkes, V., & Weiner, B. (1976). The perceived informational value and affective consequences of choices behavior and intermediate difficulty task selection. *Journal of Research in Personality, 10*, 410-423.

Michotte, A., & Prüm, E. (1910). Etude expérimentale sur le choix volontaire et ses antécédents immédiates. *Travaux du Laboratoire de Psychologie experimentale de l'Universite de Louvain, 1*, (2).

Mischel, H.N., & Mischel, W. (1983). The development of children's knowledge of self-control strategies. *Child Development, 54*, 603-619.

Nicholls, J.G. (1975). Causal attribution and other achievement-related cognitions: Effects of task outcome, attainment value, and sex. *Journal of Personality and Social Psychology, 31*, 379-389.

Nicholls, J.G. (1976). Effort is virtuous, but is's better to have ability: Evaluative responses to perceptions of effort and ability. *Journal in Personality Research, 10*, 306-315.

Nicholls, J.G. (1984). Achievement Motivation: Conceptions of ability, subjective experience, task choice and performance. *Psychological Review, 91*, 328-346.

Nicholls, J.G. (Ed.) (1984). *The development of achievement motivation*. Greenwich, Conn.: JAI Press.

Nicholls, J.G., & Miller, A.T. (1984). Development and its discontents: The differentiation of the concept of ability. In J.G. Nicholls (Ed.), *The de-*

velopment of achievement motivation (pp.185-218). Greenwich, Conn.: JAI Press.

Nisbett, R.E., & Borgida, E. (1975). Attribution and the psychology of prediction. *Journal of Personality and Social Psychology, 32,* 932-943.

Nisbett, R.E., & Wilson, T.D. (1977). Telling more than we can know: Verbal reports on mental processes. *Psychological Review, 84,* 231-259.

Nygård, R. (1981). Toward an interactional psychology: Models from achievement motivation research. *Journal of Personality, 49,* 363-387.

Patten, R.L., & White, L.A. (1977). Independent effects of achievement motivation and overt attribution on achievement motivation. *Motivation and Emotion, 1,* 39-59.

Rand, P. (1978). Some validation data of the Achievement Motives Scale (AMS). *Scandinavian Journal of Educational Research, 22,* 155-171.

Rest, S., Nierenberg, R., Weiner, B., & Heckhausen, H. (1973). Further evidence concerning the effects of perceptions of effort and ability on achievement evaluation. *Journal of Personality and Social Psychology, 28,* 187-191.

Rheinberg, F. (1980). *Leistungsbewertung und Lernmotivation.* Göttingen: Hogrefe.

Rheinberg, F. (1983). Achievement evaluation: A fundamental difference and its motivational consequences. *Studies in Educational Evaluation, 9,* 185-194.

Rheinberg, F., Dirksen, U., & Nagels, E. (in press). Motivationsanalysen zu verschiedenen riskantem Motorradfahren. *Zeitschrift fur Verkehrssicherheit, 2.*

Ross, L. (1977). The intuitive psychologist and his shortcomings: Distortions in the attribution process. In L. Berkowitz (Ed.), *Advances in Experimental Social Psychology (Vol.10)* (pp. 173-220). New York; Academic Press.

Schmalt, H.-D. (1976). *Das LM-Gitter.* Handanweisung. Göttingen: Hogrefe.

Schmalt, H.-D. (1978). Leistungsthematische Kognitionen I: Kausalerklärungen für Erfolg und Misserfolg. *Zeitschrift fur experimentelle und angewandte Psychologie, 25,*246-272.

Schneider, K. (1973). *Motivation unter Erfolgsrisiko.* Göttingen: Hogrefe.

Schneider, K. (1977). Leistungsmotive. Kausalerklärungen für Erfolg und Misserfolg und erlebte Affekte nach Erfolg und Misserfolg. *Zeitschrift für experimentelle und angewandte Psychologie, 24,* 613-637.

Schneider, K. (1984). The cognitive basis of task choice in preschool children. In J.G. Nicholls (Ed.), *The development of achievement motivation* (pp. 57-72). Greenwich, Conn.: JAI Press.

Schneider, K., & Posse, N. (1978). Der Einfluss der Erfahrung mit einer Aufgabe auf die Aufgabenwahl, subjective Unsicherheit und die Kausalerklärungen für Erfolge. *Psychologische Beiträge, 20,* 228-250.

Sohn, D. (1977). Affect-generating powers of effort and ability self attributions of academic success and failure. *Journal of Educational Psychology, 69,* 500-505.

Sohn, D. (1984). The empirical base of Trope's position on achievement-task choice: A critique. *Motivation and Emotion, 8,* 91-107.

Sorrentino, R.M. (1974). Extending initial and elaborated theory of achievement motivation to the study of group processes. In J.W. Atkinson & J.O. Raynor (Eds.), *Motivaton and achievement* (pp. 255-267). Washington, D.C.: Winston.

Sorrentino, R.M., & Field, N. (in press). Emergent leadership over time: The functional value of positive motivation. *Journal of Personality and Social Psychology.*

Trudewind, Cl. (1982). The development of achievement motivation and individual differences: Ecological differences. In W.W. Hartup (Ed.), *Review of child development research. (Vol.6)* (pp.669-703). Chicago: The University of Chicago Press.

Valle, V.A., & Frieze, I.H. (1976). Stability of causal attributions as a mediator in changing expectations for success. *Journal of Personality and Social Psychology, 33,* 579-587.

Weiner, B. (1970). An attributional analysis of achievement motivation. *Journal of Personality and Social Psychology, 15,* 1-20.

Weiner, B. (1972). *Theories of motivation.* Chicago: Markham.

Weiner, B. (1974). *Achievement motivation and attribution.* Morristown, N.J.: General Learning Press.

Weiner, B. (1980). *Human motivation.* New York: Holt, Rinehart and Winston.

Weiner, B. (1985). "Spontaneous" causal thinking. *Psychological Bulletin, 97,* 74-84.

Weiner, B., & Kukla, A. (1970). An attributional analysis of achievement motivation. *Journal of Personality and Social Psychology, 15,* 1-20.

Weiner, B., Frieze, I.H., Kukla, A., Reed, L., Rest, S., & Rosenbaum, R.M. (1971). *Perceiving the causes of success and failure.* New York: General Learning Press.

Weiner, B., Heckhausen, H., Meyer, W.-U, & Cook, R.E. (1972). Causal ascriptions and achievement behavior: A conceptual analysis of effort and reanalysis of locus of control. *Journal of Personality and Social Psychology, 21,* 239-248.

Weiner, B., Nierenberg, R., & Goldstein, M. (1976). Social learning (locus of control) versus attributional (causal stability) interpretations of expectancy of success. *Journal of Personality, 44,* 52-68.

Wendt, H.W. (1955). Motivation, effort, and performance. In D.C. McClelland (Ed.), *Studies in motivation* (pp. 448-459). New York: Appleton-Century-Crofts.

Zumkley, H. (in press). Operante versus respondente Messung von Aggressivität, Vigilanz und Wahrnehmungsabwehr bei der Identifikation von aggressionsrelevanten Wörtern. *Psychologische Beiträge.*

PART II

TASK MOTIVATION

MOTIVATION IN RELATION TO TASK CHOICE

M.J.M. Houtmans

University of Nijmegen

SUMMARY

In a free choice situation with tasks of various difficulty levels the Dynamics of Action theory predicts a shift to more difficult tasks, while episodic theories of achievement motivation predict that subjects continue to choose tasks from the same difficulty level. According to the Dynamics of Action there is a consummatory force which reduces an action tendency when this action tendency is expressed in behavior. The consummatory force is supposed to be larger when a subject succeeds at a task than when he fails. Because subjects experience more successes at easy tasks than at difficult ones, the decrease in the action tendency to choose easy tasks is therefore bigger than the decrease in the action tendency to choose difficult tasks. Accordingly subjects will choose higher levels of task difficulty during the course of the experiment. This assumption was confirmed in an experiment by Kuhl and Blankenship with university students as subjects. This finding was replicated in an experiment with elementary school children as subjects.

INTRODUCTION

The main difference between traditional episodic theories of achievement motivation (Atkinson 1957; Heckhausen 1977) and the dynamic theory of achievement motivation (Atkinson & Birch 1974) is the importance which the dynamic theory gives to changes in behavior. Whereas the traditional theory mainly studied one person performing a single task, the dynamic theory investigates the stream of behavior which a person emits. In other words whereas the traditional theory tries to pinpoint the determinants of each individual action, the dynamic theory tries to identify the determinants of a change in behavior.

All theories about achievement motivation imply that the activities performed by a subject are manifestations of underlying motivational tendencies. At any particular moment every person is motivated by a number of different tendencies simultaneously. The behavior in which a subject engages is an expression of the dominant tendency. This does not imply, however, that the other tendencies suddenly disappear. On the contrary, they will persist until a psychological force modifies them. This is the assumption of the so-called inertial tendencies (Atkinson 1964).

Every tendency which is expressed in behavior is the sum of two components: The first component is an action tendency or a tendency to actually perform the activity. The second component is the negaction tendency or a tendency *not* to perform the activity. Action and negaction tendencies wax and wane through the influence of a number of different forces. For the action tendency these are the instigating and consummatory forces, while for the negaction tendency these are the inhibitory force and the force of resistance. The instigating force represents environmental influences that cause an increase in the strength of an action tendency. This force develops when an activity has been intrinsically satisfying in the past or when the activity has been previously rewarded. Whenever an activity is expressed in behavior the consummatory force starts to increase. This force causes a decrease in the action tendency, in other words engaging in an activity causes a decrease in the action tendency to continue engaging in that activity.

The negaction tendency is influenced by the inhibitory force and the force of resistance. The inhibitory force represents environmental influences that cause an increase in the strength of a negaction tendency. This force develops when a certain activity has been frustrated or punished in the past. By definition a negaction tendency produces resistance to an activity, it dampens or blocks the performance of the activity. Analogous to the consummatory force which reduces the instigating force, there is a force of resistance which reduces the inhibitory force and thereby the resistance to an activity (Atkinson & Birch 1970, 1974).

Summarizing, there are two main differences between episodic and dynamic theories. First, the episodic theory only considers the strength of the instigating and inhibitory forces, whereas the dynamic theory complements these forces with the consummatory force and the force of resistance. Secondly, the episodic theory only considers the strength of the instigating and inhibitory forces at a particular time, whereas the dynamic theory investigates the changes of these forces over time, caused mainly by the influence of the consummatory force and the force of resistance.

Choice behavior in relation to motivation

One of the behavioral correlates of motivation is the choice behavior of people confronted with a set of different tasks. A common finding of experiments in which people are confronted with tasks of different difficulty levels is that people show a gradual shift of preference to more difficult tasks (Atkinson & Feather 1966; Atkinson, Bastian, Earl & Litwin 1960). The explanation which the episodic theory gives for this phenomenon is that the perception of the difficulty of a task changes because of improvement due to practice with the task. Through this improvement the probability of succeeding at a particular objective level of difficulty increases during the course of the experiment. A main assumption of the episodic theory is that subjects continue to choose tasks at their preferred subjective difficulty level. In order to choose tasks with the same subjective difficulty level during the entire experiment subjects have to choose tasks with an increasingly higher objective level of difficulty. If it would be possible to hold the subjective probability of success for each difficulty level constant during the course of the experiment the episodic theory predicts that subjects will choose the same difficulty level throughout the entire experiment (Atkinson & Feather 1966; Atkinson 1957; Raynor 1969).

The dynamic theory, however, can explain a shift of preference toward more difficult tasks even when the subjective probability of success at each difficulty level remains constant during the experiment. In addition to the instigating and inhibitory forces they also take the influence of the consummatory force and the force of resistance into account. One of the main assumptions of the dynamic theory is that if one works at a task of a given difficulty level a consummatory force develops which reduces the tendency to keep chosing tasks of that level of difficulty. Another assumption is that this consummatory force is supposed to be greater when one succeeds than when one fails at the task. Because subjects will experience more successes at easy than at difficult tasks, the consummatory force will be greater for tasks with a low level of difficulty than for tasks with a high level of difficulty. The result of the increase of the consummatory force is a decrease in the action tendency to choose tasks at that difficulty level and consequently a shift to more difficult tasks in the course of the experiment.

For failure-oriented subjects there is still another force that has an influence on task choice, namely the force of resistance. Resistance toward working at a given task difficulty level is supposed to be the result of fear of failure, and it consequently varies with success and failure at a task. Resistance is reduced more after success than after failure, therefore it should decrease fastest at the lowest difficulty levels. This again implies that the consummatory force can start to operate earlier on these easy tasks and this

43

again leads to a preference for more difficult tasks over time (Atkinson & Birch 1974).

In line with the above-mentioned theoretical insights with regard to the Dynamics of Action Kuhl and Blankenship (1979a and b) formulated the following hypotheses about task choice in a situation in which subjects are confronted with a set of tasks that differ in difficulty (i.e. in probability of success), a particular number of which they have to solve.

HYPOTHESIS 1: For success-oriented subjects (Ms>Mf) there is an increasing tendency to choose more difficult tasks in the course of the experiment.

This hypothesis is based on the influence of the consummatory force. Subjects experience more successes at easy than at difficult tasks and consequently the consummatory force will be greater for easy tasks. As a result subjects will gradually shift to more difficult tasks.

HYPOTHESIS 2: For success-oriented subjects the first task they will choose will be of an intermediate level of difficulty.

At the beginning of an experiment the consummatory force is not yet operative. The choice of the first task is therefore determined only by the strength of the instigating force. In line with the predictions following from the episodic theory this implies that for success-oriented individuals this choice will be a task of intermediate level of difficulty.

HYPOTHESIS 3: For failure-oriented subjects (Ms<Mf) there is also an increasing tendency to choose more difficult tasks during the course of the experiment.

Again this hypothesis is based on the influence of the consummatory force. After the initial resistance, which for failure-oriented subjects is due to a fear of failure, has been overcome the consummatory force increases more for easy tasks than for difficult ones. This results in a shift to choose more difficult tasks during the course of the experiment.

HYPOTHESIS 4: For failure-oriented subjects the first task they will choose will be at a difficulty level lower than the intermediate one.

According to the episodic theory there should be an alternation of choices between the highest and the lowest difficulty level. The dynamic theory predicts that this alternation will very quickly be replaced by a choice for the lower difficulty levels due to the influence of the force of resistance and the consummatory force.

Kuhl and Blankenship confirmed these hypotheses, both in a computer simulation (1979a) and in an experiment with male and female university students as subjects (1979b). In this paper a study will be reported in which the Kuhl and Blankenship experiment was replicated with elementary school children as subjects. The age difference between the subject groups of both experiments necessitated some changes in the design of the original experiment. For a better understanding the experiment of Kuhl and Blankenship will be briefly reviewed before the present study is described.

Kuhl and Blankenship's experiment

A group of 48 university students was divided into a group of success-oriented and a group of failure-oriented subjects on the basis of their scores on the TAT (the Thematic Apperception Test by which the strength of the motive to achieve success was determined; McClelland, Atkinson, Clark & Lowell, 1953) and the TAQ (the Mandler and Sarason (1952) Test Anxiety Questionnaire by which the strength of the motive to avoid failure was determined). The scores on the TAQ appeared to be significantly higher for female than for male subjects. Therefore the data of this experiment were analysed separately for both sexes.

In the experiment proper subjects were presented with a perceptual reasoning task where they had to connect numbered dots in order with an imaginary line (see Figure 1). Taking the arrow as a starting point they had to proceed to the highest numbered dot. The line connecting the dots should not cross, touch or retrace itself, while the borderline should not be traced or touched. The correct answer was the number of line segments in the shortest line connecting the dots. There were items on 5 levels of difficulty.

During a practice period subjects solved items of each difficulty level until the solution time for each level had stabilized. Subsequently each subject had to solve 6 items of each difficulty level. However, there was now a maximum time for each item so that subjects could solve 5 items of difficulty level 1, 4 of difficulty level 2, 3 of difficulty level 3, 2 of difficulty level 4 and 1 of difficulty level 5. In this way subjects became aware of their subjective probability of success at each difficulty level.

In the main phase of the experiment the subjective probabilities were written on cards and placed in front of 5 stacks of 50 items, one for each difficulty level. Subjects were asked to solve 50 of these items, while they were free to choose any difficulty level they liked and to switch between difficulty levels as often as they liked. During this phase of the experiment the experimenter sat facing away from the subject. In this way the experimenter could not see which trial a subject would choose and hence social desirability factors were minimized.

Figuur 1. An example of a stimulus for each difficulty level

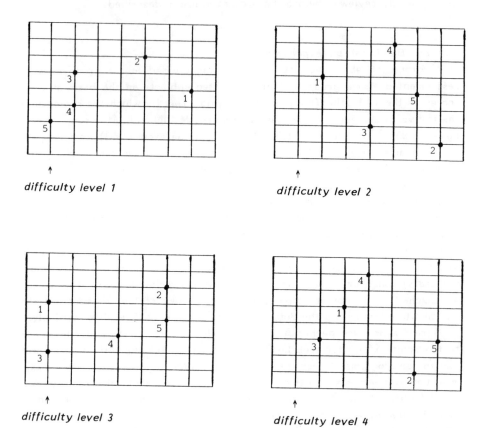

difficulty level 1

difficulty level 2

difficulty level 3

difficulty level 4

The subject indicated the fact that he had chosen an item, so that the experimenter could start a timer. As soon as the maximum time for that particular subject (i.e. the maximum time of difficulty level 3 determined during the practice period) had expired, the experimenter stopped the trial. On an answer sheet the subject subsequently indicated that he had failed at that trial, after which he could choose the next trial. If the subject solved the item before the time limit had expired he had to check his answer, again indicating on the answer sheet whether he had succeeded or failed.

After 50 trials in this way subjects had to predict their number of successes given 10 additional trials of each difficulty level. All subjects who gave different probabilities here from the ones determined during the practice period were excluded from further analysis. For these subjects the assumptions on which the hypotheses were based, namely that the subjective probability of success would remain constant during the course of the experiment, was violated.

The four hypotheses were indeed confirmed: both failure- and success-oriented subjects shift to a higher level of task difficulty during the course of the experiment; success-oriented subjects choose an item with an intermediate level of difficulty as their first trial, while failure-oriented subjects choose an item with a difficulty level lower than the intermediate one as their first item.

Changes made in the replicated experiment

There are a number of differences between the replication and the original experiment caused mainly by the age difference between the two subject groups.

In the first place the task used by Kuhl and Blankenship seemed to be too difficult for children. Therefore the children were allowed to actually draw the line connecting the dots and to correct themselves if necessary, in contrast to the adults who had to connect the dots with an imaginary line and subsequently give the number of line segments needed . In the second place the stimuli used by Kuhl and Blankenship had 4 to 9 dots. There seemed to be no objective criteria to determine the difficulty level of each individual stimulus. Instead, difficulty level seemed to depend at least in part on the time needed to solve a puzzle, which in turn depends on the number of dots of the puzzle. In the present experiment all stimuli consisted of 5 dots. The difficulty level was determined by the location of the dots within the grid and not by their number.

Instead of making subjects aware of subjective probabilities of success for different sets of stimuli in terms of proportions of trials solved during the practice period, the children were confronted with verbal labels indicating the difficulty level. Difficulty level 1 was labeled "very easy", difficulty level 2 was labeled "rather easy", difficulty level 3 was labeled "rather difficult", and difficulty level 4 was labeled "very difficult". The four levels can be characterized as follows. For difficulty level 1 the solution is more or less self-evident since the 5 dots are located in a circular pattern. The path from one dot to the next is obvious and consequently there are virtually no alternative routes. For the other difficulty levels the 5 dots are distributed more or less randomly in the matrix. To find the path from one dot to the next one has to take account of the other dots, in order to avoid a blockage of the path from one dot to the next. For difficulty level 2 only one dot is difficult to reach. For difficulty level 3 two dots are difficult to reach, while the solution is obvious if the path to these two dots is found. For difficulty level 4 at least 3 dots are difficult to reach if one does not take account of the location of the other dots. An example of a stimulus for each difficulty level is shown in Figure 1. All attempts to translate the verbal descriptions of difficulty level into quantitative measures failed, resulting in a less than 100% objective division of the stimuli. In a preliminary study therefore it was investigated whether children would agree with this a priori division of stimuli.

Another important difference between the two studies is the way in which motive strength was measured. While Kuhl and Blankenship used the TAT to determine the motive to achieve success and the TAQ to determine the motive to avoid failure, in the present experiment a Dutch version of the AMS (the Achievement Motivation Scale of Nygård and Gjesme (1973)) was used to determine both motives. The first 15 items of the AMS are used to compute the motive to achieve success, while the second 15 items are used to compute the motive to avoid failure. On the basis of these two scores subjects could be divided into 4 groups. Subjects who had a score above the median for Ms and a score below the median for Mf constituted the group of success-oriented subjects, whereas subjects who scored below the median on Ms and above the median on Mf constituted the group of failure-oriented subjects.

In the following first the preliminary study is described, in which the a priori division of stimuli in difficulty levels is compared with a division in difficulty levels of these same stimuli given by the children. After this preliminary study the actual experiment is described in which the predictions for task choice derived from the Dynamics of Action, in a situation in which a subject is confronted with a set of tasks differing in level of difficulty, are investigated with elementary school children as subjects.

THE PRELIMINARY STUDY

Subjects

Twelve girls and eight boys of the 5th and 6th grade of an elementary school took part in this preliminary investigation.

Group session

During a group session a Dutch translation of a test for measuring fear of failure and achievement motivation developed by Nygård and Gjesme (1973), the AMS, was administered in order to determine the scores for fear of failure and achievement motivation for each individual subject.

Individual sessions

The children were randomly divided into two groups of 10 children each. Each group had to solve its own set of puzzles. The children were tested in individual sessions of about one hour.

To acquaint the child with the task the individual session started with a practice period during which 8 puzzles of each difficulty level were presented. The first puzzle of each difficulty level was demonstrated by the experimenter. The child had to try to solve the second puzzle on his own. However, the experimenter would explain the solution if this still proved to be too difficult for the child. The experimenter was allowed to help when the child experienced difficulties with puzzles 3 and 4. Starting with puzzle 5 the child had to solve the puzzles on his own. The maximum time allowed for working on each puzzle was 2 minutes. If the puzzle was not solved within this time the child had to put it away and try the next one.

After the practice period the two groups of subjects had to solve their own set of 24 puzzles the difficulty level of which was unknown to them. In fact there were 6 puzzles of each difficulty level presented in a random order. Through this procedure there was a comparison between the a priori division and the children's judgment for 48 puzzles.

A maximum time of 2 minutes was allowed for the solution of each puzzle. It was our experience that puzzles which were not solved within two minutes would either take very long or could not be solved at all by the children. For each puzzle the experimenter recorded the solution time. After the child had either solved the puzzle or the maximum time had elapsed, he had to decide to which difficulty level the puzzle belonged according to him.

For each puzzle, therefore, there were two measures indicating the degree of correspondence between the a priori division and the division the children produced. Of these two measures the difficulty level chosen by the children was more subjectively oriented, while the solution time for each puzzle provided a more objective measure for the difficulty of the puzzle.

Results

To study the degree of correspondence between the a priori and the children's division in difficulty levels, both measures the children provided were taken into account. Whenever there was a serious discrepancy between the a priori and the children's judgment of difficulty level of a puzzle, this puzzle was excluded from further analyses and in addition would not be used in the main experiment. A discrepancy was defined as follows. For each child the mean solution time per difficulty level was determined, and all puzzles that had either much longer or much shorter solution times than the mean were marked. Subsequently the number of children for whom a particular puzzle had either longer or shorter solution times was counted. The puzzles for which the solution time deviated from the mean in the same direction for at least 5 children were excluded from the experiment.

This rather stringent criterium was used to avoid random factors such as the following from influencing the results. Sometimes children did not see an easy solution because they were trying to apply strategies that were only applicable to the higher difficulty levels. At other times children did not immediately find the right strategy to solve a difficult puzzle. On the other hand children sometimes solved a series of puzzles of the same difficulty level. Because they usually could apply the same strategy in this case they sometimes solved the later trials faster.

On the basis of the above mentioned criterium six puzzles were excluded out of a total of 48. Two puzzles of difficulty level 2 were consistently judged to be of a higher difficulty level, three puzzles of difficulty level 3 were consistently judged to be of a lower difficulty level and one puzzle of difficulty level 4 was excluded because no child could solve it.

In addition to the exclusion of a couple of puzzles the data of one child were also excluded. This child decided that nearly all puzzles (20 out of 24) were of difficulty level 1, while his solution times were in general very low and not consistent with the a priori difficulty levels. Obviously this child had either not understood the task or all puzzles were simply very easy for him.

A comparison of the results of the two groups of children who solved two different sets of puzzles is given in Table 1. A multivariate analysis showed that there were no significant differences between the two groups in assigning puzzles to difficulty levels ($F(4,14)=1.36$; $p>.10$) nor in the time needed to solve the puzzles of different levels of difficulty ($F(4,12)=1.39$; $p>.10$). This result implies that the two sets of puzzles are similar.

Table 1. Mean judgment of difficulty level and mean solution time for each
          a priori determined level of difficulty for the two groups of chil-
          dren

		a priori determined level of difficulty			
		1	2	3	4
group I	judgment of	1.02	1.78	2.73	3.24
(n = 10)	difficulty s.d.	0.05	0.54	0.52	0.34
	solution time	8.36	17.76	38.02	49.79
	s.d.	2.70	6.82	19.98	11.94
group II	judgment of	1.06	1.40	2.62	3.20
(n = 9)	difficulty s.d.	0.17	0.42	0.56	0.46
	solution time	11.61	21.96	47.02	59.80
	s.d.	3.74	8.46	13.34	18.17

Individual tests for trend showed that both the choice of difficulty level
and the solution times increase for every child with increasing level of difficulty of the a priori division.

In Table 2 subjects are assigned to four different motive groups of high
and low fear of failure and high and low achievement motivation. These motive groups were formed on the basis of the scores subjects had on the AMS.
Two multivariate analyses showed that neither the judgements about difficulty levels ($F(4,12)=2.77$; $p>.10$) nor the mean solution times for the four difficulty levels ($F(4,10)<1$) differed for the separate motive groups.

Discussion

This preliminary investigation was performed to study whether children
would agree with an a priori division of tasks in levels of difficulty based on
a number of qualitative criteria.

For 19 of the 20 children there was a significant linear trend, i.e. a significant increase in judged difficulty from a priori difficulty level 1 to 4, indicating that the children followed the a priori division fairly well. They
seemed to be reluctant to place puzzles in the highest level of difficulty, resulting in somewhat lower difficulty levels than the intended ones. This underestimation could be caused by a fear of appearing stupid if one admitted a

puzzle to be "very difficult" (difficulty level 4). It seems reasonable to suggest that especially subjects with a dominant fear of failure would show this
behavior. However, Table 2 shows that the division of puzzles in difficulty
levels is similar for the separate motive groups. Consequently, a dominant
fear of failure cannot be responsible for the underestimation of difficulty level.

Table 2.   Mean judgment of difficulty level and mean solution time for each
a priori determined level of difficulty as a function of motive
group

| | | a priori determined level of difficulty | | | |
		1	2	3	4
judgment of difficulty	succes-oriented (n = 5)	1.17	1.40	2.17	3.18
	failure-oriented (n = 5)	1.00	1.33	2.83	2.92
	high on both motives (n = 5)	1.00	1.60	2.62	3.01
	low on both motives (n = 5)	1.00	1.67	2.68	3.43
solution time	succes-oriented (n = 5)	11.24	20.27	41.61	59.72
	failure-oriented (n = 5)	10.50	17.07	39.78	60.75
	high on both motives (n = 5)	10.48	17.63	47.18	62.35
	low on both motives (n = 5)	8.57	20.84	35.15	45.42

Another explanation is that subjects will only judge a puzzle to be of difficulty level 4 if they are not able to solve it. During the extensive practice period, however, subjects were acquainted with all difficulty levels and they all solved one or more puzzles from difficulty level 4. This explanation also presupposes that subjects solved most puzzles of difficulty level 4 and subsequently gave them a lower level of difficulty. As can be seen in Table 3 this is not the case. In fact 56% of the puzzles of difficulty level 4 were not solved at all.

Table 3.   Percentage of trials that ended in success or failure for each a priori determined level of difficulty

| | a priori determined level of difficulty | | | |
	1	2	3	4
success trials	99.2	93.0	67.8	43.6
failure trials	0.8	7.0	32.2	56.4

According to Heckhausen (1980) it is a common finding that subjects report subjective probabilities of success that are higher than the corresponding objective probabilities of success. This finding appears to be characteristic of achievement oriented situations. It seems to reflect the wish to increase one's performance or the belief that future performance will be better due to effort and practice. Whatever the cause of this phenomenon may be, the fact remains that there is an increase in judged level of difficulty from the a priori easiest to the most difficult puzzles.

From the results of this preliminary investigation it can be concluded that the a priori division of puzzles was to a large extent in agreement with the division the children made. In the main experiment 25 puzzles of each difficulty level were needed. In this preliminary investigation 12 puzzles of each difficulty level were actually sorted by the children. Because of the high degree of correspondence between the a priori and the children's division, the remaining 13 puzzles were sorted into difficulty levels according to the a priori criteria.

THE EXPERIMENT

The main purpose of this experiment was to study whether the preferred task difficulty of a child would change if he had to choose and solve 25 tasks consecutively. Furthermore the question was whether there would be a difference between success-oriented and failure-oriented children in task choice.

Subjects
Eighteen boys and thirty-two girls of the 5th and 6th grade of two elementary schools took part in the experiment.

Group session
In a group session a Dutch translation of the AMS (Nygård & Gjesme, 1973) was administered to determine the strength of the motive to achieve success and the strength of the motive to avoid failure.

Individual sessions
The actual experiment was performed in individual sessions of approximately one hour. During an extensive practice period (that was identical to the one in the preliminary investigation) children solved 8 puzzles of each difficulty level. For difficulty level 2 and 3 the mean solution time of the last four trials was determined. The mean of these two values was taken as the maximum time the child was allowed to work on one puzzle in the main part of the experiment. The idea behind taking this measure of the maximum time was that the children should be able to solve all puzzles of difficulty level 1, most puzzles of difficulty level 2, some puzzles of difficulty level 3 and few puzzles of difficulty level 4.

During the main part of the experiment the children were confronted with four stacks of different difficulty levels of 25 puzzles each. The experimenter sat at the same table as the child but was facing away from him in order to prevent any kind of control on his choice process. The child had to choose a puzzle and to give a verbal signal at the moment at which he began to solve it. At that moment the experimenter started a timer. As soon as the maximum time had expired the child had to stop working at the puzzle and to put it away in a box in front of him. If the child solved the puzzle before the maximum time had elapsed he said "stop" himself and put the puzzle in the box. Then he had to register on a form whether he had succeeded at solving the puzzle or not. After this the whole process was repeated until 25 puzzles were solved.

54

Results

The AMS-scores showed that girls tended to have higher scores on the motive to avoid failure than boys, 2.08 versus 1.88 ($F(1,44)=2.98$; $p<.10$), while there was no difference in scores between the two sexes for the motive to achieve success (2.69 versus 2.62). Because of this difference, in addition to an analysis on the data of all subjects combined, the data were also analysed for boys and girls separately.

Table 4.   Mean preferred difficulty level as a function of motive group and block of trials for all children

	blocks of four successive trials					
	1	2	3	4	5	6
success-oriented children (n = 13)	2.5	2.5	2.5	2.6	2.5	2.6
failure-oriented children (n = 13)	2.0	2.2	2.1	2.3	2.2	2.2
children high on both motives (n = 10)	2.5	2.4	2.6	2.5	2.6	2.5
children low on both motives (n = 11)	2.5	2.7	2.5	2.8	2.8	2.8

For each individual child the mean difficulty for each successive block of four puzzles was determined. Therefore, six data-points per child were entered into a number of trend analyses. The children were divided into four separate motive groups: success-oriented children, failure-oriented children, children high on both motives and children low on both motives.

A trend analysis by means of a MANOVA (SPSS) performed on the data of all subjects with blocks of trials and motive groups as independent variables showed a significant linear trend ($F(1,44)=4.83$; $p<.05$), indicating a shift towards more difficult tasks during the course of the experiment as was expected by hypotheses 1 and 3 (see Table 4). This significant linear trend could explain 11% of the total generalized variance. There was no significant main effect for motive group ($F(1,44)<1$), indicating that there was no difference in preferred difficulty level for the four motive groups. Neither a comparison of the linear trend between success- and failure-oriented subjects ($F(1,44)<1$), nor a comparison between subjects high and subjects low on both motives ($F(1,44)<1$) showed a significant difference.

Table 5. Mean preferred difficulty level as a function of motive group and block of trials for the girls

| | blocks of four successive trials | | | | | |
	1	2	3	4	5	6
success-oriented girls (n = 7)	2.3	2.7	2.7	2.6	2.5	2.7
failure-oriented girls (n = 7)	1.7	2.0	1.8	2.2	1.9	2.0
girls high on both motives (n = 9)	2.5	2.3	2.5	2.5	2.6	2.4
girls low on both motives (n = 7)	2.6	2.8	2.5	2.9	2.0	2.9

A separate trend analysis for girls showed the same results as the analysis for all subjects. There was a significant linear trend that explained 15% of the total variance ($F(1,27)=3.99$; $p<.05$, see Table 5), no significant main effect for motive group ($F(1,27)<1$) and no difference in linear trend for either success- versus failure-oriented girls ($F(1,27)<1$) or girls high on both motives versus girls low on both motives ($F(1,27)<1$).

A trend analysis for the boys did not show any significant effect. There was no linear trend ($F(1,14)<1$), nor a difference between motive groups ($F(1,14)<1$, see Table 6), nor a difference in linear trend for either success- versus failure-oriented boys ($F(1,14)<1$) or boys high on both motives versus boys low on both motives ($F(1,14)<1$).

Table 6.   Mean preferred difficulty level as a function of motive group and block of trials for the boys

| | blocks of four successive trials | | | | | |
	1	2	3	4	5	6
success-oriented boys (n = 6)	2.6	2.3	2.3	2.5	2.5	2.5
failure-oriented boys (n = 6)	2.2	2.5	2.4	2.5	2.6	2.4
boys high on both motives (n = 1)	2.7	3.2	3.2	2.5	2.5	3.0
boys low on both motives (n = 4)	2.3	2.4	2.5	2.6	2.5	2.6

An analysis of variance comparing the mean preferred difficulty level of the first four trials for success- and failure-oriented subjects showed that failure-oriented subjects choose significantly lower difficulty levels than success-oriented subjects ($F(1,43)=6.59$; $p<.05$) as was expected by hypotheses 2 and 4 (see Table 4). When analysed separately it appeared that failure-oriented girls chose significantly lower difficulty levels than success-oriented girls ($F(1,26)=4.67$; $p<.05$, see Table 5), but although failure-oriented boys also chose lower difficulty levels than success-oriented boys this difference was not significant ($F(1,13)=2.42$; $p>.10$, see Table 6).

To see whether there is a difference in task choice for success- and failure-oriented subjects it was studied whether success or failure on a trial has a differential effect for success- and failure-oriented subjects on the choice of difficulty level of the following trial. In this task in which subjects can choose between four levels of difficulty a transition matrix can be constructed with 16 possible combinations of two consecutive difficulty levels. These 16 combinations can be combined into three main categories: subjects can choose a trial with a lower difficulty level than the previous one (i.e. the cells in the lower triangle of the transition matrix), they can choose a trial with the same difficulty level as the previous one (i.e. the cells on the diagonal), and they can choose a trial with a higher difficulty level than the previous one (i.e. the cells in the upper triangle of the transition matrix). The total number of entries for each subject is 24.

Table 7.   Mean percentage of trials with a difficulty level higher, the same or lower than the previous one as a function of success or failure on that previous trial and success or failure orientation in the subject

		subsequent difficulty level higher	subsequent difficulty level the same	subsequent difficulty level lower
previous trial successful	failure-oriented subjects	25.6	38.9	10.0
	success-oriented subjects	27.4	31.0	4.8
previous trial a failure	failure-oriented subjects	1.9	7.7	15.9
	success-oriented subjects	1.8	8.9	19.0

Table 7 shows the mean percentages of trials falling in these three categories as a function of success or failure on the previous trial for both success- and failure-oriented subjects. A multivariate test of variance with success or failure at the previous trial and motive group as independent variables and percentages of trials falling into each category as dependent variable showed that there was a significant main effect of success or failure at the previous trial ($F(3,90)=171.2$; $p<.001$). Subsequently performed univariate tests showed that a trial with a higher difficulty level was chosen significantly more often when the previous trial had been a success than when the previous trial had been a failure ($F(1,92)=174.7$; $p<.001$). A trial with the same difficulty level also was chosen significantly more often when the previous trial had been a success than when it had been a failure ($F(1,92)=36.5$; $p<.001$). Subjects chose a trial with a lower difficulty level significantly more often when the previous trial had been a failure than when it had been a success ($F(1,92)=38.9$; $p<.001$). There was no significant main effect for motive group ($F(3,90)<1$) and no significant interaction between success and failure at the previous trial and motive group ($F(3,90)<1$) implying that the differences in mean percentages between success- and failure-oriented subjects all were not significant.

DISCUSSION

In essence the results of this experiment are in agreement with the results found by Kuhl and Blankenship (1979b). The predictions about task choice derived from the Dynamics of Action (Atkinson & Birch, 1970) are thereby confirmed in an experiment in which children took part as subjects. More specifically children who were allowed to choose their preferred difficulty level, showed a predicted shift towards more difficult tasks during the course of the experiment. In addition the difficulty level preferred by failure-oriented children at the beginning of the experiment was lower than the difficulty level preferred by success-oriented children.

The main difference between the Kuhl and Blankenship experiment and the present experiment is that in the former experiment the results are especially salient for male subjects, whereas in the latter experiment they are only significant for girls, not for boys.

There are a number of factors that may have been responsible for the relative weakness of the findings of the present experiment. In the first place there were only four difficulty levels. Because of the nature of the verbal labels children may have been limited in their choice even more. They may for example have thought along the following lines: Everyone can solve a "very easy" puzzle, only the very clever can solve a "very difficult" puzzle. However, during the practice period all children had solved puzzles of difficulty level 4, so at least three difficulty levels (2 to 4) must have remained to choose from.

In the second place the composition of the success- and failure-oriented motive groups was different because in the present experiment it was based on AMS-scores, while in the Kuhl and Blankenship experiment it was based on a comparison of TAT and TAQ scores. While scores on the AMS resulted in a differentiation into four groups in which children scoring high and children scoring low on both motives were placed in separate groups, the comparison of TAT and TAQ scores as used in the Kuhl and Blankenship experiment resulted in a division into two motive groups only, namely success- and failure-oriented individuals. In order to check whether this make-up of the motive groups was responsible for the difference in the results of the two experiments, the children were separated into a success- and a failure-oriented group based on the difference between the Ms and Mf score. If the Ms score was higher than the Mf score the child belonged to the success-oriented motive group, if the Mf score was higher than the Ms score the child belonged to the failure-oriented motive group. Subsequently the data were reanalysed. Again there was a significant linear trend for the data of all subjects combined, and for the girls, but not for the boys.

In the third place there was a difference in the instruction given to both groups of subjects. The adults were told that the experimenter wanted to get information about how people felt about a new series of tasks, that their opinions concerning the tasks was sought, and that the experimenter wanted to know whether they saw any problems regarding the tasks. This could have induced a strategy to start with easy puzzles and than gradually shift to puzzles of higher difficulty levels in order to be able to supply the information the experimenter wanted. The children, on the other hand, were only told that they could choose any difficulty level they wanted. In theory they could perform this task completely in their own way. However, because of their experience with the school system children might expect the experimenter to evaluate their performance afterwards. In this way social desirability factors may have influenced the choice process of the children.

In the fourth place there was an age difference between the subject groups of the two experiments. The behavior of children in general is more variable than adults' behavior. This variability could be reflected in a number of different strategies for task choice and result in an irregular pattern of task choices. In short, the fact that the mean of a number of patterns of task choices of different children is taken could be the cause of the difference between both experiments.

The finding of the present experiment that there is a significant increase in preferred task difficulty level during the course of the experiment is supported by the results of another experiment with a different group of children (Poulie et al. 1985). At the beginning of the school year about 200 elementary school children were asked (among other things) to solve a series of six anagram tasks which they could choose from six stacks of tasks of different difficulty levels. The same group of children performed a similar task at the end of the school year. Both for the success- and failure-oriented children a small but significant increase in preferred difficulty level was found at each occassion.

Finally the question whether success- and failure-oriented subjects differ in their pattern of task choice is addressed. In the experiment by Kuhl and Blankenship the increase in preferred level of difficulty was more pronounced for success- than for failure-oriented subjects. In the present experiment there was no significant difference between success- and failure-oriented children. However, from Tables 4, 5 and 6 it appears that throughout the experiment the failure-oriented children consistently chose somewhat lower difficulty levels than the success-oriented children.

Differences between success- and failure-oriented subjects could also be caused by a differential influence of success or failure on a previous trial on the choice of task difficulty level of the next trial. From Table 7 it appears that after a success on the previous trial subjects will either choose a trial with the same or a trial with a higher difficulty level, whereas they will choose a trial with a lower difficulty level after a failure on the previous trial. This choice pattern corresponds with the pattern found by Schneider and Posse (1982). Although not significant, Table 7 shows a differential influence of success and failure on the previous trial on the choice of difficulty level of the next trial for success- and failure-oriented subjects. When the previous trial had been a success failure-oriented subjects as opposed to success-oriented subjects more often chose a trial with a lower or the same difficulty level, whereas success-oriented subjects as opposed to failure-oriented subjects more often chose a trial with a higher difficulty level. When the previous trial had been a failure success-oriented subjects as opposed to failure-oriented subjects more often chose a trial with a lower difficulty level. Together, these results suggest that success-oriented subjects used the information which a success or failure on the previous trial supplied more realistically in their decision about the difficulty level of the next trial than failure-oriented subjects did.

ACKNOWLEDGEMENT

The authors wish to thank Mrs. Grievink and Mrs. Van Zessen who developed the puzzles and collected the data used in the research described in this article.

REFERENCES

Atkinson, J.W. (1957). Motivational determinants of risk-taking behavior. *Psychological Review, 64,* 359-372

Atkinson, J.W. (1964). *An introduction to Motivation.* New York: Van Nostrand, 1964.

Atkinson, J.W., Bastian, J.R., Earl, R.W., & Litwin, G.H. (1960). The achievement motive, goal setting and probability of preference. *Journal of Abnormal and Social Psychology, 60,* 27-36.

Atkinson, J.W., & Birch, D. (1970). *The Dynamics of Action.* New York: Wiley.

Atkinson, J.W., & Birch, D. (1974). The dynamics of achievement-oriented activity. In: J.W. Atkinson & J.O. Raynor (Eds.), *Motivation and Achievement.* Washington,D.C.: Winston & Sons.

Atkinson, J.W., & Feather, N.T. (Eds.), (1966). *A theory of achievement motivation.* New York: Wiley.

Heckhausen, H. (1977).Achievement motivation and its constructs: A cognitive model. *Motivation and Emotion, 1,* 283-330.

Heckhausen, H. (1980). *Motivation und Handeln. Lehrbuch der Motivations-psychologie.* Berlin: Springer Verlag.

Kuhl, J., & Blankenship, V. (1979a). The dynamic theory of achievement motivation: from episodic to dynamic thinking. *Psychological Review, 86,* 141-151.

Kuhl, J., & Blankenship, V. (1979b). Behavioral change in a constant environment: shift to more difficult tasks with constant probability of success. *Journal of Personality and Social Psychology, 37,* 551-563.

Mandler, G., & Sarason, S.B. (1952). A study of anxiety and learning. *Journal of Abnormal and Social Psychology, 47,* 166-173.

McClelland, D.C., Atkinson, J.W., Clark, R.A., & Lowell, E.L. (1953). *The achievement motive.* New York: Appleton-Century-Crofts.

Nygård, R., & Gjesme, T. (1973). Assessment of achievement motives: Comments and suggestions. *Scandinavian Journal of Educational Research, 17,* 39-46.

Poulie, M., Bercken, J.H.L. van den, & Jansen, I. (1985). *Motivatie in het buitengewoon en gewoon lager onderwijs.* Eindrapport SVO-projekt Tp MO 642. Nijmegen.

Raynor, J.O. (1969). Future orientation and motivation of immediate activity: An elaboration of the theory of achievement motivation. *Psychological Review, 76,* 606-610.

Schneider, K., & Posse, N. (1982). Risk taking in achievement-oriented situations: Do people really maximize affect or competence information? *Motivation and Emotion, 6,* 259-271.

COGNITIONS DURING STRESSFUL ACHIEVEMENT SITUATIONS: ANALYSIS OF FACILITATION AND LEARNED HELPLESSNESS

Joachim C. Brunstein

Justus-Liebig-University Giessen

SUMMARY

The revised model of learned helplessness assumes that deficits following uncontrollable failure are mediated by attributing aversive events to global and stable factors. Studies reported in this chapter were based on an alternative explanation. Converging in coherent processes of coping with failure, the interaction of solution-oriented, motivational, and self-directed cognitions may influence characteristic changes in performance. The experimental investigations considered both approaches. Participants were exposed to learned helplessness treatments in an achievement-related context. Debilitating and facilitating cognitions were assessed by questionnaires as well as by continuously monitoring the internal dialogue of subjects during the experiments. Results demonstrated that (a) helplessness versus facilitations of performance were linked to differences in cognitive functioning; (b) differences in performance and cognition were excellently predicted by a measure of dispositional action-control; (c) predictions of helplessness theory did not receive support.

INTRODUCTION

Exposing subjects to insoluble tasks is a characteristic of achievement-behavior research. Failure induction represents a common experimental paradigm used in a variety of partly overlapping and competing theoretical conceptions (cf. Coyne, Metalsky & Lavelle 1980). One of these research traditions, the model of learned helplessness (Abramson, Seligman & Teasdale 1978), is chosen as the theoretical focus of the following investigations.

According to this approach, exposure to failure situations is conceptualized as an encounter with uncontrollable aversive events. Learned helplessness experiments are based on the assumption that perceptions of uncontrollability are linked to a deterioration of performance and efficiency in subsequent task situations. The model specifies cognitive parameters that are proposed to mediate a transfer of helplessness from an original training to a new test situation. Seligman (1975) defined the expectation of future uncontrollability as the crucial determinant of cognitive and motivational helplessness deficits that he assumed to underlie impaired test performance. Yet, the original theory, applied to human helplessness and depression, was challenged by an increasing number of conceptual inadequacies and empirical anomalies (cf. Alloy 1982, for a discussion of different stages of helplessness theory).

To resolve these problems, Abramson et al. (1978) presented an attributional reformulation of the learned helplessness hypothesis. The revision asserts that attributions people make for lack of control influence when and where deficits will occur. Following the logic of this model and some of its refinements (Pasahow, West & Boroto 1982), it is predicted that the interaction of corresponding attributional and situational dimensions influences the generalization of helplessness deficits. Attributing lack of control to global factors should lead to a generalization across different situations (pervasiveness of deficits). Furthermore, attributing lack of control to stable causes is expected to mediate a generalization of helplessness over time (chronicity of deficits). Alternatively, helplessness will most likely generalize from an original training situation to a similar and immediate test situation, regardless of what kind of causal explanation an individual prefers for uncontrollable events. Alloy, Peterson, Abramson, and Seligman (1984) reported results consistent with predictions of this model.

Dweck's research (cf. Dweck & Licht 1980) has focused on learned helplessness in the context of academic achievement situations. She investigated characteristic differences in responses to uncontrollable failure events in helpless versus mastery-oriented children. Dweck's initial work (Dweck 1975; Dweck & Reppuci 1973) demonstrated that helpless children preferred to attribute failure to stable causes, such as lack of ability, indicating their belief in the uncontrollability of outcomes and in the recurrence of new, inevitable failures. In contrast, mastery-oriented children tended to attribute failures to variable factors, such as effort. They accepted responsibility for outcomes and maintained their sense of personal control. Dweck assumed that these children show an increased motivation to rectify previous failure experience. Moreover, Diener & Dweck (1978) demonstrated that helpless and mastery-oriented children did not differ just in attributions but also in a variety of achievement-related cognitions while they worked on their tasks. Their findings indicated that helplessness (i.e., performance decrements following failure) were linked to intensive search for causal explanations, negative affective responses, and task-irrelevant cognitions. In contrast, mastery-oriented children were characterized by solution-oriented thinking.

Consistent with these findings, the model of learned helplessness has been challenged by alternative theoretical conceptions in the domain of achievement behavior. These models converge at two points. First, they refer to similar experimental manipulations, that is, they employ failure induction techniques to empirical studies. Second, they explain impaired performance following failure by self-focused attention and cognitive interference. Lavelle, Metalsky, and Coyne (1979) as well as Coyne, Metalsky, and Lavelle (1980) linked Wine's (1971, 1980) cognitive-attentional theory of test anxiety to learned helplessness. They demonstrated that only high test-anxious subjects became debilitated following helplessness induction. Moreover, they found that an imagination exercise that was expected to dissolve worry cognitions by attentional redeployment eliminated deficits following a helplessness treatment. They concluded that cognitive-attentional distraction associated with high test anxiety is the main determinant of impaired performance in helplessness experiments.

Carver (1979) considered theoretical implications of his cybernetic model of self-attention for learned helplessness research. He assumed that helplessness reactions represent a mental dissociation from task attempts. This cognitive withdrawal was proposed to mediate poor performance in helplessness studies. Carver, Blaney, and Scheier (1979) demonstrated the moderating function of self-focused attention in the expectancy - performance link of learned helplessness.

Kuhl (1981, 1984) presented a three-factor model of learned helplessness. On the basis of expectancy-value models and dynamic conceptions of human motivation (Atkinson 1964; Atkinson & Birch 1970, 1974), Kuhl specified volitional processes that intervene between intention and performance. He proposed that generalizations of helplessness are mediated by deficient action-control (action factor), even if expectancies of success and control (expectancy factor) and motivation regarding new tasks (value factor) are not reduced. Kuhl described two modes of action-control. Action orientation is defined by "cognitive activities focusing on action alternatives and plans that serve to overcome a discrepancy between a present state and an intended future one" (Kuhl 1981, p. 159). In contrast, failure-related state orientation is defined by ruminating cognitions focusing on a state created by an unpleasant outcome. State-oriented individuals are characterized by a deficit to protect goal-directed intentions against interfering task-irrelevant cognitions. Kuhl (1981) demonstrated that dispositional and experimentally induced state orientation mediate a transfer of performance decrements following failure inductions. He concluded that functional deficits, rather than reduced motivation, produce symptoms of learned helplessness. Kuhl's distinction between action and state orientation was adopted in the following studies of cognitive functioning in learned helplessness situations.

PERFORMANCE AND COGNITION IN TWO LEARNED HELPLESSNESS EXPERIMENTS: A SUMMARY OF EMPIRICAL FINDINGS

In a previous study (Brunstein & Olbrich 1985), cognitive concomitants of performance changes in success and failure situations were investigated. Participants were 32 students who were divided at the median of Kuhl's (1984) Action-Control-Scale. This is a questionnaire assessing individual responses following unpleasant outcomes. Scale scores indicate to what extent a person (a) focuses on self-evaluative aspects of a state created by an aversive event (state orientation), or (b) attempts to initiate an action aiming at a change of this state (action orientation). Kuhl (1984) reported on reliability and validity measures of this instrument.

Subjects were asked to solve 12 four-dimensional discrimination tasks (cf. Levine 1966, 1971); these tasks are frequently used in helplessness experiments. The tasks were arranged in three series of four problems each. The initial period was a mixed phase of alternating success and failure outcomes. It was followed by a failure phase of four extended failure inductions. The final period was arranged as a success phase. Each student received an ego-involving achievement induction. Moreover, participants were instructed to "think out loud", that is, to verbalize everything that would become salient to them during task attempts.

We measured three kinds of dependent variables. First, an evaluation of performance levels was derived from the path of solution hypotheses that subjects developed and stated while they worked on a task. Second, verbalizations of participants were recorded on tape and classified by two independent raters along a system of cognition categories. Third, causal explanations for success and failure outcomes as well as perceived probabilities of future success were assessed after each task. Furthermore, several rating scales were administered after each task period; these ratings referred to self-assessments of helplessness, competence, tension, hostility, and control over outcomes.

We assumed that the improvement versus deterioration of performance following failure would be associated with typical patterns of cognitions. Thus, we tried to explore the quality and timing of specific achievement cognitions and intended to study their relationship to measures of efficiency. Moreover, dispositional action-control was expected to predict discrepancies in performance and cognition, especially during a period of extended failure inductions.

The results showed that action-oriented and state-oriented subjects differed significantly in levels and changes of performance during the experiment. Whereas action-oriented participants maintained a high level of efficiency even in failure tasks and showed a continuous improvement of performance from the initial tot the final period, solution-strategies of state-oriented individuals collapsed following failure trials. Moreover, the performance level of state-oriented subjects was not raised between the initial and the final periods; this indicates helplessness and a disruption of learning.

The analysis of verbalization protocols revealed corresponding differences in action-oriented and state-oriented subjects' cognitions during failure induction tasks. Action orientation was associated with a predominance of success-related thinking. Verbalizations of efficient solution strategies, self-motivating instructions, and self-confidence in personal resources prevailed in this group. In contrast, state-oriented subjects were characterized by loss of ability cognitions, negative affects towards tasks, and unsystematic trial-and-error behavior. Furthermore, typical differences between the two groups were revealed in the development of specific cognition types over the course of the experiment. The action-oriented group responded on initial failure trials with an increase of goal-directed self-instructions. During extended failure inductions, these participants intensified their search for more efficient strategies and verbalized an increasing number of statements indicating self-competence and a strong sense of personal mastery abilities. In contrast, state-oriented subjects lapsed into inefficient solution procedures quite early. They abandoned efficient strategic plans during the failure phase of the experiment; instead, loss of ability cognitions and negative affective responses increased.

No significant group differences were found for attribution ratings and perceived success probabilities. Yet, only state-oriented students reported an increase in the perception of helplessness and a corresponding decrease of control over outcomes during the failure induction phase. In contrast, action-oriented subjects indicated a significant gain of competence during experimental experience.

These results demonstrated that action-oriented versus state-oriented individuals differed markedly in performance changes and cognitions following failure experience. Whereas action-oriented subjects focused on rectifying failures, state-oriented participants directed attention to self-evaluative aspects of the present unpleasant outcomes. Groups did not differ in expectations and attributions. In fact, 50 percent of the action-oriented group did not verbalize any attribution-related statement while performing the tasks. It can be assumed that these subjects employed an a-priori theory of causation (cf. Nisbett & Wilson 1977), when they were asked for attributions of success and failure after each task.

The findings of this study resulted in two new questions. First, it was assumed that impaired cognitive functioning rather than motivational deficits underlies learned helplessness. Thus, the question was raised as to whether generalizations of helplessness are mediated by a self-perpetuation or re-initiation of state-oriented cognitions. Second, it was proposed to analyze the influence of helplessness attributions upon a recurrence of dysfunctional cognitions during a new task situation.

These questions were addressed to a new investigation.[1] In this learned helplessness experiment, the influence of uncontrollable failure on performance and cognition was analysed during a test period. Two different approaches were considered. First, hypotheses of the attribution model of learned helplessness were tested. For this purpose, attributional preferences of participants were measured, and time and similarity between training and test administrations were manipulated. According to the reformulation, stability and globality of attributional style for negative events operate as risk factors for generalizations of helplessness. Subjects with a stable attributional style should show deficts in a delayed test; in parallel, people who exhibit a style of attributing negative events to global causes will show deficts in test situations that are dissimilar to the original training situation. A second approach focused on the distinction between action and state orientation. In Brunstein and Olbrich's study (1985), dispositional state-orientation was associated with a high degree of susceptibility to helplessness experience. It was proposed that generalizations of helplessness should be linked to the performance-interfering effect of self-perpetuating

---

[1]   This study is based on a doctoral dissertation of the author. Preliminary results are reported here. A detailed description is in preparation (Brunstein, Note 1). The author wishes to thank Thomas Kalms, Heiner Muser, Renate Steding, and Rainer Winterboer for assistance in conducting the research.

state-oriented cognitions. These cognitions are aroused during helplessness inductions and they are reinforced when subjects encounter new problem solving difficulties during a test situation. Thus, only state-oriented subjects were expected to show performance decrements during test tasks. Action-orientation, in contrast, was assumed to immunize people against helplessness experience. On the contrary, action-oriented subjects should process failure feedbacks as a challenge to increase effort expenditure, to improve efficiency, and to reestablish control in a new task situation. Thus, it was proposed that action-orientation should be associated with a facilitation of performance following helplessness training.

Participants were 100 introductory psychology students. Subjects completed a slight modification of Kuhl's Action-Control-Scale and a questionnaire of attributional preferences one week prior to participation in the experiment. Consistent with the original Attributional Style Questionnaire (Peterson et al. 1982), an instrument was employed characterized by eight positive and eight negative events in the context of academic and social competence. Subjects were asked to generate their own major cause for each event and then to rate the causes along three 7-point scales corresponding to internality, stability, and globality dimensions. Brunstein (Note 2) described the instrument in detail and reported results of reliability and validity measures.

Table 1. Design

N = 100 Questionnaires:	Action Control, Attributional Style				
	Random Assignment to Treatments				
	1	2	3	4	5
Training Period:	Discrimination learning - Phase 1 (mixed) - Phase 2 (failure)				
Treatment:	T^0/S n=20	TΔ/DS n=18	T^0/S n=21	TΔ/DS n=21	Control n=20
Test period:	Problem solving tasks				

Note. T^0 = immediate test,   TΔ = delayed test
    S = similar test,   DS = dissimilar test.

The design of the study is demonstrated in Table 1. Subjects were randomly assigned to one of the five treatment conditions. Four pretreatment groups were exposed to a training period. Again, training tasks required the solution of eight discrimination problems. An initial phase of mixed failure and success outcomes was followed by a phase of four succeeding failure inductions. Measurements of performance and cognitions followed the same procedure as in Brunstein and Olbrichs's (1985) experiment. Participants were instructed to 'think out loud' and to verbalize presentations of test tasks varied on two dimensions in a 2 (time) by 2 (similarity) factorial design. First, participants were tested either immediately after pretreatment (immediate test = T^0) or after a delay of 24 hours (delayed test = $T\Delta$); second at the onset of the test period, subjects were instructed that training and test performance measured either the same (similar test = S) or substantially different intellectual abilities (dissimilar test = DS). Manipulation checks guaranteed the efficiency of similarity instructions both, before and after tasks. A control group (C) received no pretreatment prior to test administrations.

Test tasks required the solution of three logical transformation problems adopted from Putz-Osterloh (1974) and presented in the context of a pollution control game. Each task was defined by three components: (a) an initial object A characterized by a specific combination of features, (b) a desired goal-object B characterized by a different combination of features, and (c) by a set of operators Q. Subjects were asked to find out a sequence of operations leading to a successful transformation. Participants had to consider application rules for operators, undesired side-effects of operations, and the development of subgoals in planning efficient solution programs. Dörner (1976) and Newell and Simon (1972, p. 405) described the logical structure of such tasks.

Test performance was measured on 8-point scales according to difference scores between the number of operators a subject employed to a transformation task and the minimum number of operations necessary to produce a desired change (*Additional Operations:* 0 = 'perfectly solved', 7 = 'unsolved'). Moreover, achievement cognitions during test tasks were assessed by a questionnaire administered immediately after the test period. This instrument consisted of 11 cognition categories; for each category, success versus failure related cognitions were distinguished. Table 2 presents running heads of questionnaire items. Subjects were provided with a full description of each cognition type; they were asked to rate each item on two 5-point scales according to frequency and perceived influence on performance. Questionnaire items were subsumed under two scales: (a) a scale of success-related cognitions (Co-S), and (b) a scale of failure-related cognitions (Co-F).

Table 2. Cognition Questionnaire

Success-Related Cognitions	Failure-Related Cognitions
Need for Achievement	Abandonment of Standards
Self-Instructions	Loss of Ability
Anticipating Success	Anticipating Failure
Pleasure as to Activity	Displeasure as to Activity
Positive Self-Evaluation	Negative Self-Evaluation
Confidence in Abilities	Doubts about Abilities
Internal Locus of Control	External Locus of Control
Increasing Competence	Decreasing Competence
Self-Forgetfulness	Task Irrelevancies
Relaxation	Nervousness
Low Task Difficulty	High Task Difficulty

The results of the experiment are as follows. Hypotheses of helplessness theory did not receive support. Neither stability nor globality dimensions for negative events explained differences inperformance levels during test conditions. In one analysis, subjects were divided in 'high risk' versus 'low risk' generalizers, according to the median of composite stability and globality scores. Figure 1 demonstrates the results. In sum, neither dimensions of attributional style nor experimental treatments or interactions had a significant influence on performance of subjects in this study.

In contrast, predictions derived from an action-control model of helplessness were confirmed. First, findings of Brunstein and Olbrich's study (1985) were replicated. Only a few action-oriented subjects, but a significantly greater number of state-oriented participants showed a deterioration of performance from the initial (mixed) phase to the final (failure) phase of the training period. Moreover, self-instructions to improve efficiency and verbalizations of high self-competence prevailed in the action-oriented group, whereas statements indicating loss of ability, abandonment of achievement goals, negative self-evaluations, and inefficient solution procedures were characteristic for state-oriented subjects. In summary, differences in performance of action-oriented and state-oriented subjects were associated with typical motivational, self-directed, and solution-oriented responses on failure experience. Secondly, the two groups showed different transfer effects during the test period.

73

Figure 1. Task performance of high risk and low risk generalizers: Average number of additional operations in three test tasks.

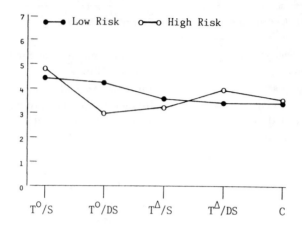

Note. Performance was measured by difference scores (0 = perfectly solved
to 7 = unsolved). Thus, the higher the score, the poorer the performance.
Test conditions: as indicated in Table 1.

Figure 2. Task performance of action-oriented (AO) and state-oriented
(SO) groups: Average number of additional operations.

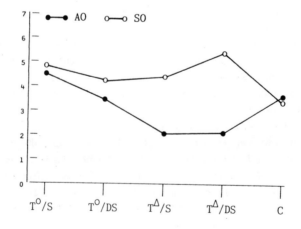

Figure 2 demonstrates results of performance measures. Group comparisons indicated a higher level of performance for action-oriented subjects. Differences between groups were especially pronounced in delayed test conditions. Whereas state-oriented subjects' debilitation remained chronic, the action-oriented group showed a facilitation of performance. In contrast, the two groups did not differ in baseline measures of performance during the control condition. In a task by task analysis, significant group differences were obtained only for the second and the third problem.

Figure 3. Predominance of success versus failure orientation in action-oriented (AO) versus state-oriented (SO) groups during immediate test (T^0) and delayed ($T\Delta$) conditions

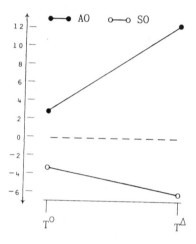

Note. Predominance was measured by difference scores between frequency ratings of success-related and failure-related questionnaire items. Scores greater than 0 indicate a predominance of success-related cognitions, scores less than 0 a predominance of failure-related cognitions.

Analysis of achievement cognitions demonstrated corresponding results. Figure 3 illustrates predominance of success versus failure orientation in action-oriented and state-oriented groups during immediate and delayed test conditions. Similarity instructions had no influence on frequency ratings. Data of cognitions scales (Co-S, Co-F) were subjected to multivariate as well as univariate analyses of variance. These tests revealed that success-related thinking prevailed in the action-oriented group, whereas state-oriented participants reported higher frequencies of failure-related cognitions. Moreover, a facilitation of performance in the action-oriented group was associated with a significant decline of negative, failure-related cognitions during the delayed test. Groups differed quite markedly in self-assessments of intellectual abilities, in expectations of success and failure, in self-evaluations, and in pleasure versus displeasure while performing the tasks. Consistent with training results, loss of ability and abandonment of standards were further typical cognitive concomitants of helplessness in the state-oriented group. In contrast, action-oriented participants indicated an increase of mastery abilities and competence during the experiment.

Finally, perceived influence of success-related versus failure-related cognitions on performance and efficiency were analysed. First of all, the debilitating effect of failure cognitions and the facilitating influence of success cognitions were intensified when reported frequencies of these cognitions increased. Yet, for influences of success-related cognitions, an additional effect for dispositional action-control was found. Even positive, success-related cognitions lose efficiency when they are embedded in a state-oriented processing style.

CONCLUSIONS AND COMMENTS

The results of these studies demonstrated that differences in performance levels and changes in failure induction and learned helplessness experiments were systematically linked to specific differences in the nature and pattern of achievement-related cognitions. Moreover, dispositional action versus state orientation was an excellent predictor of performance and cognitions in both investigations. In contrast, hypotheses of the reformulated model of learned helplessness did not receive support. Attributions did not predict performance following uncontrollable aversive outcomes, even when a measure of explanatory style dimensions was employed (cf. Alloy 1982). Pasahow (1980), Tennen, Gillen, and Drum (1982), and Tennen, Drum, Gillen, and Stanton (1982) reported similar failures to confirm the attribution model. These investigators used situation-specific measures of helplessness attributions. Thus, Wortman and Dintzer's (1978) critique has to be reconsidered as to whether the reformulated model was based on an oversimplification of the attribution - performance link.

A major shortcoming of learned helplessness research is that with a few exceptions (cf. Diener & Dweck 1978), there has been no careful analysis of the training behavior of subjects. The presented studies demonstrated significant interindividual differences in performance and in cognitive concomitants of coping with failure during helplessness induction periods. The influence of dispositional state and action orientation may be specified in terms of different degrees of susceptibility-to versus self-immunization-against helplessness experience. Provided that subjects encounter a moderate amount of failure outcomes, these dispositions are expressed in intergroup differentiations of performance and cognition and in specific intragroup courses of change. Self-immunization in action-oriented groups was characterized by subjects' success orientation in the face of failure situations. This discrepancy was expressed in self-instructions referring to an improvement of efficiency and in self-confidence in intellectual abilities and personal resources. An orientation towards future success helped action-oriented subjects to focus on a search for more efficient strategies. This constellation of cognitions underlay a continuous improvement of performance. In contrast, state orientation was characterized by the consistency of failure-oriented thinking and negative performance outcomes. Subjects were preoccupied with cognitions indicating self-concern, abandonment of goals, and self-deprecating appraisals while they worked on tasks which required the development of efficient problem solving. State orientation was associated with a shift of subjects' attentional focus from adequate solution-oriented processes to dysfunctional postactional evaluations. This interference resulted in impaired cognitive functioning and was linked to a deterioration of performance and a disruption of learning.

These results demonstrate that action-oriented and state-oriented subjects showed clear differences in efficiency and cognitive activity after leaving the training period of a helplessness experiment. Thus, different kinds of transfer effects have to be considered when these two groups enter the test period.

The discrepancy between action-oriented participants' striving for success and failure feedbacks during helplessness training should be conceptualized as a source of increased motivation to reengage in new achievement episodes, especially when evaluations of personal competence are optimistic. This assumption is consistent with two basic principles in the dynamic model of Atkinson and Birch (1970, 1974): (a) an action-tendency, once aroused, tends to persist over time, and (b) the motivation to succeed accumulates if previous attempts to solve a task have failed. Learned helplessness experiments provide action-oriented subjects with an opportunity to rectify preceding failures, and to experience success which is consistent with motivational tendencies and with positive self-conceptions. Action-oriented individuals perceive a new task situation as a challenge and respond with an increase of efficiency. It is proposed here that these motivational and evaluative processes account for the facilitation effects that have been reported in many learned helplessness experiments (e.g., Roth & Kubal 1975). Abramson, Seligman, and Teasdale's (1978) reformulation disregarded these empirical anomalies; the model did not present an explanation of improved performance following uncontrollable failure (see, Kuhl 1984, and Dweck & Wortman 1982, for related arguments to integrate achievement motivation models in learned helplessness research). The empirical findings revealed a facilitation of performance only in the delayed test condition. This indicates that an immediate test may interfere with posttraining evaluations, even in the group of action-oriented subjects. These individuals profit from a delay between failure induction and test periods; training -related cognitions have a chance to dissolve, appraisals result in a new action-orientation, and motivation to engage in substitute achievement activity is increased. Nevertheless, a comparison with control subjects demonstrated that even in the immediate test condition, action-oriented participants did not show a deterioration of performance.

In contrast, it was demonstrated that state-oriented subjects were especially vulnerable to the development and transfer of helplessness. Moreover, helplessness during training and test periods was linked to similar patterns of cognitions underlying performance decrements. Nevertheless, both situations differ in an important characteristic. Whereas helplessness during training depends on an intensive and extensive induction of uncontrollable failures, a far lower problem solving barrier is sufficient to revive helplessness during the test period. Helplessness training provides state-oriented subjects with a prototypical failure experience which results in a decline of future helplessness thresholds. The studies demonstrated that a generalization of helplessness was associated with a reinitiation of state-oriented cognitions instigated during the training period. Provided that subjects are challenged to develop new solution programs while working on test tasks, state-oriented individuals will tend to appraise the emergence of new complications as a replication of their preceding training experience. Subsequently, even surmountable tasks are perceived as a threat of new, inevitable failures. Typical cognitive concomitants of helplessness are reactivated and reinforced in a self-perpetuating vicious circle of failure orientation and negative outcomes. If a test is administered immediately after pretraining, a generalization is mediated by state-oriented subjects' rumination on self-deprecatory training evaluations. Moreover, state-oriented participants showed performance decrements, even if a delayed test was administered. On the basis of results of a task by task analysis, it is suggested that the initial problem indicated new solution barriers and risks of failure which triggered a reinitiation of discrepancies in helplessness and mastery-orientation. This conclusion is consistent with a finding reported in Pasahow's (1980) study; a transfer of helplessness depended on the difficulty of the first test task. Thus, learned helplessness research should consider the interaction of task characteristics and transfer effects more carefully.

Similarity instructions did not influence performance and cognitions of action-oriented and state-oriented subjects. This finding is consistent with Kuhl's (1981) assumption that effects of increased substitutional motivation and of perseverating state-orientation may generalize to any task that serves the same goal as the one aspired during preceding failure situations. Moreover, Kuhl speculated that excessive state-orientation following academic failure should impair efficient cognitive functioning in subsequent situations, even if they are not related to an achievement-goal.

Given an extreme disposition towards state orientation, preceding failure inductions might not even be necessary to demonstrate learned helplessness. A new task may spontaneously be interpreted in terms of personal failure experiences. In fact, state-oriented subjects frequently remembered earlier failure-related achievement episodes during helplessness inductions. This is an argument for an intensive exchange of ideas between learned helplessness and mood and memory research (Bower 1981; Teasdale 1983). Finally, these data and conclusions should instigate new research on the learned helplessness model of depression.

REFERENCE NOTES

(1) Brunstein, J.C. *Learned helplessness in achievement situations.* Manuscript in preparation. Justus-Liebig-University, Giessen, FRG, 1985.
(2) Brunstein, J.C. *Attributionsstil und Depression: Erste Befunde zur Reliabilitat und Validitat eines deutschsprachigen Attributionsstil-Fragebogens.* Manuscript submitted for publication. Justus-Liebig-University, Giessen, FRG, 1985.

REFERENCES

Abramson, L.Y., Seligman, M.E.P., & Teasdale, J.D. (1978). Learned helplessness in humans: Critique and reformulation. *Journal of Abnormal Psychology, 87,* 49-74.

Alloy, L.B. (1982). The role of perceptions and attributions for response-outcome noncontingency in learned helplessness: A commentary and discussion. *Journal of Personality, 50,* 443-479.

Alloy, L.B., Peterson, C., Abramson, L.Y., & Seligman, M.E.P. (1984). Attributional style and the personality of learned helplessness. *Journal of Personality and Social Psychology, 46,* 681-687.

Atkinson, J.W. (1964). *An introduction to motivation.* Princeton, N.J.: Van Nostrand.

Atkinson, J.W., & Birch, D. (1970). *The dynamics of action.* New York: Wiley.

Atkinson, J.W., & Birch, D. (1974). The dynamics of achievement-oriented activity. In J.W. Atkinson & J.O. Raynor (Eds.), *Motivation and achievement* (pp. 271-325). Washington, D.C.: Winston.

Bower, G.H. (1981). Mood and memory. *American Psychologist, 36,* 129-148.

Brunstein, J.C., & Olbrich, E. (1985). Personal helplessness and action-control: Analysis of achievement-related cognitions, self-assessments, and performance. *Journal of Personality and Social Psychology, 48,* 1540-1551.

Carver, C.S. (1979). A cybernetic model of self-attention processes. *Journal of Personality and Social Psychology, 37,* 1251-1281.

Carver, C.S., Blaney, P.H., & Scheier, M.F. (1979). Reassertion and giving up: The interactive role of self-directed attention and outcome expectancy. *Journal of Personality and Social Psychology, 37,* 1859-1870.

Coyne, J.C., Metalsky, G.I., & Lavelle, T.L. (1980). Learned helplessness as experimenter-induced failure and its alleviation with attentional redeployment. *Journal of Abnormal Psychology, 89,* 350-357.

Diener, C.I., & Dweck, C.S. (1978). An analysis of learned helplessness: Continuous changes in performance, strategy, and achievement cognitions following failure. *Journal of Personality and Social Psychology, 36,* 451-462.

Dörner, D. (1976). *Problemlosen als Informationsverarbeitung.* Stuttgart: Kohlhammer.

Dweck, C.S. (1975). The role of expectations and attributions in the alleviation of learned helplessness. *Journal of Personality and Social Psychology, 31,* 674-685.

Dweck, C.S., & Licht, B.G. (1980). Learned helplessness and intellectual achievement. In J. Garber & M.E.P. Seligman (Eds.), *Human helplessness: Theory and applications* (pp. 197-221). New York: Academic Press.

Dweck, C.S., & Reppucci, N.D. (1973). Learned helplessness and reinforcement responsibility in children. *Journal of Personality and Social Psychology, 25,* 109-116.

Dweck, C.S., & Wortman, C.B. (1982). Learned helplessness, anxiety, and achievement motivation: Neglected parallels in cognitive, affective, and coping responses. In H. Krohne & L. Laux (Eds.), *Achievement, stress, and anxiety* (pp. 93-125). Washington, DC: Hemisphere.

Heckhausen, H. (1963). *Hoffnung und Furcht in der Leistungsmotivation.* Meisenheim: Hain.

Heckhausen, H. (1982). Task-irrelevant cognitions during an exam: Incidence and effects. In H. Krohne & L. Laux (Eds.), *Achievement, stress, and anxiety* (pp. 247-274). Washington, DC; Hemisphere.

Kuhl, J. (1981). Motivational and functional helplessness: The moderating effect of state versus action orientation. *Journal of Personality and Social Psychology, 40,* 155-171.

Kuhl, J. (1984). Volitional aspects of achievement motivation and learned helplessness: Toward a comprehensive theory of action control. In B.A. Maher (Ed.), *Progress in experimental personality research* (Vol.13, pp. 99-171). New York: Academic Press.

Lavelle, T.L., Metalsky, G.I., & Coyne, J.C. (1979). Learned helplessness, test anxiety, and acknowledgement of contingencies. *Journal of Abnormal Psychology, 88,* 381-387.

Levine, M. (1966). Hypothesis behavior by humans during discrimination learning. *Journal of Experimental Psychology, 71,* 331-338.

Levine, M. (1971). Hypothesis theory and nonlearning despite ideal S-R reinforcement contingencies. *Psychological Review, 78,* 130-140.

Newell, A., & Simon, H.A. (1972). *Human problem solving.* Englewood Cliffs, N.J.: Prentice Hall.

Nisbett, R.E., & Wilson, T.D. (1977). Telling more than we can know: Verbal reports on mental processes. *Psychological Review, 84,* 231-259.

Pasahow, R.J. (1980). The relation between an attributional dimension and learned helplessness. *Journal of Abnormal Psychology, 89,* 358-367.

Pasahow, R.J., West, S.G., & Boroto, D.R. (1982). Predicting when uncontrollability will produce performance deficits: A refinement of the reformulated learned helplessness hypothesis. *Psychological Review, 89,* 595-598.

Peterson, C., Semmel, A., Baeyer, C.v., Abramson, L.Y., Metalsky, G.I., & Seligman, M.E.P. (1982). The attributional style questionnaire. *Cognitive Therapy and Research, 6,* 287-300.

Putz-Osterloh, W. (1974). Über die Effektivität von Problemlösetrainung. *Zeitschrift fur Psychologie, 182,* 253-276.

Roth, S., & Kubal, L. (1975). Effects of noncontingent reinforcement of tasks of differing importance: Facilitation and learned helplessness. *Journal of Personality and Social Psychology, 32,* 680-691.

Seligman, M.E.P. (1975). *Helplessness: On depression, development, and death.* San Francisco: Freeman.

Teasdale, J.D. (1983). Negative thinking in depression: Cause, effect, or reciprocal relationship? *Advances in Behavior Research and Therapy, 5,* 3-25.

Tennen, H., Gillen, R., & Drum, P.E. (1982). The debilitating effect of exposure to noncontingent escape: A test of the learned helplessness model. *Journal of Personality, 50,* 409-425.

Tennen, H., Drum, P.E., Gillen, R., & Stanton, A. (1982). Learned helplessness and the detection of contingency: A direct test. *Journal of Personality, 50,* 426-442.

Wine, J. (1971). Test anxiety and direction of attention. *Psychological Bulletin, 76,* 92-104.

Wine, J. (1980). Cognitive-attentional theory of test anxiety. In I.G. Sarason (Ed.), *Test anxiety: Theory, research, and applications* (pp. 349-385). Hillsdale, N.J.: Erlbaum.

Wortman, C.B., & Dintzer, L. (1978). Is an attributional analysis of the learned helplessness phenomenon viable?: A critique of the Abramson-Seligman-Teasdale reformulation. *Journal of Abnormal Psychology, 87,* 75-90.

THE VALIDITY OF MOTIVE MEASUREMENT:
A THEORETICAL ANALYSIS AND AN EMPIRICAL STUDY
OF THE EFFECTS OF TEST- AND SELF-CONSCIOUSNESS

Julius Kuhl
Lothar Stahl

Max-Planck-Institut für Psychologische Forschung Munich

SUMMARY

This paper has two aims. First, a theoretical analysis of the motivational processes mediating motive-test behavior is given. Second, the results of an empirical study are reported which was designed to investigate two psychological conditions that may affect the validity of questionnaire scores, namely the degree to which subjects are aware what personality attribute is to be assessed by the questionnaire ("test-consciousness") and the degree to which subjects attention is focused on some aspects of the self rather than on the external situation ("self-consciousness").

THEORETICAL ANALYSIS OF MOTIVE MEASUREMENT

The original theory of achievement motivation (Atkinson 1957) comprised only two independent parameters - success-orientation (M) and failure-orientation (M), that is the two tendencies that enter into the achievement motive, and the subjective probability of success (P). The measurement methods elaborated subsequently, concentrated on these two parameters.

Unfortunately the problems arising from methods of measurement are too often separated from the theory-building process. This is made evident by the emergence of a separate discipline in psychology-test theory and test construction (Lienert 1961; Fischer 1974). Moreover, test constructors and test users are rarely identical.

83

This separation did not take place in achievement motivation research, however. McClelland and his coworkers recognized early on that questions related to measurement theory and measurement methods cannot be dissociated from those posed by motivation theory. An instrument developed to measure motives must be based on the theory relating to the motivational process involved in test behavior. Theory development, by the same token, is decisively affected by the development of testing procedures. True, a test can but roughly approximate the theoretical content of a psychological construct. Yet as motivation research produces new knowledge test revisions are likely to emerge. Nonetheless, this necessity is too often disregarded. Established tests seem to disconnect themselves from the general process of theory construction as if it was perfectly clear how the construct could be described and assessed, and all that remained was to specify what the new construct could explain and predict. In view of the close correspondence between measurement theory and methods on the one side and motivation theory on the other, we will discuss the problems arising in the measurement of motivational parameters in some detail. Subsequently, we will present one specific study in which various aspects of the test situation in conjunction with the measurement of the achievement motive were investigated.

The research program developed by McClelland during the late forties with the intention of finding a measure system. This technique makes it possible to extract the achievement-related content from fantasy stories that subjects are asked to make up about various pictures presented to them. Typically the picture material is ambiguous in order to minimize the impact of firmly established habits on the fantasies produced through the pictures. The more unusual the situation that is presented, the less likely is it that learned habits rather than actual motives will determine the content of the fantasy stories (McClelland 1951; McClelland et al. 1953).

In McClelland's scoring key, success-oriented and failure-oriented ways of dealing with achievement goals. It soon became evident that such a distinction was, however, necessary as it was shown that the validity of motive scores differed for different terciles of the frequency distribution - a result also reported in a more recent investigation (Sorrentino & Short 1977). These results prompted Heckhausen (1963) to develop a separate scoring key for fear of failure. The two parameters for hope for success (HS) and fear of failure (FF) were now to be determined by the number of HS and FF categories found in the stories subjects made up about 6 pictures. According to Heckhausen's (1963) scoring system, 'global motivation' (GM) was defined as the sum of both motive components (GM=HS+FF), while the difference between the two components was defined as 'net hope' (NH=HS-F). The correlation between the HS scores and the n Ach scores came to .60 and .73 in one investigation while only low correlations were found between n Ach and NH (Heckhausen 1963, p. 74).

Construct Validity

In constructing the TAT-procedure the primary focus was on the explanatory value of the construct to be assessed, rather than on the technical aspects connected to the degree of precision needed. Later developments actually revealed that it paid off to leave some of the psychometric details related to internal consistency of the test for future research. We will therefore first discuss the evidence in support of the validity, thereafter the evidence relating to the objectivity and reliability of motive measurement.

Projective Procedures

Three behavioral parameters were related to motive parameters: Persistence, risk-taking (level of aspiration and preferred task difficulty), and performance. These behavioral criteria were not selected at random but evolved from the components of the motive construct, as they have been discussed by McClelland (1951) for instance. On these terms a motive differs from other personality variables (habits, traits) in that it drives, directs, and selects behavior. Persistence is taken to express the drive function of the motive, while level of aspiration and risk-taking should be affected by the directing function of the motive. The selective function of the motive should be crystallized in performance scores since the quality of performance can be conceived of as resulting from the successive selecting out of successful responses (see McClelland 1980). Atkinson and Litwin (1960) have described an experiment which demonstrated the relationship between these three behavioral measures with the TAT motive parameters. The subjects were divided into four groups according to the medians of the n Ach and the TAQ scores. The next step was to find out how many subjects in each group preferred intermediate risks in a ring-toss game, how many subjects showed above-average persistence in a written final test and how many obtained above-average grades in the test. As Table 1 shows, subjects with high versus low n Ach averaging across high and low anxiety groups, revealed high divergence in all behavioral measures: Subjects with high achievement orientation more frequently preferred intermediately difficult levels and showed higher persistence and higher performance in the final test.

Table 1: Three parameters of achievement-oriented behavior measured within the same sample of male college students (after Atkinson & Litwin 1960)

need achieve- ment	test anxiety	n	preference of intermediate difficulty levels	High persist- ence in test	High perform- ance in test
High	Low	13	77%	73%	67%
High	High	10	40	40	60
Low	Low	9	44	43	43
Low	High	13	31	25	25

The three relative frequencies are highest for subjects with
above-average motive strength and low test anxiety, and lowest for subjects
with high test anxiety and low motive strength. The findings were similar in
an investigation by French and Thomas (1958). Persons with a difficulty levels and made better use of the time allotted than persons with a low n Ach
score. A higher preference for intermediate difficulty levels was also demonstrated in five-year-old children having a strong achievement motive (McClelland 1958).

The relationship between motive strength and performance presents particular problems for the construct validation of motive. Obviously there
should be a relationship between the achievement motive and the behavioral
outcome that the definition of the motive implicates. Early studies revealed
significant performance differences between high- and low-motive groups at
the complex tasks, not so much in the initial performance, but rather in the
slope of the learning curve. These differences appeared on the initial task,
however, at simple, overlearned arithmetic tasks (Lowell 1952). In an extra-
ordinarily sharp and polemic critique of the TAT-method of motive measurement, Entwisle (1972) pointed out that the TAT-measure often shows little or
no correlation with school performance while questionnaire measures have
been successfully validated precisely on the basis of school performance.

It must first be acknowledged that positive relationships between projective motive measures and school performance were indeed found (e.g., Heckhausen 1963; McClelland et al. 1953; Meyer, Heckhausen & Kemmler 1965;
Sader & Specht 1967). On the other hand, the absence of (positive) relationships between motive strength and performance is about as frequent. Inver-

sion of the expected relationship tends to be the exception (Wasna 1972). However, a simple linear relationship between motive strength and perform-ance is theoretically not expected. Rather the relationship between the two terms will be a curvilinear one in that performance only tends to increase un-til it reaches the critical value of motive strength and then tends to decrease (Atkinson 1974), something that has been empirically demonstrated long ago (Yerkes & Dodson 1908). Beyond this, no generally valid relationship be-tween motive strength and performance is to be expected for the simple rea-son that this relationship is essentially determined by the achievement-relat-ed incentives inherent in each particular situation.

As may be expected from Atkinson's (1957) model, and as has been dem-onstrated empirically by the early studies of incentive effects (e.g., McClel-land, Clark, Roby & Atkinson 1949), however strong the motive, it will be effective only in association with a corresponding motive-specific incentive. There are still no investigations of the incentive conditions that prevail in classrooms where no relationship was found between projective motive meas-ures and students' grades (Klinger 1966; Entwisle 1972). What we do know, on the other hand, is that many teachers make no effort to adjust their task demands to the achievement levels of individual students - although such ad-justment is absolutely necessary to arouse the achievement motive (deCharms 1976; McKeachie 1961; Rheinberg 1980). As a result students' expectancy of success may deviate substantially from the point of optimal arousal, so that on the basis of Atkinson's model we cannot expect a full arousal of the achievement motive. Low correlations between motive and performance scores are therefore not surprising.

There is a propensity to use school performance as the criterion in vali-dating questionnaire measures (e.g., Mehrabian 1969; Rand 1978). As a rule, however, this tendency does not give any clear indication of whether questionnaire methods may be held to be superior, for in most cases no at-tempt is made to use any projective method for purposes of comparison. Even a correlation between motive scores and school performance can in no way be taken as proof that the achievement motive actually influences school per-formance. The notion that the direction of causation works in the opposite direction is at least as plausible, in which case school performance appears to influence the questionnaire responses most decisively. Presumably, subjects who have high grade sat school have those in mind when expressing their at-titude toward scholastic achievement. A favorable attitude toward achieve-ment need not be associated with a strong achievement motive. This motive may perfectly well be rooted in the social learning history experienced and the resulting motive disposition, which may be inaccessible to conscious awareness (Heckhausen 1972).

One other reason reduces expectations of any general relation between motive strength and performance: It can not be taken for granted that a source of strong motivation will also manifest itself in subsequent performance, even in cases of strong situational arousal, for the degree to which motive strength and performance go together depends on the cognitive mediators of this relation. Such mediators enable the individual to perceive what action he/she must undertake during the execution of an intention (Kuhl 1983, 1984, 1985).

Questionnaire Procedures

In a recent analysis of an investigation into the n-achievement motive measure, McClelland pointed out that none of the studies comparing the validity of TAT-motive parameters with the validity of self-report measures presented questionnaire measures which passed the "drive, direct, and select" criteria for pinpointing a motive measure. In spite of intensive efforts by the constructors of the TAT-method (e.g., Atkinson 1969; Heckhausen 1968; McClelland 1980) as well as by other authors (Edwards 1959; Jackson 1966; Mehrabian 1968; Gjesme & Nygård 1970; Hermans 1970), no questionnaire has been thus far devised, which exemplifies a construct validity comparable to that of the TAT-measure. To demonstrate the construct validity of a measure, it is not sufficient to simply show that the test yields significant correlations with given behavioral measures. Whether a questionnaire or TAT-measure actually does measure motives, rather than a habit, a disposition, an ideal self-image or some other variable can only be determined if the empirical evidence itself reveals that the technique applied satisfies all the criteria essential to interpreting test behavior as an indicator of a latent motive disposition. In the study referred to above (Atkins & Litwin 1960), dividing the subjects into a high and low motive group on the basis of a questionnaire (Edwards 1959) did not yield validity correlates comparable to those shown in Table 1. On the contrary, those who described themselves as particularly achievement-motivated exhibited behavior in the experiment which was more typical of low-motivated individuals. They preferred at a significantly higher rate extremely easy or extremely difficult tasks, thus making it more difficult to meet achievement standards. These results led McClelland (1971) to assume that questionnaire measures represent a different personality trait than do TAT-measures, an assumption supported by the typically low correlation between self-report measures and TAT-parameters (e.g., Atkinson & Litwin 1960; DeCharms, Morrison, Reitman & McClelland 1955). In this regard, questionnaires assess the value an individual (consciously) attaches to achievement (hence: v ach = value achievement), while operant procedures such as the TAT actually assess the motive variables which influence behavior.

The real problem is perhaps not so much that a questionnaire measures a different kind of variable than does an operant procedure but rather that the validity of questionnaires is more susceptible to fluctuations than the validity of operant procedures. A questionnaire may actually yield a perfectly valid motive measure; however, interindividuality and intraindividuality, at different times and in different situations, this measure could possibly assess something quite different from what the questionnaire was originally designed to measure. Psychometricians tend to pursue what I term trait-monism, and with such singleness of purpose that they ascribe unalterable 'traits' not only to their subjects, but also to their tests.

Moreover, in test test construction, efforts required to elaborate a psychological theory of the processes underlying test behavior tend to be delayed, in favor of simple and psychometrically handy assumptions concerning test behavior. The TAT-method of motive measurement is based on a psychological theory that seeks to explain and predict the relationship between the latent construct to be measured and the observable behavior, a theory that has been painstakingly elaborated over many years, and has a solid basis in empirical evidence (Atkinson 1958, Chapter 42; Atkinson & Birch 1970; Atkinson, Bongort & Price 1977; Heckhausen 1963; McClelland et al. 1953; Murray 1938). No comparable theoretical efforts were undertaken by various authors of questionnaire measures. For the most part they have confined themselves to formulating their questions either on the basis of TAT scoring keys or of behavioral correlates of projective motive measures. However, both procedures have unmistakable disadvantages, all of which tends to substantiate the earlier argument that person and situation specificity must be taken into account, and moreso than hitherto in the validation of questionnaire measures.

The transpostion of the scoring from the TAT-system to questionnaire items is for theoretical reasons a highly questionable procedure. Beginning with Freud and Lewin, motivation theory has made a clear distinction between the motivational principles which underlie imaginative behavior and those which influence questionnaires. Regardless of whether the focus is on such explanatory principles as the pleasure principle or the primary process, or whether following Lewin, the concern is with the distinctiveness of mental systems constituting "life space", there is agreement to the extent that the entire thinking process, on the 'irreality level' of fantasy productions, is not only less differentiated bad also primarily determinant by the pleasure principle or by a value-focused principle.

From a measurement theory point of view, all the heterogeneous imaginative contents produced through fantasy can be used as indicators of one unifying, value-related parameter: Expectations, such as subjective probability, are geared to the possible fulfillment of wishes whereby the expectancy scores and the scores for affective or value-related categories (e.g., praise) point to one common underlying motive disposition. This theoretical proposition is clearly not applicable to questionnaires, for the expectations stated in response to a questionnaire are undoubtedly based more on real experience, and thereby relatively undetermined by value-related processes. In a later section we will discuss an investigation that was designed to check this hypothesis with regard to the construct-related equivalence of scoring categories through the application of the Rasch-model.

The transition from operant to respondent measures not only produces construct-related heterogenity of response categories as a consequence of the greater realism which characterizes questionnaire responses, but also involves yet another disadvantage. In view of the definition stated earlier, motives should explicate above all how operant behavior is driven, directed, and selected. It stands therefore to reason that a respondent measure is less effective in capturing the causes underlying operant behavior than an operant measure. It can not simply be assumed that individuals would show the same response under questionnaire conditions as by spontaneous activity.

The second principle underlying the construction of questionnaire methods for motive assessment involves the formulation of questions based on the empirically obtained behavioral correlates of TAT-scores. The same method has also been applied by the constructors of the TAT-scoring system (e.g., Atkinson 1969); Heckhausen 1965; McClelland 1980). This method, however, contains a serious disadvantage. An empirical relationship between a motive score and behavior is not sufficient for the interpretation of behavior as an indicator of motive strength as behavioral variables are affected by numerous factors. Preference for intermediate risk levels may for instance be determined by many other factors than by just a strong achievement motive. Moreover, the relationship between motive scores and behavioral indices, as a basis for the measurement of motive strength, is based on group data. In using such a behavioral index as a motive measure more error variance is permitted than would be the case if one were to attempt to isolate the motive by direct tapping of the subjective evaluation of achievement-related situations. The questionnaire measure for motives as developed on the basis of similar considerations (Gjesme & Nygård 1970), seems to yield very promising results (Rand 1978).

Replacing the TAT-method with a questionnaire, involves the loss of another important advantage of the operant method: The accessibility of the variable to be measured, regarding conscious awareness, is not a factor premised by the TAT scoring system, but is indeed presupposed by the respondent procedures. A questionnaire is valid only to the extent to which the respondent is willing and able to offer valid information concerning the motives governing his actions. This critical problem, however, has rarely been the object of systematic theoretical or empirical analysis. In any event it can be assumed that this type of motivation varies across and within individuals.

Empirical studies in all areas of motivation research demonstrate that situational variables, substantially affect the course of motivational tendencies through the arousal of motives (e.g., Heckhausen 1980). This fact undoubtedly applies equally well to the individuals' readiness to provide information in answering questionnaires. The TAT scores are, of course, affected by the conditions of arousal inherent in the test situation (achievement-related arousal). However, such factors have been thoroughly investigated and can be carefully controlled upon administration of the test, (e.g., Atkinson 1958; Heckhausen 1963; McClelland et al. 1953). The situational conditions of arousal by TAT fantasy productions are also largely commensurate with the measurement in question for they relate to the same motivational dimension. With respect to the respondents' readiness to offer information in answering questionnaires, however, the situational conditions of arousal cannot be identified with the (motivational) dimension measured, as the former includes motive-unrelated factors (e.g., social desirability). One factor affecting the subjects' readiness to offer information may relate to an awareness of the personality disposition being assessed by the test at hand. In a study presented later in this paper, we explored the effects of 'test-consciousness' on the validity of questionnaire measures.

In addition to variance in the motivation to offer valid information, differences in the ability to provide such information may reduce the validity of a questionnaire. Variation in both general mental abilities and specific abilities (such as "self-knowledge") may also produce fluctuations of questionnaire validity. However, the validity of a questionnaire, as expressed in the correlation between a questionnaire score and a behavioral criterion, is higher when the respondent's attention is focused on the 'self', either by means of a large mirror placed opposite during the test, or by presenting self-related questions immediately prior to the administration of the questionnaire (Duval & Wicklund 1972); Wicklund 1982). In our study reported below, the degree of self-consciousness was experimentally manipulated in order to test the effect of self-focused attention on questionnaire validity.

The ability of respondents to describe the behaviorally relevant variables incorporated into a questionnaire certainly depends in part on the way specific items are formulated, i.e., on the demands an item makes on self-knowledge. Accessibility can be improved by taking three aspects into account in formulating the items: The language and content of the questions asked, context-specificity, and phenomenological representativeness (Kuhl 1980).

Predictive Validity

According to the theory, motives drive, direct, and select behavior. The influence of motives on behavior is expected to manifest itself most in relatively unstructured situations, in which the subjects themselves can determine the goals to be achieved. Skinner (1938) referred to such units of behavior that are not evoked by any specific stimulus as operant responses. The assumption that motives are especially effective in controlling operant behavior was the main reason prompting the development of an operant method of motive measurement (McClelland et al. 1953). Hence, to the extent that our concern lies in finding construct-related behavioral correlates the focus of interest is not so much on achievement-related behavioral measures that are preeminently evoked in laboratory or school conditions, but rather on variables which relate to operant behavior in real-life settings.

In a number of studies, McClelland and his associates have found significant correlations between operant thought measures (motive scores) and life outcome measures, taken some 16 years later. McClelland & Boyatzis (1979) presented the results of a recent retest of a study undertaken with the 1956-196- management trainees for the American Telephone and Telegraph Company (AT & T) (see Bray, Campbell & Grant 1974). TAT scores were obtained for achievement-, affiliation-, and leadership motive patterns. The post-test confirmed the theoretical expectations: The management trainees with high achievement motivation on the TAT during training sessions (1956-60) initially had the greatest success in their profession, particularly as long as promotion depended primarily on superior performance. In later years, as the management level attained coincided more with leadership qualities, those trainees who had written TAT stories containing many more power-related and fewer affiliation-related ideas while in training reached higher levels. The eventual slowdown in the attainment of higher management levels on the part of the highly achievement-motivated is consistent with the theory that managers must involve themselves with helping or influencing others to perform well rather than seeking to do better themselves. This longitudinal study also included two respondent motive measures and 18 other highly reliable measures obtained from self-report questionnaires, none of which, however, predicted significantly levels of management advancement in the course of employment at AT & T.

92

Reliability

According to classical test theory (e.g., Gulliksen 1950; Lienert 1961), the reliability of a measure determines the upper limit of its validity. A test can only be valid to the extent that it is reliable. The lack of validity in self-report measures as found in the study by McClelland and Boyatzis (1979) does not contradict this principle, for high reliability in no way guarantees high validity. Nonetheless, a number of indications point to the possibility that even highly reliable measures also effect a partial loss of validity.

The critics of operant measures of motive patterns tend to justify their preference for questionnaire methods with reference to the higher retest reliability and the higher internal consistency of questionnaires (Entwisle 1972). However, questionnaires often require respondents to pass what could be termed sweeping retrospective judgments on their earlier habits. In view of the fact that the elements of an individual's past as well as his/her memory of it are not apt to change, it is not surprising that respondents tend to respond the same way to the same questions in a second test-run even when the latent personality trait to be measured has changed in the meantime. A former delinquent, for example, always answers the relevant questions in the same way - provided he is willing and able to give valid information - even under the condition that his delinquent tendencies have completely subsided (McClelland 1980). Unmistakably, high reliability at the level of manifest test responses can only be obtained at the cost of validity. The more a respondent refers to past experiences and events in statements about achievement-related habits the less tendency there is for recent changes in the motive pattern to be manifested in the questionnaire scores.

In the event that a question is actually explicitly related to current rather than past behavior, the need to appear consistent in one's own eyes and in those of the experimenter (Festinger 1957) may result in that changes in the latent variables that are nevertheless not shown in manifest responses. Similarly indistinguishable questions in somewhat modified formulations enhances response consistency, but to the detriment of validity. The effort here not to fall into obvious contradictions may actually be more responsible for determining test behavior than the latent dimension to be assessed.

The partial incompatibility between the reliability and validity of questionnaire responses is due to well-known response tendencies, which involve giving either positive or negative answers, or socially desirable answers (Edwards 1957). Such tendencies obviously have a negative effect on validity but may in fact increase test reliability. In contrast to questionnaire methods, the TAT is based on a theory which assumes that valid results will be produced, even with low consistency at the level of overt behavior. It is self-evident that respondents who have been instructed to invent stories rich in fantasy and original in content will not consistently repeat the same topics or substance. Heterogeneity in story content, however, reduces internal consistency. If the instruction is such as to allow repetitiveness, retest reliability of values under 0,30 will approach values of 0.60 (Heckhausen 1963; Winter & Stewart 1977).

An important theoretical reason for expecting low behavioral consistency in spite of high consistency in latent behavioral determinants, is simply that motivational processes do not operate to meet the expectations of test theoreticians. Admittedly, it is much easier to make the mathematical derivations both in terms of classical and modern test theory, if it is assumed that the responses to the various test items are stochastically independent (Gulliksen 1950; Fischer 1974; Lord & Novick 1968; Rasch 1960). One of the basic assumptions of motivation theory, however, suggests that exactly the contrary should be the case. Freud's assumption concerning the persistence of wishful thinking until the wishes themselves are fulfilled, which reappears in a modified form in Lewin's (1935) theory, and which modern motivation theories also take into account (Atkinson & Birch 1970, 1978), contradicts the assumption regarding stochastic independence of test items. What a person does at a given point in time depends on what he/she was doing prior to that moment. Whether the TAT-story told involves achievement-concerns will depend on whether the previous story was related to achievement. Both examples fall under the common assumption that the behavioral expression of a motivational tendency. This assumption was confirmed by the "saw-tooth effect" (Atkinson 1950; Reitman & Atkinson 1958). The number of achievement-related categories expressed in stories decreases in accordance with the degree to which the previous story contained such contents.

Questionnaires responses may actually prove to be more consistent with the assumption of stochastic independence, for the answering of a questionnaire presumably does not arouse any motives that could be consummated by the answers given, that is if we disregard the 'motive' to answer the questions presented. The respondent test situation in particular, involves a minimal arousal of the motive to be measured, and offers virtually no possibilities for its expression. This method is clearly advantageous, for it assures stochastic independence of the responses and high consistency of the answers. However, one major disadvantage relates to the fact that the motive to be measured is scarcely aroused in the test responses to a limited extent. Once again, measures taken to increase reliability jeopardize validity.

In considering the significance that literally all test theories ascribe to the assumption of stochastic independence in test responses, it would appear that operant procedures used to measure the achievement-motive could only yield partial validity. It remains unclear how the consistent latent determinants premised can be deduced on the basis of inconsistent observable behavior? Personality theorists have claimed time and again that such is possible, and that all of us do so quite successfully in our every day perception of others (e.g., Allport 1949; Alker 1972). Atkinson and Birch (1970) are to be credited with putting together the theoretical foundation proving the truth of this assertion. In their "Dynamics of Action" (Atkinson & Birch 1970), they combine the basic assumptions of motivation theory into a formalized model of action. The degree of formalization is such, that the theoretically expected temporal changes in several competing action tendencies can be simulated on the computer (Bongort 1975); Kuhl & Mader 1980; Sletzer 1973; Seltzer & Sawusch 1974). One of the simulation studies derived the theory's predictions for a typical TAT-situation (Atkinson, Bongort & Price 1977). How much time does a subject (with a priori-defined motive strength) need to produce achievement-related contents for a picture (with a specific arousal value) and how often will he/she shift to contents related to other motives? The simulation confirmed one expectation: If the fundamental principles of motivation theory are taken into account, especially persistence of action tendencies until these are consummated by appropriate actions the internal consistency of imaginative contents found in successive stories is extremely low.

The most important finding of the simulation above reveals that the pessimistic view suggested by psychometricians, according to which valid measurement presupposes sufficiently high consistency, has no justification. In spite of extremely low or even negative internal consistency, the initially specified motive strength of the hypothetical subjects could reliably be derived from the behavioral parameters (length and frequency of achievement-related contents). There is no point in criticizing the lack of empirical evidence in this study (Brody 1980) - the intention was solely to demonstrate that what is unthinkable in terms of the conceptual system of test theory is in reality perfectly conceivable: Low internal consistency can theoretically perfectly well be associated with high validity.

The study by Atkinson, Bongort and Price (1977) also demonstrates that motivation theory is perfectly capable of explaining why in spite of absolutely consistent latent determinants, overt behavior may seem to exhibit a high grade of inconsistency. To deduce that the inconsistency of overt behaviors implies inconsistency of the latent determinants of behavior is jumping to conclusions. This fallacy (see Mischel 1968) is rooted in confounding overt behavior and its latent determinants. However, as classical test theory makes no distinction between these two levels, the methods derived from it can not but produce the same error. Modern test models avoid this misinterpretation. Rasch's stochastic test model explicitly distinguishes the level of overt responses from the level of latent determinants. True, Rasch's model still upholds the untenable assumption of stochastic independence of test responses. Nevertheless, the consequences of this assumption are mitigated by the stochastic structure of the model: Deviations from stochastic independence can be tolerated within certain limits.

In an analysis of 1034 TAT protocols, the compatability of Heckhausen's (1963) scoring key for the assessment of the achievement motive with the Rasch-model was examined (Kuhl 1978). At that time, we were particularly interested in investigating the property of the model which implies the consistency of the *latent* determinants (i.e., achievement motive of the subjects and arousal value of the pictures). Rasch called this test property 'objective specificity', for it indicates that latent person parameters are invariant across situations. Independent of the respective items of a test, latent person parameters consistently determine test behavior. Conversely, the item parameters to be measured must also be invariant in relation to changes in the subject sample. The data was highly consistent with the Rasch-model. In spite of the large sample, there were no significant deviations from the model by the measurement of the success-oriented achievement motive. On the other hand, the analysis of failure-related responses did not yield any compatability with Rasch's model. The scoring key for fear of failure seems to confound two types of coping with failure: A more state-oriented way of dealing with an experienced failure and its (affective) outcomes and a more action-oriented endeavour to overcome such failure or at least its outcomes, by appropriate action. Factor-analytic investigations produced very similar results (Sader & Keil 1968; Kuhl 1972; Schmalt 1976) in which the failure categories produced two separate factors that can be interpreted in terms of state- versus action-orientation is not just confined to coping with failure, but is relevant for a motivational construct, which alongside traditional expectancy and value constructs is an essential element in any motivation process (Kuhl 1983, 1984, 1985).

EXPERIMENTAL STUDY

Method

The following experiment was conducted to investigate the effects of test- and self-consciousness: 103 students (age 14-17) from 4 classes in a German Gymnasium (tenth grade) were administered the TAT-technique (Heckhausen 1963) and several questionnaires (Gjesme & Nygård 1970; Mehrabian 1968) to assess individual differences in the achievement motive. On a subsequent occasion, several measures of achievement-related behavior were obtained, i.e., level of aspiration, risk-taking, persistence, effort invested in an achievement task, performance, and subjective evaluation of outcomes. Each session took about 90 minutes. The experiment was conducted in a normal class environment. Before administering the questionnaires, the experimental manipulation was introduced.

Design

To avoid a confounding of class and experimental manipulation, each of the four experimental conditions was introduced within each class. Since the seats were arranged in four parallel rows, written instructions containing the experimental manipulation could be administered easily: Students in each row received one of the four instructions. The four types of instruction resulted from crossing two test-consciousness versus control) with two self-consciousness conditions (induced self-consciousness versus control).

Subjects assigned to one of two induced test-consciousness conditions (i.e., high test-consciousness / high self-consciousness and high test-consciousness / low self-consciousness) received the following (written) instruction: "You just finished a so-called "indirect" test of various personality traits. It is possible to assess certain traits with these tests, without the subjects' knowing what traits are being assessed. Now, we would like to find out how well you are able yourself to estimate to what extent one of the traits applies to you. Please complete the following questionnaire. Most subjects find it very easy to infer from the questions what trait is being assessed". Subjects assigned to one of the two low test-consciousness conditions did not receive this instruction.

Subjects assigned to one of the two high self-consciousness conditions (i.e., high self-consciousness / high test-consciousness and high self-consciousness / low test-consciousness) received ten items from the private-self-consciousness scale (Scheier, Buss & Buss 1978). It has been shown that the administration of this scale raises the level of self-awareness in a similar way as exposing subjects to a mirror (Wicklund 1975, 1982). Subjects assigned to the two low-self-consciousness groups were not administered this questionnaire.

Dependent Variables

In the second session, all subjects were given a modified version of the symbol-digit-substitution task (Wechsler 1952). Five difficulty levels of this task had been constructed. These levels differed with regard to the number of digits that had to be substituted by a symbol within the time allotted (15 sec). After several practice trials on each difficulty level *risk-perference* was assessed by the following question: "Suppose you are asked to work on 100 "digit-symbol" tasks. How many tasks from each of the five difficulty levels would you choose? Subsequently, subjects were given a sheet containing 12 digit-symbol tasks. It was made clear to the subjects that they could not substitute all 26 digits contained in a task within the time allotted (15 sec). They were asked to indicate their *level of aspiration* (=number of symbols completed) before starting a new task. After time was up subjects wrote down the number of symbols actually completed. The number of errors made was computed later as a second *performance* measure. After the 12 tasks had been completed subjects were asked to indicate (on 7-point rating scales) the average amount of *effort* invested in the tasks an the amount of *dissatisfaction* experienced when their performance fell short of their level of aspiration. Finally subjects were asked to work on an allegedly difficult "perceptual reasoning task" (Feather 1964) which was actually unsolvable. The number of trials attempted until they switched to a second (solvable) puzzle was taken as a measure of *persistence*.

Results and Discussion

In order to compare the validity of operant and respondent measures, product-moment correlations were computed between ten behavioral correlates and five motive scores, i.e. a respondent (AMS) and an operant (TAT) measure of hope for success (HS), a respondent (AMS and an operant (TAT) measure of fear of failure (FF), and a respondent measure of need achievement (MAS) which does not differentiate between approach and avoidance motives.

As can be seen from Table 2 correlations are generally low, but in the expected direction. With an increasing motive to achieve success there is an increase in speed of performance (and a corresponding decrease in accuracy), an increase in typical shifts following success (i.e., raising one's level of aspiration), an increased preference of tasks of intermediate (P =0.5) or moderate (P =0.3) difficulty, and decreased persistence at a difficult problem. The negative correlation between resultant motive strength ("net hope"=HS-FF) and persistence has been derived for *difficult* tasks from Atkinson's (1957) theory of achievement motivation by Feather (1962, 1964). A subsequent ·computation of non-linear correlations did not yield better predictions. Despite the fact that all correlations are very low it is interesting to note that operant and respondent measures of the success-oriented motive yielded comparable results. McClelland's (1980) claim that operant and respondent methods *inevitably* assess different dispositions is not corroborated by our findings. It cannot be concluded, however, that projective and respondent measures are equivalent (cf. the many discrepant results summarized by McClelland, 1980). Our results suggest that operant and respondent measures may at least occasionally assess similar dispositions. This does not contradict McClelland's (1980) claim that operant methods assess *needs* whereas respondent methods assess *values*. There is no theoretical reason to deny that needs and values coincide, at least occasionally. The expression of value in a questionnaire may be subject to many situational factors inherent in the setting. Some of these influences will be analyzed in the next section.

Table 2: Significant product-moment correlations ($p<0.05$) between five measures of achievement motive and ten behavioral criteria

Predictor	Hope for success (HS)			Fear of Failure (FF)	
	TAT[1]	AMS[2]	MAS[3]	TAT	AMS
Criterion					
Performance (DSS)[4]					
Speed	.20	.20			
Accuracy	-.18				
Typical shifts					
following success		.23			
Typical shifts					
following failure				.20	
Rated satisfaction					
following success					
Rated dissatisfaction					
following failure					
Risk-preference					
at Ps=0.5	.27		.17		
Risk-preference					
at Ps=0.3			.19		
Rated effort					
at DSS-task					
Persistence					
at a difficult					
task	-.20[5]				

Notes: [1] TAT = Thematic Apperceptive Test
(Heckhausen 1963)
[2] AMS = Achievement Motive Scale
(Gjesme & Nygard 1970)
[3] MAS = Mehrabian Achievement Scale
(Mehrabian 1968)
[4] DSS = Digit-Symbol-Substitution Task
(Wechsler 1952)
[5] Obtained with "Net-Hope" Score (=HS-FF)

Table 3: Significant product-moment correlations (p<0.05) between three self-report measures of achievement motives and ten behavioral criteria for four experimental conditions

Experimental condition Induced test-consciousness	High			High			Low			Low		
Induced self-consciousness	High (n=28)			Low (n=26)			High (n=24)			Low (n=25)		
Predictor	HS	FF	MAS	HS	FF	MAS	HS	FF	MAS	HS[1]	FF[2]	MAS[3]
Criterion												
Performance (DSS)[4]												
Speed				-.33						.55		.43
Accuracy							-.33		-.38			
Typical shifts following succes												
Typical shifts following failure											.46	
Rated satisfaction following succes										-.36		
Rated dissatisfaction following failure						.35						
Risk-preference at Ps=0.5												.36
Risk-Preference at Ps=0.3									.35	.47		
Rated effort at DSS-task						-.42						-.37
Persistence				.63		.63						

Notes: [1] HS = Hope for success score from Achievement Motive Scale (Gjesme & Nygard 1970)
[2] FF = Fear of failure score from AMS
[3] MAS = Mehrabian Achievement Scale (Mehrabian 1968)
[4] DSS = Digit-Symbol-Substitution Task (Wechsler 1952)

The assessment of the failure-oriented motive was *not* successful. Except for one significant correlation between the AMS-score for FF and typical shifts following failure (i.e. lowering the level of aspiration), no significant correlation involving the FF-measure was found. With regard to the operant measure (i.e., Heckhausen's TAT scoring key for FF), one reason might be that fear of failure is associated with avoidance rather than with the expression of fear-related imagery in TAT-stories (Atkinson 1958, p. 622; Clark, Teeyan & Ricciuti 1958; Moulton 1958; Scott 1958). A similar argument can be made with regard to respondent assessment of fear-related motives.

Many subjects may be reluctant to admit their fears in a questionnaire (Asendorpf 1981; Byrne 1964). The degree to which situational factors affected the validity of self-report measures can be seen from Table 3. Expected correlations were only found in the control group that was not subjected to any experimental manipulation (i.e., the low test-consciousness / low self-consciousness group). In this group, some correlations considerably exceed those computed across the entire sample (cf. Table 2). The *negative* correlation between hope of success (HS) and rated satisfaction following success is inconsistent with theoretical expectations. This correlation might be attributable to the fact that success-oriented subjects have future-oriented long-term rather than short-term goals which may reduce their interest in immediate success (Gjesme 1981).

Surprising results were obtained in the high test-consciousness / low self-consciousness condition. The rather strong relationship between speed of performance and hope of success (.55 and .43) disappear totally. Instead, three correlations were found whose sign is opposite to theoretical expectations. Subjects having a high HS- (or MAS-) score in this condition report high dissatisfaction with failure, low invested effort, at the task (MAS), and high persistence at a very *difficult* problem. Since these are normally behavioral indicators of failure-orientation, it seems that the HS- and MAS-scales assess fear of failure when subjects are aware of what is being tested. According to one plausible explanation, this phenomenon results from the fact that failure-oriented subjects are reluctant to admit to failure-related symptoms when they are aware of the fact that their anxiety is being tested. A simple way to express their achievement concerns without admitting to their anxieties is to endorse the positive statements contained in the success-oriented scale.

To test the hypothesis that expression of fear-oriented responses was inhibited in the high test-consciousness (low self-consciousness) condition, fear-of-failure scores (AMS) were subjected to a 2 x 2 (test-consciousness x self-consciousness) analysis of variance. A significant interaction was obtained (Figure 1).

The results are in line with the hypothesis. FF-scores were lower in the high test-consciousness / low self-consciousness group compared to the low-low control group. This difference approaches statistical significance, $t(49)=1.56$, $p<.07$.

Figure 1.   Fear of failure score as a function of experimental manipulation of test- and self-consciousness

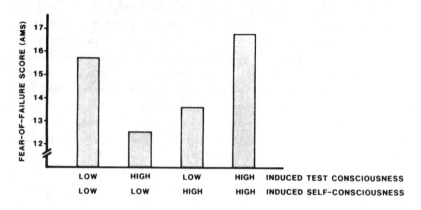

Further inspection of Table 3 reveals that both high self-consciousness groups do not show the expected validity-enhancing effect (cf. Wicklund 1975). Instead, the number of significant correlations is considerably reduced compared to the low-low control group. Conceivably, high self-consciousness does not increase the accessibility of every personal disposition. This might be especially true for motive disposition. Moving one's self-concept into focus may actually blur the view into one's genuine needs and desires. One reason for this effect may be that self-consciousness often activates people's *ideal* self, i.e., the needs and desires people would like to possess. The tendency to access one's ideal desires and needs might overlap with McClelland's construct of value as opposed to need. This interpretation leads us to go one step beyond McClelland's need-value distinction: Even if his claim is true that respondent methods tap values and operant methods assess (genuine) needs, the degree to which values and needs overlap remains an open question. McClelland (1980) suggests that values and needs are necessarily discrepant. Our results suggest that they may be congruent *or* discrepant depending on certain cues inherent in the testing situation.

CONCLUSION

In the first part of this paper we have given an overview of the theoretical issues involved in operant ("projective") and respondent methods to assess achievement motives. One of the most critical issues is whether both methods provide convergent information about the same construct or whether they assess different constructs, for example needs and values. Our results suggest that these two alternatives may be reconcilable. The degree to which the two methods assess overlapping constructs depends on certain cues inherent in the testing situation in which self-report scales are administered.

Our finding s add an additional item to the list of factors (discussed in the first part) that may attenuate linear correlations between motive measures and their behavioral correlates, namely the degree of test and self-consciousness aroused in the testing situation. One might be tempted to circumvent the problems arising from our findings by simply ignoring the test and self-consciousness manipulations which resulted in reduced validity coefficients. This view is not tenable, however, because under "normal" testing conditions test and self-consciousness are usually uncontrolled. Even within our control condition validity coefficients might be attenuated because several subjects had been test- or self-conscious without experimental induction. Unless we succeed in isolating situational cues affecting these factors in future studies, the validity of questionnaire measures might be subject to random variations in testing conditions. After confining ourselves to the analysis of the motivational determinants of operant analysis of the motivational determinants of operant motive measures for more than three decades, it is time to replace our naivite regarding respondent measures by a well-designed research program exploring the psychological determinants of their validity.

REFERENCES

Alker, H.A. (1972). Is personality specific or intrapsychically consistent? *Journal of Personality, 40*, 1-16.

Allport, G. (1949). *Personlichkeit: Struktur, Entwicklung und Erfassung der menschlichen Eigenart.* Stuttgart: Klett.

Asendorpf, J. (1981) *Affektive Vigilanz: Eine psychologische Untersuchung der defensiven Abwehr von Angst und Arger unter besonderer Berucksi-*

chtigung nichtverbalen Affektausdrucks. Dissertation Universität Giessen.

Atkinson, J.W. (1950). *Studies in projective measurement of achievement motivation*. Unpublished doctoral dissertation. University of Michigan.

Atkinson J.W. (1957). Motivational determinants of risk-taking behavior. *Psychological Review, 64*, 359-372.

Atkinson, J.W. (Ed.) (1958). *Motives in fantasy, action, and society*. Princeton, NJ: Van Nostrand.

Atkinson, J.W. (1969). *Measuring achievement-related motives*. Unpublished final report, NSF Project GS-1399, University of Michigan.

Atkinson, J.W. (1974). Strength of motivation and efficiency of performance. In J.W. Atkinson & J.O. Raynor (Eds.), *Motivation and achievement*. New York: Wiley.

Atkinson, J.W., & Birch, D. (1970). *The dynamics of action*. New York: Wiley.

Atkinson, J.W., & Birch, D. (1978). *An introduction to motivation*. New York: Van Nostrand.

Atkinson, J.W., Bongort, K., & Price, L.H. (1977). Explorations using computer simulation to comprehend thematic apperceptive measurement of motivation. *Motivation and Emotion, 1*, 1-27.

Atkinson, J.W., Litwin, G.H. (1960). Achievement otive and test anxiety conceived as motive to approach success and motive to avoid failure. *Journal of Abnormal and Social Psychology, 60*, 52-63.

Bongort, K. (1975). *Most recent revision of computer program for dynamics of action*. Unpublished program: University of Michigan.

Bray, D.W., Campell, R.J., & Grant, D.L. (1974). *Formative years in business: A long-term study of managerial lives*. New York: Wiley.

Brody, N. (1980). Social motivation. In M.R. Rosenzweig & L.W. Porter (Eds.), *Annual Review of Psychology, 31*, 143-168.

Byrne, D. (1964). Repression-sensitization as a dimension of personality. In B.A. Maher (Ed.), *Progress in experimental personality research (Vol. I)*. New York: Academic Press.

Clark, R.A., Teevan, R., & Ricciuti, H.N. (1958). Hope of success and fear of failure as aspects of need for achievement. In J.W. Atkinson, (Ed.), *Motives in fantasy, action, and society*. Princeton, NJ: D. van Nostrand.

DeCharms, R. (1976). *Enhancing motivation: Change in the classroom*. New York: Irvington.

DeCharms, R., Morrison, H.W., Reitman, W., & McClelland, D.C. (1955). Behavioral correlates of directly and indirectly measured achievement motivation. In D.C. McClelland (Ed.), *Studies in motivation*. New York: Appleton-CenturyCrofts.

104

Duval, S., & Wicklund, R.A. (1972). *A theory of objective self-awareness.* New York: Academic Press.

Edwards, A.L. (1957). *The social desirability variable in personality assessment and research.* New York: Dryden.

Edwards, A.L. (1959). *Edwards Personal Preference Schedule.* New York: Psychological Corporation.

Entwisle, D.E. (1972). To dispel fantasies abot fantasy-based measures of achievement motivation. *Psychological Bulletin, 77,* 377-391.

Feather, N.T. (1962). The study of persistence. *Psychological Bulletin, 59,* 94-115.

Feather, N.T. (1964). Persistence at a difficult task with alternative task of intermediate difficulty. *Journal of Abnormal and Social Psychology, 66,* 604-609.

Festinger, L. (1957). *A theory of cognitive dissonance.* Evanston, IL: Row & Peterson.

Fischer, G.H. (1974). *Einfuhrung in die Theorie psychologischer Tests.* Bern: Huber.

French, E.G., & Thomas, F.H. (1958). The relation of achievement motivation to problem solving effectiveness. *Journal of Abnormal and Social Psychology, 56,* 46-48.

Gjesme, T. (1981). Is there any future in achievement motivation? *Motivation and Emotion, 5,* 115-138.

Gjesme, T., & Nygård, R. (1970). *Achievement-related motives: Theoretical considerations and construction of a measuring instrument.* Unpublished paper: University of Oslo.

Gulliksen, H. (1950). *Theory of mental tests.* New York: Wiley.

Heckhausen, H. (1963). *Hoffnung und Furcht in der Leistungsmotivation.* Meisenheim: Anton Hain.

Heckhausen, H. (1965). Leistungsmotivation. In H. Thomae (Ed.), *Handbuch der Psychologie (Bd. II).* (pp. 602-702). Göttingen: Hogrefe.

Heckhausen, H. (1968). Achievement motive research: Current problems and some contributions towards a general theory of motivation. In W.J. Arnold (Ed.), *Nebraska Symposium on Motivation (Vol. 16).* Lincoln: University of Nebraska Press.

Heckhausen, H. (1972). Die Interaktion der Sozialisationsvariablen in der Genese des Leistungsmotivs. In C.F. Graumann (Ed.), *Handbuch der Psychologie (Bd. 7/2)* (pp.955-1019). Göttingen: Hogrefe.

Heckhausen, H. (1980). *Motivation und Handeln.* Berlin, Heidelberg: Springer.

Hermans, H.J.M. (1970). A questionnaire measure of achievement motivation. *Journal of Applied Psychology, 54,* 353-363.

Jackson, D.N. (1966). A modern strategy for personality assessment: the personality research form. *Research Bulletin*. London, Canada: University of Western Ontario.

Kliner, E. (1966). Fantasy need achievement as a motivational construct. *Psychological Bulletin, 66,* 291-308.

Kuhl, J. (1972). *Zum Problem der Eindimensionalitat der Messung von Leistungsmotivation mittels des Heckhausen-TAT.*Diplomarbeit, Psychologisches Institut der Ruhr-Universität, Bochum.

Kuhl, J. (1978). Situations-, reaktions- und personbezogene Konsistenz des Leistungsmotivs bei der Messung mittels des Heckhausens-TAT. *Archiv fur Psychologie, 130,* 37-52.

Kuhl, J. (1980). Leistungsmotivation. In H. Werbik & H.J. Kaiser (Eds.), *Kritische Stichworter zur Sozialpsychologie.* München: Fink.

Kuhl, J. (1983). *Motivation, Konflikt und Handlungskontrolle.* Heidelberg: Springer.

Kuhl, J. (1984). Volitional aspects of achievement motivation and learned helplessness: Toward a comprehensive theory of action control. In B.A. Maher (Ed.), *Progress in Experimental Personality Research (Vol. 13)* (pp. 99-171). New York: Academic Press.

Kuhl, J. (1985). Volitional mediators of cognition-behavior consistency: Self-regulatory processes and action versus state orientation. In J. Kuhl & J. Beckmann (Eds.), *Action control: From cognition to behavior.* Berlin, New York: Springer-Verlag.

Kuhl, J. & Mader, N. (1980). *Systemubergreifendes Computerprogramm zur Simulation der dynamischen Handlungstheorie.* Unveröffentlichtes Programm, Ruhr-Universität Bochum.

Lewin, K. (1935). *A dynamic theory of personality.* New York: McGraw-Hill.

Lienert, G.A. (1961). *Testaufbau und Testanalyse.* Weinheim: Beltz.

Lord, F.M., & Novick, M.R. (1968). *Statistical theories of mental test scores.* Reading, MA: Addison-Wesley.

Lowell, E.L. (1952). The effect of need for achievement in learning and speed of performance. *Journal of Psychology, 33,* 31-40.

McClelland, D.C. (1951), *Personality.* New York: Holt, Rinehart and Winston.

McClelland, D.C. (1958). Risk taking in children with high and low need for achievement. In J.W. Atkinson (Ed.), *Motives in fantasy, action, and society* (pp. 7-42). Princeton, NJ: Van Nostrand.

McClelland, D.C. (1971). *Assessing human motivation.* New York: General Learning Press.

McClelland, D.C. (1980). Motive dispositions: The merits of operant and re-spondent measures. In L. Wheeler (Ed.), *Review of Personality and Social Psychology*. Beverly Hills: Sage Publications.

McClelland, D.C., Atkinson, J.W., Clark, R.A., & Lowell, E.L . (1953). *The achievement motive*. New York: Appleton-Century-Crofts.

McClelland, D.C., & Boyatzis, R. (1979). *Motivational predictions of pro-motion in the American Telephone and Telegraph Company: A longitudinal study*. Vortrag gehalten auf dem APA-Kongress, New York.

McClelland, D.C., Clark, R.A., Roby, T.B., & Atkinson, J.W. (1949). The projective expression of needs. IV. The effect of need for achievement on thematic apperception. *Journal of Experimental Psychology, 39*, 242-255.

McKeachie, W.J. (1961). Motiyation, teaching methods, and college learning. *Nebraska Symposium on Motivation, 9*, 111-142. Lincoln: University of Nebraska Press.

Mehrabian, A. (1968). Male and female scales of the tendency to achieve. *Educational and Psychological Measurement, 28*, 492-502.

Mehrabian, A. (1969). Measures of achieving tendency. *Educational and Psychological Measurement, 29*, 445-451.

Meyer, W.U., Heckhausen, H., & Kemmler, L. (1965). Validierungskorrelate der inhaltsanalytisch erfassten Leistungsmotivation guter und schwacher Schüler des 3. Schuljahres. *Psychologische Forschung, 28*, 301-328.

Mischel, W. (1968). *Personality and assessment*. New York: Wiley.

Moulton, R.W. (1958). Notes for a projective measure of fear of failure. In J.W. Atkinson (Ed.), *Motives in fantasy, action, and society* (pp. 563-571). Princeton, NJ: Van Nostrand.

Murray, H.A. (1938). *Explorations in personality*. New York: Oxford Uni-versity Press.

Rand, P. (1978). Some validation data for the achievement motives scale. *Scandinavian Journal of Educational Research, 22*, 155-171.

Rasch, G. (1960). *Probability models for some intelligence and attainment tests*. Kopenhagen: Nielson und Lydicke.

Reitman, W.R., & Atkinson, J.W. (1958). Some methodological problems in the use of thematic apperceptive measures of human motives. In J.W. At-kinson (Ed.), *Motives in fantasy, action, and society* (pp.664-684). Princeton, NJ: Van Nostrand.

Rheinberg, F. (1980). *Leistungsbewertung und Lernmotivation*. Göttingen: Hogrefe.

Sader, M., & Keil, W. (1969). Faktorenanalytische Undersuchungen zur Pro-jektion der Leistungsmotivation. *Archiv fur die gesamte Psychologie, 120*, 25-53.

Sader, M., & Specht, H. (1967). Leistung, Motivation und Leistungsmotivation: Korrelationsstatistische Untersuchungen zur Leistungsmotivmessung nach Heckhausen. *Archiv fur Psychologie, 119,* 90-130.

Scheier, M.F., Buss, A.H., & Buss, D.M. (1978). Self-consciousness, self-report of aggressiveness, and aggression. *Journal of Research in Personality, 12,* 133-140.

Schmalt, H.-D. (1976). *Die Messung des Leistungsmotivs.* Göttingen: Hogrefe.

Scott, W.A. (1958). The avoidance of threatening material in imaginative behavior. In J.W. Atkinson (Ed.), *Motives in fantasy, action, and society.* Princton, NJ: D. van Nostrand.

Seltzer, R.A. (1973). Simulation of the dynamics of action. *Psychological Reports, 32,* 859-872.

Seltzer, R.A., & Sawusch, J.R. (1974). A program for computer simulation of the dynamics of action. In J.W. Atkinson & J.O. Raynor (Eds.), *Motivation and achievement.* Washington, DC: Winston.

Skinner, B.F. (1938). *The behavior of organisms.* New York: Appleton-Century-Crofts.

Sorrentino, R.M., & Short, J.A.C. (1977). The case of the mysterious moderates: Why motives sometimes fail to predict behavior. *Journal of Personality and Social Psychology, 35,* 478-484.

Wasna, M. (1972). *Motivation, Intelligenz und Lernerfolg.* München: Kösel.

Wechsler, D. (1952). *The measurement of adult intelligence (3rd ed.).* Baltimore: Williams & Wilkins.

Wicklund, R.A. (1975). Objective self-awareness. In L. Berkowitz (Ed.), *Advances in Experimental Social Psychology (Vol. 8)* (pp. 233-275). New York: Academic Press.

Wicklund, R.A. (1982). Self-focused attention and the validity of self-reports. In M.P. Zanna, E.T. Higgins & C.P. Herman (Eds.), *Consistency in social behavior.* Hillsdale, NJ: Erlbaum.

Winter, D.G., & Stewart, A. (1977). Power motive reliability as a function of retest instructions. *Journal Consulting and Clinical Psychology, 45,* 436-440.

Yerkes, R.M., & Dodson, J.D. (1908). The relation of strength of stimulus to rapidity of habit-formation. *Journal of Comparative and Neurological Psychology, 18,* 459-482.

GLOBAL AND SPECIFIC MOTIVE MEASUREMENT IN RELATION TO TASK PERFORMANCE:
Behavioral criteria for validating differences in achievement motivation

John H.L. van den Bercken

University of Nijmegen

INTRODUCTION

Measurement problems in achievement motivation research are mainly concerned with 'motive constructs', witness the questions addressed during the past decade: How should we measure 'motives', by means of operant, projective techniques, or by means of respondent, questionnaire techniques (Atkinson et al. 1977; Kuhl 1983)? Should we not abandon the view of 'achievement motivation' as a unitary construct (Heckhausen 1977a, b)? What is the psychometric quality of the various measurement methods (Fineman 1977; De Bruyn 1979)? What about the state-trait distinction, should we not resort to 'situation-specific' measurement; and should we not incorporate 'domain-specificity' also in our measurements (see examples in Roede & Bergen 1981)? These questions tend to obscure the fact that motivation theories are meant to explain *behavior*. "The questions of traditional interest that concern the motivation of behavior are questions about the contemporaneous determinants of activities. What factors account for the selection, initiation, intensity, persistence, and cessation of a particular activity?" (Atkinson & Birch 1970, p. 1-2).

The apparent polarity between the endeavours of refining conceptual matters and (re-)establishing a firm empirical basis for achievement motivation theory is the background of the research reported in this paper. The paper addresses the question of the relationships between three kinds of measures: motive scores on a trait-level, obtained by standard questionnaires, situation-specific motive scores, assessed by questions directly related to the actual execution of a task, and behavioral responses that are supposed to be indicators of achievement motivation: 'choice', 'effort' and 'persistence'.

The general orientation of the paper is predominantly empirical and explorative. The following specific questions are addressed. (1) Are behavioral indicators of motivation sensibly correlated? (2) Are behavioral indicators of motivation related to situation-specific motive scores? (3) Are situation-specific motive scores related to dispositional motive scores? (4) Are task-specific motive scores and task behavior affected by task conditions?

METHOD

The present study is part of a larger project in which motivational processes of normal and (educably) learning disabled children in elementary schools are explored (SVO TP MO 642). The description of the methods will be tailored to the research questions listed above. For a complete description of the scope and the methods of the project see Poulie et al. 1985.

In this report data are presented obtained from about 230 normal elementary school children (4th and 5th grade). The children filled out a number of questionnaires in their classrooms and completed two experimental tasks, one in the classroom and one individually. Questionnaires included Harter's scale for intrinsic motivation (Harter 1980, 1981) and the achievement motive scale of Gjesme and Nygård (1970). The first questionnaire provides a score for 'intrinsic motivation' (IM), based on 24 items tapping curiosity, challenge seeking, and mastery attempts. The second questionnaire measures 'hope of success' (MS), based on 15 items, and 'fear for failure' (MF), based on 15 items. These motive scores are of primary concern in this paper. Some related scores were obtained by means of additional questionnaires. A questionnaire of Buhrmester (1980) was used to measure 'school anxiety' (BU), and Hermans's achievement motive questionnaire for children (Hermans 1971) provided scores for 'achievement motivation' (PMS) and 'fear for failure' (PMF). In addition, intelligence scores were obtained, from the primary mental abilities tests (PMA) and from Raven's progressive matrices (RAV, Raven 1958). Scholastic achievement in language and arithmetics was assessed by a special subset of the primary abilities tests (VERB and AR) and by corresponding teacher ratings (TVERB and TAR).

The tasks consisted of anagrams of five types or difficulty levels; 'easiest' were 3-letter words, and 7-letter words were 'most difficult'. The difficulty levels had been validated in a pilot study by recording ratings of perceived difficulty, number of solving subjects, and solution time. The classroom task had two sets of six anagrams and was administered according to the following procedure. After a short introduction and demonstration of the kind of problem on the blackboard the children tried to solve two items of each difficulty level, for 12 minutes in all. Then they were asked to rate the difficulty of each type of anagram on a 5-point scale. After a specific *instruction* a few questions were asked in order to obtain situation-specific motive scores. To this end a few items of the pertaining questionnaires were used in task-related wordings. The children then chose a first set of six anagrams, and tried to solve them in 12 minutes. They completed various questions on individual goal-orientation and on perceived source of reward. Then the experimenter provided *feedback* on the children's performance. The children reported their dominant feelings and their attributions of success or failure. Next they completed a *second set* of six items, again answered various questions, were offered *feedback*, and reported their feelings and attributions. The classroom task took about 75 minutes. The procedure for the individual task was in general similar to that of the classroom task. This task, however, consisted of only one set of six separately chosen anagrams. There was no task-specific measurement of motives; instead, some other questions were asked. The recording of answers and of task performance was more detailed (for instance, solution time was recorded). A specific feature of the individual task was a so called persistence item: an anagram of modal preferred difficulty level. During the completion of this item the child had the opportunity of asking help at successive points during the solution process, i.e. the first letter of the word, the second one, and so on.

The subjects, or rather the classrooms participating in the study were randomly assigned to two groups that only differed in the way the classroom task was presented. The differences were created by manipulating the procedural aspects that are marked in the above description (by means of italics). The two groups will be labeled the 'no evaluation'-group (NE) and the 'evaluation'-group (EV). First, the specific instructions were different. In the NE-group the task was presented as an opportunity for learning experience and pleasure of performance. In the EV-group the children were asked to state the expected number of solved items (out of six), and the task was presented with emphasis on accomplishment and evaluation of outcome. The two groups also differed in the way feedback was given, and in the nature of the second set of anagrams. In the NE-condition the children were given sheets with the correct answers and they verified their results all by themselves; then they could freely choose a second set of anagrams. In the EV-group the children's results were checked together with the experimenter and explicitly recorded on the worksheet. The children rated their satisfaction, and were asked to indicate the type of anagram that they perceived as being of intermediate difficulty. Before starting on the indicated set they had to state their personal norm for success.

In line with the tradition of achievement motivation research the following measurements of task performance were taken as behavioral indicators of motivation in the classroom task: the (objective) difficulty level of the first and second set of six anagrams (= 'choice', CHC1 and CHC2, with scores ranging from 1 to 5), and the number of correctly solved items weighed by (subjective) difficulty level (= 'effort', EFC1 and EFC2, range 0-30). The individual task provided scores for 'choice', by the difficulty level of the first chosen item (CHI1, range 1-5), and for 'persistence', by the time spent on the first failed item (PE1, range 0-120 secs), the number of times asked for help at the 'persistence item' (PEH, range 0-7 letters, more letters asked meaning less persistence), and the average time spent on all failed items (PEX, range 0-120 secs). The individual and the classroom task, and most of the questionnaires were administered on two occasions: either at the beginning and at the end of the school year, or in the middle and at the end of the school year.

The data relevant to the questions of this paper consist mainly of correlations and averages obtained in the NE- and the EV-groups. Due to missing values the actual number of observations entering a statistic may vary around 120 for the NE-group and around 100 for the EV-group. Except for a few t-tests, no statistical tests are used to evaluate the results. As to the correlations, the size of the matrices is more or less arbitrary (depending on the variables selected to be included) and the individual coefficients are based on a varying number of cases (due to pair-wise deletion of missing values; list-wise deletion would entail a greater loss of degrees of freedom). This obviates testing the correlation matrix as a whole. The following information may provide a substitute: with df=100 and α=.025 critical values of r are .195, .241, .274, .300, .322 and .341, for correlations between up to 7 variables, and .374 for 9 variables (one-tailed) (Guilford 1954).

RESULTS

The first question to be dealt with is the relationship among the various behavioral indicators of task motivation. The relevant data are presented in Table 1.

In order to facilitate the discussion of the results we have oriented the various scales in a common semantic direction (higher scores meaning more difficult choices, more effort spent, and more persistence, i.e. presumably stronger motivation). Before elucidating the pattern of the correlations we note two points. First, the values of the coefficients are in general rather low, ranging up to .62. Secondly, in some cases the direction of the relationship is inconsistent with expectation. In the NE-group the correlations between PE1 and PEH is negative (-.12); similarly, in the EV-group there are negative correlations between PEX and other variables, and between PEH and CHC1. As these negative values are rather low, we may, for the time being, proceed on the assumption that they are effectively zero.

Table 1. Product-moment correlations between behavioral indicators of 'choice', 'effort' and 'persistence' (× 100)

	EFC1	EFC2	CHC1	CHC2	CHI1	PE1	PEH	PEX
EFC1		37	32	29	37	17	14	-11
EFC2	35	-	40	50	29	14	9	-15
CHC1	21	21	-	50	45	8	- 2	-22
CHC2	37	27	62	-	32	25	12	- 0
CHI1	7	32	54	57	-	31	6	- 8
PE1	5	15	26	30	36	-	25	16
PEH	1	7	26	26	27	-12	-	29
PEX	13	6	23	27	34	58	62	-

Note: below diagonal = No evaluation group (n ± 120)
     above diagonal = Evaluation group (n ± 100)
EFC1, EFC2 = first and second 'effort' measurement in classroom task; CHC1, CHC2 = first and second 'choice' measurement in classroom task; CHI1 = first 'choice' in individual task; PE1 = time to first failed item (individual task); PEH = number times asked for help (individual task); PEX = mean time spent on unsolved items.

The correlation matrix may be seen to reveal the following pattern. The highest values are found between the various measurements of one index within one task. The correlation between the difficulty levels of the first and second choice in the classroom task is .62 in the NE-condition, and .50 in the EV-group. The effort measures in the classroom task correlate .35 and .37 respectively. The average correlation for the persistence measures in the individual task in both conditions is .40 and .23. The only variable that can be compared over tasks is 'choice'. The average correlation for the choice measures is .55 in the NE-group, and .38 in the EV-group.

Turning to the correlations between different variables within one type of task, we note that the average correlation between 'choice' and 'effort' measures in the classroom task is .27 in the NE-group, and .38 in the EV-group. For 'choice' and 'persistence' in the individual task the values are .32 and .10 respectively.

The last category of correlations is that between alternative indicators across the two types of task. Between 'choice' in the individual task and 'effort' in the classroom task the average correlation is .20 and .33; similarly, between 'persistence' and 'effort' measures the average correlation is .08 and .09; between 'persistence' in the individual task and 'choice' in the classroom task it is about .26 and .07.

Finally we observe that in general the correlations tend to be higher in the NE-condition, particularly the within-measures correlations.

The next question is whether the behavioral measurements are correlated with task-specific motive measurements. The data are in Table 2.

Table 2.   Correlations between task-specific motive scores and behavioral indicators (× 100)

	IM		MS		MF	
	NE	EV	NE	EV	NE	EV
EFC1	21	36	22	38	-20	-20
EFC2	30	21	24	22	- 8	-22
CHC1	35	40	39	26	-13	-40
CHC2	35	27	38	22	-17	-21
CHI1	30	26	31	11	0	-23
PE1	17	-10	18	- 6	1	-10
PEH	10	20	14	3	- 5	- 8
PEX	15	-15	2	0	- 6	- 1

Note: IM = 'intrinsic motivation', MS = 'hope of success', MF = 'fear for failure', NE = no evaluation group, EV = evaluation group. Other abbreviations as in Table 1.

Again the values of the correlations are rather low, ranging from -.40 to .40; and again there are some inconsistently directed values, in this case also mainly in the EV-group, associated with the measurement of 'persistence'. This variable however, does not seem to be related at all to the motive measures. Only the various 'choice' indicators are likely to covary with motive scores, at least weakly (up to 16% of common variance).

On average there doesn't seem to be much difference between the NE- and the EV-group. If there is any difference at all, it is in the first place with respect to 'choice' and 'fear of failure' (MF); the pertinent correlation is on average somewhat stronger in the EV-group than in the NE-group (-.28 vs -.07). The correlations between 'choice' and 'success orientation' (MS) appear to corroborate such a difference: in the EV-condition the values are lower than in the NE-group (.20 vs .36).

The third question focuses on the relationship between situation-specific motive measures obtained in actual task performance and global measures obtained by means of questionnaires. The data are presented in Figure 1.

Figure 1. Correlations between various kinds of motive measurements (n = ± 225)

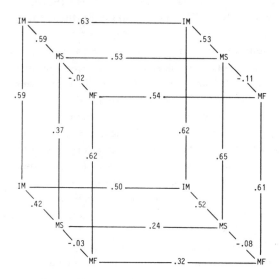

Left plane vs right plane: first measurement occasion vs second measurement occasion (test-retest reliability).

Upper plane vs lower plane: trait measurement (questionnaires) vs state measurement (tasks).

IM = intrinsic motivational orientation, MS = success orientation,

MF = failure orientation.

For a better understanding of the psychometric qualities of the questionnaires figure 1 includes data from both the first and the second measurement occasion (in this case the beginning and the end of the academic year).

One indication of the quality of the various questionnaires is provided by their internal consistencies (Cronbach's alpha); the pertinent figures satisfactorily range from .82 to .91. The corresponding figures for the task-specific measures are lower: from .52 to .73 (note that the latter figures are based on 'tests' consisting of 4 to 6 'items'!). The test-retest correlations are fairly good, indicating a common variance of 53% to 63% (assuming equal error variances on both occasions). For the task measures these figures are much lower: 24% to 50%.

The validity of the measures can be evaluated by means of multitrait multimethod-like approach to the data from each occasion. We note that the correlation between the 'hope of success' and the 'fear for failure' scales of the AMS(-.02 and -.11) is in agreement with other reported findings (e.g. Rand 1978). Harter's 'intrinsic motivational orientation' to a large extent covers the same behavioral domain as 'hope of success' does: the data suggest a common variance of about 28% to 35%. The figures for the situation-specific measures are essentially the same.

The crucial correlations are of course those between questionnaire measures and task-related measures. For the data of the second occasion the values are fairly substantial, at least compared with the correlations between the behavioral measures and the task-specific motive scores reported above.

The next question to be addressed in this paper concerns the distinction between global and situation-specific motive measurement. This distinction rests on the assumption that actual motivation is to a large extent determined by situational factors, and that global measures sort of smooth away situational sources of variation. If this assumption is valid, the difference between the two conditions of task performance (emphasis on evaluation of results versus no evaluation), should be reflected in the task-specific motive scores. The relevant data are presented in Table 3.

We first note that the two groups are not differing in their mean level of motive strength. They are different however, with respect to the behavioral measures, particularly with respect to 'choice'. Subjects in the EV-group prefer tasks of a difficulty level that is somewhat lower than in the NE-condition. They also appear to be less persistent: they spend less time and ask more help. With respect to 'effort' the picture is ambiguous: subjects in the EV-group show less effort in the first classroom task, but not in the second one. The first result is consistent with the reduced persistence in the individual task.

Table 3.   Mean values of behavioral measures 'effort', 'choice' and 'persist-
            ence' in the No Evaluation group (NE) and the Evaluation group
            (EV)

	NE	EV	t	p
EFC1	10.83	9.52	2.11	.036
EFC2	11.15	11.38	-1.39	.70
CHC1	2.68	2.42	2.13	.034
CHC2	2.48	2.24	2.07	.039
CHI1	2.35	2.08	2.48	.014
PE1	106.88	97.68	2.07	.04
PEH	.83	1.11	-1.96	.052
PEX	103.05	82.50	7.59	.000
IM	2.96	2.88	1.13	.26
MS	2.69	2.71	- .24	.81
MF	1.73	1.80	-1.00	.32

In order to appreciate these figures properly, they must be related to the
results in Table 2. Those variables on which the mean level of both groups is
significantly different (Table 3), also appear to be differentially correlated
with task-specific motive measures in each group (Table 2). As the groups
are not different on the motive measures, this means that emphasising evaluation of outcomes does not affect the degree of motivate strength by itself
(means of motive scores), but rather the effect of motive strength on task
behavior (correlations between motive scores and behavioral variables).
This effect is seen most clearly with 'choice' and the AMS-cores. The
NE-group consistently prefers more difficult tasks than the EV-group; at the
same time the mean correlation of chosen difficulty level and 'hope of success'
is .36 in the NE-group, and .20 in the EV-group, whereas the mean correlation of 'choice' and 'fear for failure' is -.07 in the NE-group, and -.28 in
the EV-group.

To complete the picture with respect to the meaning of motive measures
obtained by questionnaires, we finally present in Table 4 some data that are
conventionally presented in validation studies (e.g. Rand 1978).

Table 4. Correlations between 'intelligence' (PMA, RAV), 'achievement motivation' (IM, MS, PMS), 'avoidance motivation' (BU, MF, PMF), and 'scholastic achievement' (VERB, TVERB, AR, TAR) (n = 144) (× 100)

	PMA	RAV	IM	MS	PMS	BV	MF	PMF	VERB	TVERB	AR	TAR
PMA	-	48	17	18	04	-23	-19	-23	39	36	56	47
RAV		-	15	13	06	-34	-23	-05	30	27	39	33
IM			-	53	26	-41	-45	-34	14	23	26	32
MS				-	45	-07	-15	01	14	13	25	20
PMS					-	-22	-24	-10	24	23	27	21
BU						-	69	51	-12	-24	-32	-39
MF							-	42	-14	-26	-26	-36
PMF								-	01	-06	-16	-22
VERB									-	64	53	50
TVERB										-	50	69
AR											-	66
TAR												-

Table 4 contains the correlations between the scores on the intelligence tests and motive questionnaires (2nd occasion) and various indicators of scholastic achievement. A regression analysis was performed (by means of Jöreskogs LISREL-program), with intelligence scores and motive scores as (latent) predictors, and scholastic achievement as the criterion. The results are presented in Figure 2.

It should be stressed that there were no restrictions in the structural part of the model. The goodness-of-fit measures therefore only pertain to the measurement model implied by Figure 2. The regression results should be interpreted accordingly.

'Scholastic achievement' turns out to be mainly determined by 'intelligence' (β = .64), and, to a lesser extent, by 'hope of success' (β = .20). Both factors account for 58% of the variance in scholastic achievement. The squared loadings of each manifest variable on the latent factors offer another reliability estimate, conditional of course on the validity of the measurement model. The motive questionnaires are clearly not very congeneric: The PMT-k of Hermans has substantially lower loadings on the latent variables than the other questionnaires (.43 and .56 vs .64 to .89).

Figure 2. A latent-variable model for regression of scholastic achievement on intelligence and motivation (LISREL, n = 144)

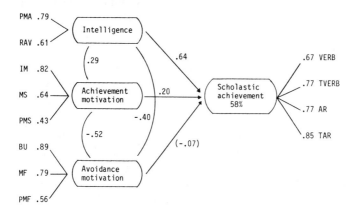

For abbreviations see text. Chi-square = 134.06, df = 48, Goodness of fit index = .87, adjusted GFI = .80, mean resident correlation = .073.

DISCUSSION

Before commenting upon the validity and the implications of the results we first summarize them in the following statements. (1) Alternative operationalizations of each behavioral indicator of motivation (e.g. of 'choice') correlate only moderately. Indicators of 'choice', 'effort', and 'persistence' within each task correlate on average .23 to .62; 'choice' operationalizations across tasks correlate on average .38 to .55. (2) Between the various behavioral variables there is a rather low association within tasks (.10 to .38 on average), and a still lower association over tasks (.07 to .33). (3) Behavioral motivation indicators do not appear to be very substantially related to task-specific motive scores (correlations below .40). (4) Motivation indexes may be affected by task conditions (e.g. evaluation of outcome), whereas motive scores are not (Table 2). (5) Relationships between motive scores obtained from questionnaires appear to be more substantial (Figure 1) than relationships between motive scores and other tests (Figure 2).

How should we evaluate these results? First of all we must consider some methodological points. Disappointingly low correlations are often attributed to various 'technical' causes, such as low reliabilities, non-linearity, restriction of range and selection, and a limited number of scale values. As to the behavioral measures, we prefer to regard variability (stochasticity) of responses as something to be explained, rather than as a de facto explanation of deviations from some unknown but allegedly true score; so we cannot held measurement error responsible for the low correlations. Unreliability seems to be more of a problem for the various questionnaire measures, since the questionnaires have been conceived in the spirit of classical test theory. But even with a correction for attenuation the correlations between task-specific motive measures and the behavioral indicators of motivation remain low, as may be seen in the following example. From Figure 1 we take 'hope of success' as the variable having the lowest (retest) reliability (.53). Since task-specific motive measures may vary over time by definition, it seems reasonable to assume that their intrinsic unreliability, due to measurement error, is equal to that of the questionnaire measures. Assuming perfect reliability for the behavioral measures, the lowest and the highest observed correlations of 'choice' and 'hope of success' (.11 and .39 in Table 2) become .20 and .54 respectively, when corrected for attenuation. These figures would not substantially alter our summary statements above.

The presentation of the results thus far has been relatively 'theory free', in that 'choice', 'effort', and 'persistence' have been taken at face value as behavioral expressions of task motivation. On the assumption that strength of motivation is reflected in various behavioral responses, it is certainly legitimate to investigate the association between these responses in the way it was done above. Quite another matter is the question of HOW actual behavioral reflects task motivation, or the way in which actual behavior is related to various determining factors, e.g. task properties and personality characteristics. It is precisely this question that is addressed by theories of achievement motivation such as Atkinson's risk-taking model (Atkinson 1964) and Vroom's effort model (Vroom 1964). That question is not the subject-matter of our study; we have been focusing instead on a preliminary one, the implicit assumption of theories of achievement motivation THAT particular behaviors are indeed reflecting motivational tendencies. As long as the various theories do not specify exactly the way in which different behavioral responses should reflect motivation strength, we may proceed on the assumption that different behaviors should correlate when they share a 'common cause'. Now there is one theory that indeed specifies a relation between a behavioral response ('choice') and task factors, particularly 'difficulty level'. Atkinson's model predicts (indirectly) the kind of choice that is made by subjects differing in motive strength. Relevant to our discussion is the fact that a non-linear relation is implied. If Atkinson's theory is correct, it does not make sense to correlate 'choice of difficulty level' and 'motive score' in the way we did. We therefore also computed these correlations according to Atkinson's model; the coefficients ranged from .28 to .45, again not dramatically different from the figures in Table 2.

As to the remaining problems, our sample clearly involves selection, in that only 4th and 5th grade pupils were included. It is, however, not very likely that the ensuing restriction of range with respect to age is responsible for the low values of some critical correlation coefficients, as there is also a large number of coefficients that have quite acceptable values (e.g. Figure 1 and Figure 2). It is difficult to see how restriction of range could affect only a subset of the coefficients, and then again precisely the ones that are crucial to our argument!

The final problem is that of the small number of scale values. This problem would apply particularly in the case of 'choice', where only 5 discrete values are possible. (The motive scores range from 1 to 4 but are not discrete). The possibility that this limited number of values would have a negative affect on the degree of correlation with other variables cannot be completely ruled out. This possibility can, however, at least partially be refuted by pointing out that precisely the alternative 'choice'-measurements are comparatively strongly correlated. So it is not likely that the problem is very serious.

As a result of the foregoing argument, we are confronted with a rather paradoxical situation. On the one hand we have motive measurements, either global, at the level of general dispositions or traits, or more specific, as task-induced states. These measures, obtained by questionnaires, appear to behave fairly well, at least in terms of the conventional criteria for convergent and discriminant validity. On the other hand, we have behavioral measures of task performance, presumably reflecting certain motivational states. These measures do not behave as they should: they correlate poorly within themselves and they also correlate very weakly with motive measures at the state level. In the following paragraphs we will in particular comment upon the predicament of the behavioral measures of task motivation.

Barring methodological shortcomings, and faced with similar findings from other studies (De Bruyn and Van den Bercken 1983), we are forced to the conclusion that the implicitly assumed behavioral domain of achievement motivation theory is very ill defined, to say the least.

Without going into a detailed analysis, we would like to point out one factor that certainly has contributed to this predicament: the tendency to emphasise 'theoretical constructs' in some areas of psychological research. The focus of research in achievement motivation has long been 'n Ach', and its derivative constructs like 'hope of success' and 'fear for failure'. Much effort went in the development of measurement methods: the constructs had to be 'operationalized' and 'validated'. The problems of that enterprise are well known (for reviews see: Fineman 1977; De Bruyn 1979). Discussions of the relative merits of 'operant' versus 'respondent' measurement (Atkinson et al. 1977; Kuhl 1983; see also Kuhl in this volume), or of 'behavioral decision tasks', for that matter, are apt to get lost in some kind of infinite regress: constructs are validated by referring to other constructs, instead of by actual behavior.

The prevalence of 'constructs' over 'behavior' is nicely illustrated by the review article of Kleininga and Kleininga (1981) on motivation. "In an attempt to resolve the terminological confusion, 102 statements defining or criticizing the concept were compiled". The authors tried to find common denominators on a conceptual level; they did not attempt to delimit a common behavioral domain. Another illustration, more specific to the area of achievement motivation, is provided by the vicissitudes of a recent proposal for a 'new' measurement method: the use of a decision task or a scenario. Some years ago it was felt that 'behavioral decision theory' might be used in motivation research in order to study the factors affecting 'intended choice' and 'intended effort'(e.g. Stahl & Harrell 1981). In this method respondents are asked to indicate what they would prefer to do and how much effort they would spend in well-defined situations the description of which was systematically varied by the experimenter. The data obtained by this procedure seem to be closer to actual behavior than 'global motivational orientations or attitudes' and 'phantasies, thoughts and feelings' are, in the sense that the causal links to be specified by a theoretical mechanism might be shorter. One would expect that this method would indeed be used for bridging the gap between motivational constructs and actual behavior. It comes therefore as a surprise, when people are using the method in order to measure constructs again (Harrell & Stahl 1983), thereby again moving away from behavior and again facing the problem of behavioral validity.

Instead of searching behavioral correlates for theoretical constructs it may be more fruitful to search constructs that are able to explain observed behavior (cf Roskam 1981). The choice between (a) having constructs and being in need of behavior, and (b) having having behavior and being in need of constructs should not be difficult. Before constructing any explanation of behavior, one should know exactly what behavior one wants to explain. Concentrating upon the behavioral domain may have the advantage of facilitating (not necessarily ensuring) consensus among researchers: it is easier to agree on what can be seen than on what can be thought or 'constructed' - unless of course the constructs are completely embodied in the formalism of mathematical equations.

The relevance of this argument may appear to be weakened by some of the data reported in this paper. Figure 2 seems to witness the very fact that it is possible to obtain results on relationships between variables (constructs) that are easy to understand: it does make sense that 'intelligence' and 'motivation' account for some 60% of variation in scores for 'scholastic achievement'. It is, however, not at all clear what such figures are actually telling us. The scores for 'intelligence' and for 'scholastic achievement' are different from the 'motive' scores: they are based on actual behavior, i.e. on the outcomes of actual tasks, whereas the 'motive' scores are based on subjective descriptions of how children think they are (which is certainly 'behavior' too, but of a different level, and not easily related to actual task motivation). So it is not quite clear what these figures are in effect proving: Our capacity to organize data in a meaningful way (i.e. congruent to our intuitive notions)? The capacity of 'normal' respondents to offer a consistent picture of their own self-perception (consistency increasing with 'intelligence')? Or the fact that the only possible set of empirical data (admitted by our theory or 'constructs') has indeed been realized?

This is not the place however, to elaborate alternative approaches to achievement motivation research. As a matter of fact, much of the position outlined above is in the spirit of the program presented by Atkinson and Birch (1970). Unfortunately, despite their intentions, they do not fulfill their promise: they offer a theory for behavioral tendencies (another construct), not for actual behavior, and they do not specify a mechanism that predicts actual behavior. The work of Blankenship and Kuhl (1979 a,b) partly makes up for this neglect. Moreover, various competing attempts are being made to develop (formal) models starting from well-defined response domains (e.g. Thomas 1983 for 'effort'; Myers and Miezin 1980 for 'choice'). Perhaps still more promising are approaches explicitly dealing with a problem that has been recognized for a long time by intelligence theorists (Thurstone 1937), although only recently it received some attention from motivation theorists (Atkinson 1981): the intricate relationship between intelligence (ability) and motivation (effort, persistence) in task performance (skills, problems) (e.g. White 1982).

ACKNOWLEDGEMENTS

The research reported in this paper was supported by a Grant from the Dutch Foundation of Educational Research (SVO TP MO 642).

123

Thanks are due to mrs Margreet Poulie and mrs Inge Jansen, who translated several questionnaires and prepared the material for the individual and the classroom task.

REFERENCES

Atkinson, J.W. (1964). *An introduction to motivation.* Princeton, N.J.: Van Nostrand.

Atkinson, J.W. (1980). Motivational effects in so-called tests of ability and educational achievement. In: L.J. Fyans (Ed.), *Achievement motivation.* New York: Plenum Press.

Atkinson, J.W., & Birch, D.A. (1970). *The dynamics of action.* New York: Wiley.

Atkinson, J.W., Bongort, K., & Price, L.H. (1977). Explorations using computer simulation to comprehend thematic apperceptive measurement of motivation. *Motivation and Emotion, 1,* 1-27.

Buhrmester, D. (1980). Assessing elementary-school aged children's school anxieties: The rationale, development and correlations of the school concerns scale. Denver: University of Denver (Unpubl. Masters Thesis).

De Bruyn, E.E.J. (Ed.) (1979). *Ontwikkelingen in het onderzoek naar prestatiemotivatie. Theorie, meetmethoden en toepassing in het onderwijs.* Lisse: Swets & Zeitlinger.

De Bruyn, E.E.J., & Bercken van den (1982). Components of achievement motivation in young children. *International Journal of Behavioral Development, 5,* 467-489.

Fineman, S. (1977). The achievement motive construct and its measurement: Where are we now?. *British Journal of Psychology, 68,* 1-22.

Gjesme, T., & Nygård, R. (1970). Achievement-related motives: Theoretical considerations and construction of a measuring instrument. Unpublished manuscript. University of Oslo.

Guilford, J.P. (1954). *Psychometric methods.* New York: McGraw-Hill.

Harter, S. (1980). *A scale of intrinsic versus extrinsic orientation in the classroom. Manual.* Denver: University of Denver.

Harter, S. (1981). A new self-report of intrinsic versus extrinsic orientation in the classroom: motivational and informational components. *Developmental Psychology, 17,* 300-312.

Harrell, A.M., & Stahl, M.J. (1983). A behavioral decision theory approach for measuring McClelland's trichotomy of needs. *Journal of Applied Psychology, 66*, 242-247.

Heckhausen, H. (1977a). Achievement motivation and its constructs: A cognitive model. *Motivation and Emotion, 1*, 283-329.

Heckhausen, H. (1977b). Motivation: Kognitionspsychologische Aufspaltung eines summarischen Konstrukts. *Psychologische Rundschau, 28*, 175-189.

Hermans, H.J.M. (1971). *Prestatiemotief en faalangst in gezin en onderwijs.* Amsterdam: Swets & Zeitlinger.

Kleininga, P.R., & Kleininga, A.M. (1981). A categorized list of motivation definitions, with a suggestion for a consensual definition. *Motivation and Emotion, 5*, 263-291.

Kuhl, J. (1983). Leistungsmotivation: Neue Entwicklungen aus modeltheoretischer Sicht. In: H. Thomae (Ed.), *Enzyklopaedie der Psychologie, Bd. 2.* Göttingen: Hogrefe.

Kuhl, J., & Blankenship, V. (1979a). The dynamic theory of achievement motivation: From episodic to dynamic thinking. *Psychological Review, 86*, 141-151.

Kuhl, J., & Blankenship, V. (1979b). Behavioral change in a constant environment: Moving to more difficult tasks in spite of constant expectations of success. *Journal of Personality and Social Psychology, 37*, 551-563.

Meyers, J., & Miezin, F.M. (1980). The kinetics of choice: an operant system analysis. *Psychological Review, 87*, 160-174.

Poulie, M., Bercken, J.H.L. van den, & Jansen, I. (1985). *Motivatie in het buitengewoon en gewoon lager onderwijs.* Eindrapport SVO-projekt Tp Mo 642. Nijmegen.

Rand, P. (1978). Some validation data of the Achievement Motives Scale (AMS). *Scandinavian Journal of Educational Research, 22*, 155-171.

Raven, R.C. (1958). *Standard progressive matrices.* London.

Roede, E., & Bergen, Th.C.M. (Eds.) (1983). *Motivatie gemeten?* Harlingen: Flevodruk.

Stahl, M.J., & Harrell, A.M. (1981). Modelling effort decisions with behavioral decision theory: toward an individual differences model of expectancy theory. *Organizational Behavior and Human Performance, 27*, 303-325.

Thomas, E.A.C. (1983). Notes on effort and achievement-oriented behavior. *Psychological Review, 90*, 1-20.

Thurstone, L.L. (1937). Ability, motivation and speed. *Psychometrika, 2*, 249-254.

Vroom, V.H. (1964). *Work and motivation.* New York: Wiley.

White, P.O. (1982). Some major components in general intelligence. In: H.J. Eysenck (Ed.), *A model for intelligence.* Berlin: Springer.

THE INTERPLAY BETWEEN COGNITIONS AND MOTIVATION IN EARLY INFANCY

Stein Erik Ulvund
University of Oslo

SUMMARY

Based on a previous theoretical study on the interplay between cognition and motivation in early infancy (Ulvund 1980), the present report suggests an explorative empirical approach to this issue. A longitudinal study of infants (n=23) from 6 tot 13 months was made to investigate infants' engagement in their attempts to solve tasks which represented moderate and large degrees of discrepancy from the subjects' adaptation level (level of cognitive competence). Adaptation level was assessed by the Uzgiris-Hunt scales (IPDS). The results showed that the infants were significantly more intensely engaged in tasks which were moderately discrepant from the subjects' adaptation level as compared with tasks with large discrepancy.

THEORETICAL CONSIDERATIONS

Elsewhere (Ulvund 1980) a theoretical discussion on the interplay between cognition and motivation in early infancy is presented. Referring among other things to some selected aspects of Piaget's (1952) theory of the development of cognitive competence and Hunt's (1965) theory of the development of intrinsic motivation, it is argued that there seems to be a continuous interaction between cognition and motivation in infancy, and it is pointed out that the two processes cannot be clearly distinguished from each other.

A main line of argument for the above suggestion is as follows: In both Piaget's and Hunt's theories the motivational principle is closely related to a *discrepancy hypothesis*. According tot Piaget motivation is related to a disturbance in the individual's cognitive equilibrium, i.e., to a discrepancy between the individual's existing cognitive structure (schemas) and the problem or situation encountered by the individual. A base level of cognitive organization is a necessary precondition for the operation of the motivational principle. Those situations which represent a moderate discrepancy from the individual's schemas are assumed to be most strongly motivating. The momentary disequilibrium caused by a recognition of discrepancy between the individual's cognitive structure and the encountered situation is called by Piaget a "functional need". These needs ".... appear during functioning" (Piaget 1952, p. 44). According to Piaget, a sine qua non of an optimal development of the individual's cognitive structure (schemas) is that the individual at each developmental level repeatedly has the possibility of encountering situations which represent a moderate discrepancy from the individual's cognitive structure.

Thus, the problem of motivation in Piagets's theory of cognitive development is conspicious at two points. Firstly, in the situation where the individuals encounters a problem and secondly, in the individual's development from one cognitive stage to another. The basic assumptions (a) that a moderate discrepancy between the individual's present cognitive structure and the situation the individual encounters is a necessary precondition for the development of cognitive structures and further, (b) that a certain level of cognitive structures (schemas) must exist prior to the assimilation, imply that there must be a close interplay between cognition and motivation in early infancy.

Like Piaget Hunt has also based his theory on a discrepancy hypothesis. One of the key concepts in Hunt's theory is the *incongruity* principle. In line with Piaget Hunt assumes that behavior is most strongly activated when there is a moderate discrepancy between the individual's standards and the ongoing input. These standards "... may take the form of adaptation levels ... of expectations ..." (Hunt 1965, p. 202), and these expectations are derived from previous experiences. Thus, the epigenesis of standards becomes an important aspect of motivational development. One aspect of what Hunt (1965) has labelled "the problem of the match" constitutes "... the problem of arranging a proper relationship between circumstances and existing schemata to produce accomodative modification in the structure of schemata for intellectual growth" (Hunt 1965, p. 230). Hunt assumes that such arrangements will foster the development of intrinsic motivation.

It should be emphasized that the incongruity principle implies a judgemental procedure concerning the extent to which there is a discrepancy between the input and the standard, and whether this discrepancy is conceived as optimal or not (e.g., Weizmann 1977). The individual is not reacting to an absolute level of stimulation, and it is implicit in the concept of optimal incongruity that the individual spontaneously evaluates and compares inputs with existing cognitive standards. This judgement represents a cognitive

function, and the crucial point here is that cognitive functions play a decisive part both in the activation and the development of intrinsic motivation.
Thus, Hunt's theory of intrinsic motivation represents another example of a
theory of interplay between cognition and motivation in infancy.

However, an empirical approach to the interplay between cognition and
motivation in early infancy is, from a methodological point of view, a highly
complicated issue. Elsewhere (Ulvund 1980) it has tentatively been suggested
that when *ordinal* scales of psychological development are used, it may be
possible to study the relationship between cognition and motivation by an exploration of infant's responses to items which represent different degrees of
discrepancy from the adaptation level expressed through the items which the
infant masters at a given time. Based on the above considerations it will in
the following be explored to what extent infants are more motivated for problems represented by items which are of moderate degrees of discrepancy from
the subjects' adaptation level, than for items which represent a large discrepancy.

PROCEDURE

Subjects
   Subjects were 23 first-born medically healthy infants, 13 boys and 10
girls, who were 6 months old upon entrance in the study. The subjects were
selected from the card index of two Centres of Child Welfare in Oslo.

Instruments
Cognitive Adaptation Levels
   The subjects' cognitive *adaptation level* was defined as the highest mastered task on the Ordinal Scales of Psychological Development (IPDS) constructed by Uzgiris and Hunt (1975). These scales can be used
independently of each other, and in the present study the following four scales were used: The development of visual pursuit and the permanence of ob-
jects (Scale 1); The development of means for obtaining desired
environmental events (Scale 2); The development of operational causality
(Scale 3); and The construction of object relations in space (Scale 4). The
IPDS were scored according to the manual.

Tasks of Moderate and Large Discrepancy from the Adaptation Level

129

The IPDS are to a large extent of *ordinal* nature, and tasks of *moderate* discrepancy from the subjects' adaptation level were defined as tasks *one* step above the tasks which the subjects were mastering at each age level. Further, tasks which were assumed to represent a relatively *large* degree of discrepancy from the subjects' adaptation level were defined as tasks three steps above the task which were correctly solved.

In some cases the subjects got zero or ceiling scores on the scales. In such cases it was impossible to present items of any discrepancy from the adaptation level, and these subjects were later excluded from the analysis of data.

Motivation

Motivation was assessed by the subjects' *engagement* in their attempts to solve tasks of, respectively, moderate and large discrepancy from the subjects' adaptation level. Engagement was rated by the author on a three point scale, ranging from high, to moderate, to low according to the following criteria: high when the subjects clearly showed a strong interest and persistence in the situation and a lot of relevant responses were observed; moderate, when the subjects showed some interest in the situation and some relevant responses were observed, but were easily disturbed and the attention was often directed towards the examiner or things in the room; and low when the subjects showed no interest in the situation, no relevant responses were observed, and they looked at the examiner or things in the room. As yet here are no data on the reliability of the rating procedure.

General Procedure

A longitudinal study from 6 to 13 months was conducted. The infants were observed by the author in their homes once a month (on their monthly birthday ± 5 days). The observations were made at different times during the day, but appointments for observations were at a time when the infant usually was alert and active. During nearly all testing sessions the infants were highly alert and active, and it was never necessary to interrupt the testing because of tiredness or lack of motivation. However, three observation sessions were lost; two at 10 months and one at 11 months.

During each testing session first the child's adaptation level was established (phase 1), and then the discrepancy tasks were given. Since session 1 represents a determination of the highest mastered task on the IPDS for each subject, the time for reaching this level was varying for the different subjects, and the time was also varying from one scale to another. How long time the subjects used to reach their level of mastery was not assessed. However, in phase 2 the basis for scoring motivation was a time period of three minutes, and motivation was only assessed during phase 2. The final motivation score was based on the three point scale described above. The time basis for this scoring was the subjects behavior in phase 2 during three minutes.

RESULTS

In Table 1 mean values and standard deviations for the subjects' engagement in tasks which were of moderate, respectively large discrepancy from the adaptation level are presented.

On scale 1 the infants clearly show a stronger engagement in connection with items which were moderately discrepant from the adaptation level compared with items with large discrepancies. This strong tendency is stable over age, and a sign test (Siegel 1956) shows that the result is highly significant (p=.004, one-tailed test). The Table shows that, except for engagement at 12 months, there is no variation in scores for items of large discrepancy from the adaptation level, i.e. nearly all subjects have the lowest possible score.

Even the results for Scale 2 show that the subjects were clearly more engaged when confronted with tasks which had moderate degrees of discrepancy from the adaptation level than those of large discrepancy. This result is consistent over the eight age periods, and again a sign test shows that the result is highly significant (p=.004, one-tailed test). On this scale for five out of eight age levels there is also a certain variation in scores for items of large discrepancy from the adaptation level.

The results for Scale 4 deviate from the former ones. On this scale only three of the six age periods which were investigated show a tendency in the expected direction. (At 12 and 13 months ceiling performances were nearly obtained for the majority of subjects, and consequently it was impossible to present items with large discrepancy from the adaptation level). For the other age periods no differences were found between items of moderate and large degrees of discrepancy from the adaptation level. Thus, for this scale the differences between mean values did not exceed chance expectations.

However, the results for Scale 5 are in agreement with the results for Scale 1 and 2. On Scale 5 subjects at seven of the eight age levels were more engaged in tasks of moderate discrepancy than in those of large discrepancy. This result is significant (p=.035, one-tailed test).

Table 1. Mean values and standard deviations at different age levels for the sujects' engagement on items at the IPDS with moderate and large discrepancies from the adaptive level

		6			7			8			9			10			11			12			13		
		X	N	SD	X	N	SD	X	N	SD	X	N	SD	X	N	SD	X	N	SD	X	N	SD	X	N	SD
Scale I	Moderate	1.65	(23)	0.83	1.57	(23)	0.84	1.87	(23)	0.87	2.00	(22)	0.82	2.62	(21)	0.67	2.00	(21)	0.78	1.83	(23)	0.89	1.96	(23)	0.88
	Large	1.00	(23)	0.00	1.00	(23)	0.00	1.00	(23)	0.00	1.00	(22)	0.00	1.00	(21)	0.00	1.00	(21)	0.00	1.09	(23)	0.42	1.00	(21)	0.00
Scale II	Moderate	2.14	(22)	0.83	2.22	(23)	0.74	2.09	(23)	0.73	1.86	(22)	0.64	2.05	(21)	0.81	1.86	(21)	0.85	2.35	(23)	0.83	2.43	(23)	0.79
	Large	1.00	(22)	0.00	1.00	(23)	0.00	1.22	(23)	0.60	1.09	(22)	0.43	1.00	(21)	0.00	1.05	(21)	0.22	1.13	(23)	0.46	1.09	(22)	0.43
Scale IV	Moderate	2.00	(20)	0.56	1.71	(21)	0.56	1.81	(21)	0.40	1.79	(19)	0.42	1.92	(13)	0.28	2.00	(02)	0.00	-	(00)	-	-	(00)	-
	Large	1.70	(20)	0.57	1.71	(21)	0.56	1.80	(20)	0.41	1.74	(19)	0.45	1.77	(13)	0.44	2.00	(02)	0.00	-	(00)	-	-	(00)	-
Scale V	Moderate	1.87	(23)	0.69	1.91	(23)	0.73	1.83	(23)	0.65	1.68	(22)	0.65	1.71	(21)	0.72	1.95	(21)	0.87	1.78	(23)	0.52	1.96	(22)	0.90
	Large	2.13	(23)	0.69	1.26	(23)	0.45	1.09	(23)	0.29	1.09	(22)	0.29	1.00	(21)	0.00	1.05	(21)	0.22	1.00	(23)	0.00	1.00	(19)	0.00

132

DISCUSSION

For three of the four scales it has been shown that infants are significantly more engaged in connection with items which are assumed to represent a
moderate degree of discrepancy from the adaptation level, compared with
items which are assumed to represent a large discrepancy.

As far as Scale 4 is concerned there seems to be no obvious explanation of
why the results for this scale deviate from the other ones. However, the fact
that this scale consists of only seven steps, and that a majority of subjects
almost obtained ceiling performances at 11 months, may have influenced the
results.

The above results give an illustrative example of the interplay between
cognition and motivation in infancy. They demonstrate that infants at different developmental levels are more strongly motivated in terms of engagement
in situations which represent a moderate degree of discrepancy from the infants' existing cognitive structure. Thus, the extent to which an infant's *motivation* to solve a task is aroused, depends on the infant's level of cognitive
competence as well as situational factors. Furthermore, the quality of an item
(stimulus) must be individually defined in relation to the degree of discrepancy between the new input and the infant's level of cognitive competence.
On the other hand, the fact that new stimuli or problems must always be
compared with the individual's level of competence implies that cognition is an
active process, and this means that *motivational* functions are considered to
be important aspects of the individual's *cognitive functions.*

The suggested interplay between cognition and motivation in early infancy
indicates among other things that it is essential to reconsider the problem of
how to identify critical factors which are of primary importance for the development of cognitive competence in infancy. To the extent that motivation
is dependent on the infant's encounters with "perturbing" events, the *quality* of the environmental stimulation becomes a decisive factor in cognitive development. Generally, one of the most important variables in the environment
is probably the total variation of environmental stimulation, because variation
increases the possibility for individuals at different levels of cognitive competence to encounter situations (problems) which represent a moderate discrepancy from the individual's existing cognitive structure at a given time.
Restricting examples to the physical environment, a recent study (Ulvund,
paper submitted for publication) has shown that variables in the infants'
home environment such as variety, complexity and responsiveness are significantly related to the infants' cognitive competence assessed by the Uzgiris-Hunt scales (IPDS).

ACKNOWLEDGEMENT

This study was supported by the Norwegian Research Council for Science and Humanities. Thanks to Roald Nygard and Per Rand for their comments on the paper. The author is also grateful to Olav Skard for his assistance in the treatment of the data.

REFERENCES

Hunt, J. McV. (1965), Intrinsic motivation and its role in psychological development. In D. Levine (Ed), *Nebraska symposium on motivation* (pp. 189-282). Lincoln: University of Nebraska Press.

Piaget, J. (1952). *The origin of intelligence in children.* New York: International Universities Press

Siegel, S. (1956). *Nonparametric statistics for the behavioral sciences.* New York: McGraw-Hill.

Ulvund, S.E. (1980). Cognitions and motivation in early infancy: An interactionistic approach. *Human Development, 23,* 17-32.

Ulvund, S.E. Physical environmental parameters and the development of cognitive competence in infancy. Paper submitted for publication.

Uzgiris, I.C. & Hunt, J. McV. (1975). *Assessment in infancy. Ordinal scales of psychological development.* Urbana: University of Illinois Press.

Weizmann, F. (1977). Praxis and interaction. The psychology of J. McVicker Hunt. In I.C. Uzgiris & F. Weizmann (Eds.), *The structuring of experience* (pp. 1-23). New York: Plenum Press.

PART III

MOTIVATION IN EDUCATION

THE CONTENT-ORIENTED TASK-MOTIVE AND ITS EFFECTS ON THE ACQUISITION OF KNOWLEDGE AND SKILLS

Peter Nenniger

University of Freiburg

SUMMARY

A motivational analysis of instructionally guided learning requires some modifications of the general expectancy x value model of motivation. Hereby the dynamic aspects of motive development and learning are examined in a 3-dimensional model. The results lead to the supposition that the "domain of learning" is the predominant dimension on which all other aspects of learning largely depend.

INTRODUCTION

In general, achievement motivation and content-oriented task motivation are conceived within the framework of expectancy x value models of motivation (Atkinson 1957; Feather 1982), and in addition Heckhausen's process-model of motivation (Heckhausen 1973, resp. Heckhausen 1977). For several reasons however, the analysis of content - oriented motivation requires some modifications of the general model, especially when used for a motivational analysis of instructionally guided learning. The most important reasons are the following:

Firstly as we noticed in our own studies (e.g. Eigler, Macke & Nenniger 1982) in ordinary learning situations (not in examinations etc.) with respect to instructional conditions, explained variances most commonly amount to about 30% for cognitive variables, and to about 20% for motivational variables, 3-7% of which are for achievement oriented, but 8-20% content oriented variables. This might suggest that, in such environments, achievement motivation has to be conceived as a stable framework surrounding content oriented interactions between cognitive and motivational aspects of learning. Therefore it is necessary to pay special attention to cognitive conditions in motivational settings, and to specify properly the type of situational determinants interacting with the motive considered.

Secondly, There is some empirical evidence that content-oriented motives are not as stable as the achievement motive (cf. Nenniger 1985) Therefore the aspect of motive development must be considered with increasing attention.

Thirdly, although problems of future time perspective have already been developed in achievement motivation (e.g. Atkinson & Raynor 1974; Lens & De Volder 1982), this view needs some more specification with respect to content orientation (e.g. Lind 1975; Schiefele et al. 1979; Schiefele 1980) and meaningfulness of learning (e.g. Lehwald 1982; Matushkin 1980; Nenniger 1985). Content-oriented motivation of meaningful learning should not be explained only with regard to the final outcome of learning (or more precisely, due to the final reaching of specific goals), the dynamic aspect of instructional guidance in the acquisition of knowledge or skills has also to be taken into consideration. According to these desiderata, motivation conceptualized as a condition for goal-reaching in meaningful learning needs to be expanded to a concept that also reflect the correspondences between motive development and the dynamics of learning during the period of instructional guidance.

Finally, on the basis of theories of learning and instruction (Bruner 1966; Gagne 1977; Lompscher 1982; Aebli 1980), as well as from research in cognitive learning (originating e.g. from Lindsay & Norman 1977, Anderson 1980), the supposition may be put forward that the domain of learning, and most probably also its content, merit to be taken into consideration more seriously. Hereby the distinction between an informative and an operative domain of learning (i.e. between knowledge and skills) seems of particular use, since it covers the most important variables for the description of cognitive learning (cf. Kluwe & Spada 1981). For that reason, in content-oriented motivation a separate analysis of motivational effects on knowledge and in skills acquisition may be recommended.

A cubic model for motivation in meaningful learning
With respect to the above four arguments a cubic model with the dimensions "aspect of motive", "aspect of learning" and "domain of learning" might be useful for an analysis of content-oriented motivation of meaningful learning.

136

Figure 1. Cubic model for the analysis of motivation in instructionally guided learning

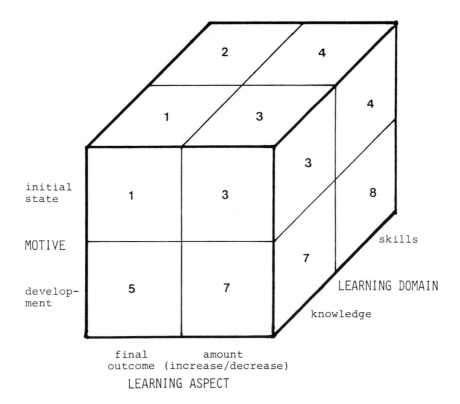

The first dimension (aspect of motive) differentiates between initial motive strength and motive development, the second dimension (aspect of learning) between final learning outcome and acquired amount of learning, and the third dimension (domain of learning) between learning in the informative domain (knowledge) and learning in the operative domain (skills)

Thus, the cubic model contains the following eight octants (see Figure 1): (1) Initial motive strength on the final informative level (knowledge), (2) Initial motive strength on the final operative level (skills), (3) Initial motive strength on the acquired amount (increase/decrease) of knowledge (4) Initial motive strength on the acquired amount of skills, (5) Motive development on the final informative level, (6) Motive development on the final operative level, (7) Motive development on the acquired amount of knowledge, (8) Motive development on the acquired amount of skills.

Following the order of the eight octants, the three aspects of motivated meaningful learning are easily detected: first, a static view of motivational effects in the first four octants (1-4) versus a dynamic view in the second four octants (5-8); secondly, motivational effects on the final level of learning outcomes (octants 1,2,5,6) versus effects on the amount of learning (octants 3,4,7,8); and finally, motivational effects in the informative domain of learning (octants 1,35,7) versus effects in the operative domain (octants 2,4,6,8). Within this heuristic model, it is possible to analyse different questions about motivational effects of instructional settings. In this paper, however, the main question only deals with contributions of content-oriented motives to instructionally guided meaningful learning in the acquisition of knowledge and skills

What contributions may be expected in the different octants? First, as results of research in content-oriented motivation indicate (e.g. Eigler, Macke & Nenniger 1985, in press), an analysis of the correspondence between motive development and meaningful learning may more sensitively reflects the various contrasts between different instructional settings than the analysis of single effects of initial motive strength on the final outcomes of learning. Moreover, on the basis of research in learning and instruction (e.g. Macke 1978), the supposition may be put forward that - instead of the final level of learning outcomes - the different amounts of meaningful learning are the more useful variables for the study of motivational effects of different instructional settings. Finally, recent theories of learning, reflecting the different underlying cognitive and metacognitive processes more and more (cf. Weiner & Kluwe 1984), may lead to the conclusion that the most important motivational effects in instructionally guided learning will be found in the operative domain of learning.

On the basis of the above arguments, the following three hypothesis may be put forward: differential effects of instructional settings are more important. When associated with motive development (effects in octants 1-4 inferior to effects in 5-8); when gauged by the amount of learning (effects in octants 1,2,5,6 inferior to effects in 3,4,7,8); when affecting the operative domain of meaningful learning (effects in octants 1,3,5,7 inferior to effects in 2,4,6,8). As a consequence, motivational effects in instructionally guided learning should be detected with increasing probability from octant 1 to octant 8. In order to evaluate the hypothesis with regard to instructional settings a field experiment that took place at different high schools (Gymnasiums) in the Region of Freiburg i.Br (F.R.G.) in 1981 is reported.

METHOD

312 pupils, aged 12-13 years, participated in an introductory course of geometry. Three groups of learners were submitted to different instructional conditions: two experimental groups with different but relatively strong and systematic instructional guidance (E1 with guided discovery after the systematic elaboration of knowledge, E2 with systematic elaboration of previously discovered knowledge), and C, a control group without systematically elaborated instruction. Measures of the content-oriented motive on the basis of a two-dimensional questionnaire (interest in mathematics and readiness for work in mathematics) on the one hand, and, measures of operational skills and measures of knowledge, (both in geometry of angles) on the other hand, were taken at the beginning and at the end of an instructional period of two weeks. We used in our analyses several measures of the motive: factor-scores of a first (factor-analytical) motive dimension "interest in the subject matter", factor-scores of a second motive dimension "readiness for work in the subject matter" and the resulting vector of the two dimensions as a compound measure. The developmental aspect is accounted for by the difference of the measures taken at the beginning and at the end of the instructional period. For further details see Nenniger 1986 and Eigler et al. 1986.

The design has one between-subjects factor, instructional setting (IS), giving rise to three groups as indicated above (E1, E2 and C). Measures of motive strength and of operational knowledge and skills were taken before the treatment (M1, K1 and S1) and after the treatment (M2, K2 and S2). The data were analyzed by means of various (univariate) linear models with final knowledge (K2), final skills (S2), increase in knowledge (K2-K1), or increase in skills (S2-S1) as the dependent variable. In each model the treatment variable (instructional setting, IS) was variously combined with other independent variables; motive strength (M1 and M2, as within-subjects factor), and increase or decrease in motive strength (M2 < M1 or M2 > M1, M±, a dichotomous variable). In some models covariables were included: initial motive strength, knowledge and skill (M1, K1, S1) or, change in motive strength (M2-M1). The various linear models were formulated in accordance with the octants of the cubic model for motivation. For instance, the model (K2-K1) = IS and M± corresponds to the 7th octant; it reveals the effect of instructional setting on the relation between motive development and the acquired amount of learning.

The results are presented with respect to two important aspects of the main question: the validity of the model (i.e. the interaction of instructional setting and motive strength) and the significance of the main effects (i.e. the influence of instructional setting and the influence of the content-oriented motive strength).

RESULTS

(A) Results with respect to the validity of the model

In the first evaluation the amount of variance explained by the interaction of instructional setting and motive strength are taken as a measure of validity for the statistical model. The results are given in Table 1.

Table 1. Variances explained by the interaction of instruction and motive for each of the octants of the cubic model

Octant	1	2	3	4	5	6	7	8
variance explained	.04	.15	.07	.16	.06	.15	.08	.17

In general, the explained variances are not very high, but there are nevertheless some important differences between the octants. The explained variances are lower bound estimations. They show the minimal variance explained by the statistical models used and are therefore considered as an indicator for the minimal importance of that model in view to explain differential effects on the dependent variable.

With respect to the first supposition, there are only very slight differences between the amount of explained variances in the different octants. No impressive differences between models starting from initial motive strength and models starting from motive-development are observable.

With respect to the second supposition, there are also very slight differences. The aspect of learning is certainly not independent of the learning conditions as imposed by different instructional settings. The increasing importance of the developmental aspect of learning is of considerable stability throughout the octants regarded, but it is certainly not of considerable differential power.

In contrast to the first two suppositions, there are very important differences in favor of the third supposition: The domain of learning is a very important factor for effect strength and moreover the operative domain is apparently more sensitive to instructional settings than the informative.

Summing up these results, the following conclusions remain: in general, the model conditions only partially explain the learning criterions, and the domain of learning is (perhaps in relation with the learning aspect) the only, but very important factor differentiating model validity.

(B) Results with respect to the most important effects in the model
In the following paragraph, the results of the significance tests (error probabilities) for the relevant sources of variation are compared between the octants. The results for the effect of instructional setting are given in Table 2.

Table 2. Results due to the influence of the instructional setting

Octant	1	2	3	4	5	6	7	8
err-prob.	.10	.01	.01	.01	.03	.01	.01	.01

In all eight octants there are highly significant effects due to the instructional settings. Almost no differences in error probability are observable throughout the octants, with one exception: for the final level of knowledge, there is a tendency of lower significance for differences in instructional settings. This result may be understood as a hint for a probable interaction of effects between the learning aspect and the learning domain. So, not surprisingly, instructional settings remain the principal sources for differences in learning.

But what about the influence of the motive? Subject-matter oriented motive is a compound measure of two dimensions: "interest in the subject matter" and "readiness for work in the subject matter". As there was no significant or unambiguous result in the compound measure separate analyses were made for each of the two dimensions. The relevant results are presented in Table 3.

Table 3. Results due to the influence of the motive (initial motive-strength and motive-development)

Octant	1	2	3	4	5	6	7	8
err-prob.	n.s.	n.s.	n.s.	.05*	.02**	n.s.	n.s.	.06***

* The significance refers only to initial interest as a covariate to the acquired amount of skills.

** The significance refers only to the development of interest whereby initial readiness is considered as a significant covariate.

*** The significance refers only to the development of readiness whereby initial interest is considered as a significant covariate.

The only significant effect of initial motive strength was found in octant 4, on the acquisition of skills. In octant 5 there was only a significant effect of "readiness" as a covariate of the increase/decrease of interest as a main effect and of the interaction of this latter variable with instructional settings. specifically on the motive dimensions and instructional settings.

With respect to the first supposition, the results clearly indicate that more differential motivational effects may be expected from differences in motive development. With reference to initial motive strength, there is only one significant effect: the increase in operative skills depends on the initial interest (octant 4). However, with respect to the other two suppositions, the above results may, in addition, lead to the conclusion that motivational effects on learning also depend on some other, relatively complex interactions with the remaining dimensions in the cubic model. Obviously the domain of learning seems to play the most important role in this context. Nevertheless, there is also some relation with the learning aspect and the motive dimension: Differences in the final level of knowledge depend on the initial level of readiness and the (instructionally differential) development of interest (octant 5), while differences in the increase/decrease of skills depend on the initial level of interest and the development of readiness (octant 8).

The above results can be summed up in the statement that motive development differentially affects the final level of knowledge and the increase of (operative) skills. A differential effect to be described by a two-sided interaction between the dimension and the aspect of the content-oriented motive on the one hand, and between the dimension of the motive and the learning domain on the other hand.

Regarding the three dimensions of the cube, the results clearly indicate that instruction is of general importance for learning.

However, the results also indicate that differences due to motivational conditions are predominantly in close relation to the learning domain, and that additional effects should only be judged with respect to this dimension.

DISCUSSION

Reconsidering the three suppositions stated at the beginning of this contribution we must concede that, although the results do not contradict our expectations, they do not support them unconditionally either.

First of all, the importance originally assigned to the different suppositions must be reordered. Without doubt, differential effects of instructional settings largely depend on the learning domain and the operative domain is the most sensitive to pedagogical interventions. The other effects are far from playing a comparable role. However there is also some evidence that motivational effects in meaningful learning may be better understood with regard to the developmental aspect of learning and motivation. In addition, some interaction can be detected between learning domain and learning aspect, and even a considerable interaction between the motive and the learning domain. But, surprisingly, it is not the motive aspect (motive strength versus motive development) that affects learning, it is the motive dimension (interest versus readiness).

So finally domain specificity is encountered in a double sense, since the observed interaction refers simultaneously to domain specific motives and to domain specific learning, a result that is very close to the outcomes of recent research in metacognitive processes (e.g. Prenzel 1984) and also of a number of studies in structural learning under specific instructional settings (e.g. Macke & Nenniger 1984).

Even if this final conclusion seems premature at the moment, - we still must know further details about the nature of the differential effects - there are good reasons to assume that specific expectancies as emerging in content-oriented motivation are differently processed when refering to knowledge or to skills and it may be recommended to encourage future research in that direction.

REFERENCES

Aebli, H. (1980/81). *Denken: das Ordnen des Tuns.* Stuttgart: Klett.

Anderson, J.R. (1980). *Cognitive psychology and its implications.* San Francisco: Freeman.

Atkinson, J.W.d (1957). Motivational determinants of risk-taking behavior. *Psychological Review, 64,* 359-372.

Atkinson, J.W., & Raynor, J.O. (1974) (Eds.), *Motivation and achievement.* Washington, D.C.: Winston.

Bruner, J.S. (1966). *Towards a theory of instruction.* Cambridge, Mass.: Harvard University Press.

Eigler, G., Macke, G., & Nenniger, P. (1982). Mehrdimensionale Zielerreichung in Lehr-Lern-Prozessen. *Zeitschrift fur Padagogik, 28,* 397-423.

Eigler, G., Macke, G., & Nenniger, P. (1986). *Studien zur Mehrdimensionalitat von Lehr-Lern-Prozessen.* Weinheim: Beltz.

Feather, N.T. (1982). *Expectations and actions - expectancy-value models in psychology.* Hillsdale, N.J.: Lawrence Erlbaum Associates.

Gagné, R.M. (1977, 2nd ed.) *The conditions of learning.* New York: Holt.

Heckhausen, H. (1972). Die Entwicklung des Erlebens von Erfolg und Misserfolg. In C.F. Graumann & H. Heckhausen (Eds.), *Padagogische Psychologie (Vol. 1)* (pp. 95-122). Frankfurt: Fischer.

Heckhausen, H. (1977). Motivation: Kognitionspsychologische Aufspaltung eines summarischen Konstrukts. *Psychologische Rundschau, 28,* 175-189.

Kluwe, R., & Spada, H. (1981). Wissen und seine Veränderungen - einige psychologische Beschreibungsansätze. In K. Foppa & R. Groner (Eds.), *Kognitive Strukturen und ihre Entwicklung* (pp. 284-327). Bern: Huber.

Lehwald, G. (1982). Aspekte der Zielbildung aus der Sicht der Handlungs- und Motivationspsychologie. In H. Schröder (Ed.), *Psychologie der Personlichkeit und Personlichkeitsentwicklung.* Berlin: Gesellschaft für Psychologie der DDR.

Lind, G. (1975). *Sachbewogene Motivation und Handeln.* Weinheim: Beltz.

Lens, W., & De Volder, M.L. (1982). Academic achievement and future time perspective as a cognitive-motivational concept. *Journal of personality and social psychology, 42,* 566-571.

Lindsay, P.H., & Norman, D.A. (1977). *Human information processing.* New York: Holt.

Lompscher, J. (1982). Conditions and potentialities on the formation of learning activities. In R. Glaser & J. Lompscher (Eds.), *Cognitive and motivational aspects of learning* (pp. 45-55). Berlin: VEB Deutscher Verlag der Wissenschaften.

Macke, G. (1978). *Lernen als Prozess.* Weinheim: Beltz.

Macke, G., & Nenniger, P. (1984). Zur Korrespondenz von inhaltsspezifischer Motivenentwicklung und Lernzuwachs unter alternativen Lehrbedingungen. In K. Ingenkamp (Ed.), *Sozial-emotionales Verhalten in Lehr- und Lernsituationen.* Landau: University Press.

Matushkin, A.M. (1982). Psychological structure, dynamics and stimulation of learning activity. *Woprossi psychologii, 4,* 5-17 (russ.).

Nenniger, P. (1986 in press). Stabilité et fluctuation de dimensions motivationelles pendant l'acquisition de connaissances en mathématiques. *Cahiers de psychologie cognitive.*

Nenniger, P. (1986). *Das Padagogische Verhaltnis als motivationales Konstrukt in der Lehr-Lern-Forschung.* Weinheim: Beltz.

Prenzel, M. (1984). Ein theoretisches Modell zur Wirkungsweise von Interesse. *Arbeiten zur Empirischen Padagogik und Padagogischen Psychologie* (Gelbe Reihe Nr. 9). München: University Press.

Schiefele, H. (1980). *Interesse als spezifische Handlungsbedingung - Ein aktualgenetisches Prozessmodell -.* München: University Press.

Schiefele, H., Hauser, K., & Prenzel, M. (1979). "Interesse" als Ziel und Weg der Erziehung. *Zeitschrift fur Padagogik, 25,* 1-20.

Weinert, F.E., & Kluwe, R.H. (Eds.) (1984) *Metakognition, Motivation und Lernen,,* Stuttgart: Kohlhammer.

CLASSROOM CLIMATE AND CONTINUING MOTIVATION

Daniel Brugman
A. Leo Beem

University of Leyden

SUMMARY

What Maehr has called continuing motivation is a motivational index *par excellence* from an educational point of view.

A theoretical model based on the valuation theory is presented for the instigation of continuing motivation. Lessons for a specific social studies subject were developed so as to be contiguous to pupils' valuations. It will be argued that problem-based instructional designs can be used to stimulate valuation processes. Classroom climate variables may facilitate the development of valuations of pupils and influence continuing motivation.

The predictability of continuing motivation for history and geography and for the specific social studies subject is investigated from classroom climate variables. The predictability of achievement on this subject-matter is also investigated. The predictability is assessed in a non-random sample of 39 classes, with a total of over 900 pupils. Continuing motivation for history and geography was predictable from pleasure in school, empathy of teacher and openness in the classroom. Achievement was predictable from specific subject-matter continuing motivation measures, and relationships between pupils. It is suggested that this subject-matter may satisfy important personal and social needs for the majority of the pupils.

RESEARCH ON CONTINUING MOTIVATION AND ITS EDUCATIONAL ANTECEDENTS

When children enter elementary school at the age of 6 or 7, most of them seem to like learning, or at least not to dislike it. It is for example a common experience that children of that age like to read or write at home when not obliged to do so. This attitude, however, often changes during elementary school years. Although for most children the motivation to achieve need not become less, they lose their continued interest in learning activities. Following Maehr (1976), this continuing motivation in learning activities may be broadly defined as "the tendency to return to and continue working on tasks away from the instructional context in which they were initially confronted".

As Maehr argues, "the continued willingness of students to learn" (p. 444) may well be the critical outcome of any learning experience for at least two reasons. First, continuing motivation is related to permanent education, which is of national interest for a changing, complex society. Secondly, it is highly probable that it affects the pupils' achievement.

If one accepts the importance of continuing motivation, two questions seem immediately relevant:
1. what factors are related to continuing motivation, and
2. how can continuing motivation be aroused and maintained.
   Some research pertaining to these questions has already been conducted.

The impact of the *classroom climate* has been investigated by Pascarella, Walberg, Junker and Haertel (1981). Teacher enthusiasm and encouragement appeared to be positively related to continuing motivation for early adolescents. For both early and late adolescents, class morale, utility of science content and science classes were positively related to continuing motivation and achievement, while teacher control over, and structuring of, classroom learning activities were negatively related to continuing motivation, but positively to science achievement. Hence, on the basis of these results achievement in the classroom and continuing motivation outside the classroom seem to demand to some extent educational conditions that are inconsistent with each other.

In line with research on *intrinsic motivation* (Deci 1975; Lepper 1983), continuing motivation has been shown to be negatively related to external evaluation (Maehr & Stallings 1972). The controlling aspects of external evaluation thwart pupils' self-determination in goal setting and feelings of competence.

Another line of educational research has paid attention to *instructional strategies*. One such strategy is controversy within learning groups (Johnson & Johnson 1979). Johnson and Johnson define controversy as the incompatibility of one person's ideas, information, conclusions, theories, or opinions with those of another person, and the two seek to reach an agreement. When people attempt to resolve the disagreement, controversy creates conceptual conflict. In an attempt to reduce the uncertainty accompanying the conflict, persons engage in information-seeking behavior, i.e. epistemic curiosity is induced. Several experiments (Lowry & Johnson 1981; Smith, Johnson & Johnson 1981; Tjosvold & Johnson 1978) have confirmed the hypothesis of controversy as a source of continuing motivation in content-related activities.

One purpose of this paper is to add to the evidence for the first question, i.e. about the factors that are related to continuing motivation. Results will be presented on the relationship between classroom climate and continuing motivation for history and geography and on the relationship between continuing motivation for, and knowledge acquired about, a specific subject matter. Another purpose is to tackle the second question, i.e. how continuing motivation may be aroused and maintained, from a theoretical point of view. This point will be taken up first.

THEORETICAL FRAMEWORK

As is implied by its definition, the concept of continuing motivation applies when pupils, having the opportunity to choose among alternatives, prefer a schooltask related activity. Maehr (1976, 1984) has stressed the differences between continuing motivation and persistence. Contrary to the case of persistence, continuing motivation requires an interruption of and spontaneous return to the task.

As a unifying principle different motivational patterns (i.e. continuing motivation, persistence, direction, activity and performance), Maehr (1984) suggests the term personal investment. This term signifies that a person is "in effect investing his or her personal resources in a certain way" (p. 121). As Maehr goes on: "Whether or not persons will invest themselves in a particular activity depends on what the activity means to them" (p. 123). So, according to Maehr, it is the meaning of the situation to the person that is of primary motivational significance. To the pupil, it is the meaning of a task-related activity compared with meanings of other activities in a particular situation and at a particular moment, that determines if the task activity will be taken up again.

Maehr's starting point in theorizing is compatible with ours, which is based on Hermans' valuation theory (1976). The central concept in this theory is that of a value area or valuation, which is defined as anything persons find of importance in their situation. A value area is linked with an affective and a behavioral component. According to the valuation theory, the involvement of a person in a value area depends on the strength of the affective component, i.e. the sum of frequencies of positive and negative affects associated with a value area.

The totality of value areas together with their mutual relations is called a system of value areas. In this system it becomes visible how the self-as-person looks at the self-as-object. The system may be viewed as a "local" theory of persons about their life-situation. This local or ideographic theory is developing in interaction with local theories of other persons and with a general or nomothetic theory (Hermans 1985).

The development of value areas related to subject-matter is defined as the execution of four valuation processes (cf. Van der Plas 1981):

1. Making explicit one's own subject-related value areas and affects connected with them;
2. Making explicit subject-related value areas of others (of persons, groups, institutions, etc. presented in the subject-matter as well as of pupils) and affects connected with them;
3. Relating values areas and affects, a) within the system of the persons, b) between different systems, one of which may be the pupils' own system;
4. Validating value areas and affects, by comparing symbolizations of value areas and affects with the actual execution of behaviors linked with the value areas.

Discrepancies induced by these processes, create motivational tendencies because of people's need to strive after congruence between experience and symbolization (process 1, 2), different symbolizations (process 3), and symbolization and behavior (process 4).

In accordance with the proposition that people strive after congruence, a person's local theory may, like a scientific, general theory, be evaluated on its representativeness, parsimoniousness, coherence and verifiability. These criteria together determine the flexibility of the system. We assume that the more flexible the system, the more the motive for self-definition is satisfied.

According to Kagan (1972), the motive for self-definition, i.e. the knowledge of self-as-object to the self-as-person, is an important basis for the motive for mastery. As Kagan points out, psychologists have narrowed the motive for mastery down to the intellectual domain. The same holds for many educators. Generally, education concerns knowledge of the physical world and cultural artefacts at the expense of knowledge of the social world. Besides, these classes of knowledge are seldom related to the pupils' valuations of them, i.e. their local theories. Hence, the motive for mastery, and thereby the motive for self-definition, is only fractionally gratified in schools.

If, however, schools would pay more attention to knowledge in the social domains, and relate the general theories on the different domains to pupils local theories, they could satisfy the motive for self-definition better. In case of absence of external evaluation, this might stimulate continuing motivation.

At the moment we are engaged in a research project in which thematic lessons in a social studies subject were developed which were aimed at being contiguous to pupils' positive value areas. Besides, cooperative learning activities were encouraged. Lessons and learning activities may satisfy the motive for self-definition better and are regarded as a *first step* in developing a pupil's local theory about the theme in interaction with the local theories of other pupils and the global theory as it is presented in the lessons and by the teacher.

The effects of these lessons may be strengthened by a *second step*, the stimulation of what is called the content-centered development of value areas (cf. Stahl 1979, 1981), or personalizing subject-matter (Howe & Howe 1975).

As Stahl (1979) has noted, problem-based instructional designs may be useful in the values domain. For instance, in the textbook "The struggle for the whale", pupils are given a problem based on environmental and work-employment valuations. This approach is in line with the approach of Johnson and Johnson (1979) in creating controversy. We suggest that such designs are especially useful in stimulating the process of relating value areas or values between pupils. However, instead of creating consensus by controversy one also can try to create group value areas by dialogue.

With the valuation processes, we think, more attention is paid to the development of value areas and local theories of pupils related to the subject. Such a viewpoint on content-centered development of value areas is related to the development of "mindful action" (Kruglanski & Klar 1985), and the construction of "personal knowledge" (Pope 1982).

PRESENT RESEACH

In our present research two groups of classes receive different treatments, based respectively on step 1 supplemented by different cognitive activities requiring cooperation between pupils, and on step 1 supplemented by step 2, which also requires cooperation. However, in the presentation of our results here, we will not differentiate between these two groups. At the moment only part of the treatment is finished and as our former research indicates, differential effects can only be expected after a prolonged treatment (Beem & Brugman 1983).

Thus, in initiating continuing motivation for both groups, only the first step has been taken into account. This step, however, might be of great importance to the pupils compared with more traditional approaches. From the general enthusiasm with which the lessons were received by most pupils, we infer that topics and activities were indeed contiguous to their positive value areas. Because of that, we expect that pupils more often spontaneously return to contents and task activities related to them.

Classroom climate may be of interest for any learning activity (cf. Moos 1979), but they seem of special relevance in the case of developing pupils' value areas. It has been suggested that a helping and personal, encouraging relationship by the teacher and dialogues between pupils and between teacher and pupils would be most desirable in stimulating the development of value areas (Hermans 1976; Van der Plas 1981).

The relationship between teacher control and encouragement with continuing motivation (Pascarella et al. 1981) might be due to the increase of dialogues between pupils about the subject, i.e. the satisfaction of pupils' needs for self-definition.

The following aspects of classroom climate were measured by means of pupil questionnaires: *pleasure in school* which refers to the attitude of pupils towards the school as an institution; most items in this scale refer to the cognitive and affective evaluation of school (learning) activities. *Relations between pupils:* friendship and acceptance between pupils; *openness/diversity in the classroom:* the opportunity for novel, unusual activities; *friction in the clasroom:* the existence of quarrels, conflicts; *empathy of teacher:* the acceptance and understanding of pupils by the teacher.

Three of these scales are related to scales used by Pascarella et al. (1981): *openness in the classroom* to their *teacher control, empathy of teacher* to *class moral* and *utility of science content and science classes.*

Relationships between pupils and friction in the classroom will be important in carrying out group learning activities. However, they might be heavily influenced by situations outside the classroom. Because of that, we do not hypothesize a direct relationship between these variables and continuing motivation or achievement.

Hypotheses
The following hypotheses will be tested:

1. Classroom climate (pleasure in school, openness/diversity in the class-room, empathy of teacher) will be positively related with continuing motivation for history and geography, and for a specific subject-matter.
2. Continuing motivation for history and geography, and for a specific subject-matter will be positively related with achievement on that subject-matter.

METHOD

At the moment a research project to study the effects of content-centered values development based on the valuation theory is carried out. During the study, classroom climate scales are used as pre- and posttest measures, while measures on specific subject-matter are used for content-related continuing motivation and achievement.

Here we are interested in the relationship between the classroom climate, continuing motivation, and achievement scales. To investigate this relationship, pretest measures on classroom climate and continuing motivation, and an achievement measure for a first textbook aimed at personalizing social studies subject-matter were available.

Subjects

39 out of 500 6th grade teachers agreed to participate in a research study on personalizing subject-matter in social studies. The schools were located in the province of South-Holland, or near it. A total of over 900 pupils participated in the study. The subjects' age was about 12.

Procedure

About 6 weeks after the start of the first term, the classroom climate scores and a general continuing motivation measure were obtained (CM1). Two weeks later the classes could start on the first textbook "The struggle for the whale". Teachers were recommended to finish the textbook, which took about 10 hours, within three weeks. After that, scores were obtained at two content-specific continuing motivation measures (CM2 and CM3) and an achievement test, in that order, on the same day. Most teachers did, but some teachers did not work as intensively on the textbook as was asked, with the result that measurement dates for continuing motivation and achievement for this specific subject-matter were wide apart.

153

Classroom climate

Classroom climate was measured by means of an 81-item questionnaire, containing five subscales.

Table 1 contains two items from each scale, the reliabilities of classroom mean scores, and eta squared as a measure of the differences between the mean scores.

Table 1. Classroom climate scales, reliabilities, and eta-squared

Questonnaires	Items	Reliabilities	eta-squared
1 Relations between pupils (11 items)	My classmates are not nice to me.	.91	.12
	I get along well with most pupils.		
2 Pleasure in school (17 items)	I think time passes quickly at school.	.95	.16
	I like to go to school.		
3 Empathy of teachers (11 items)	The teacher frankly admits if he does not know something.	.96	.18
	The teacher is interested in me.		
4 Openness/diversity (15 items)	We think of new things to do at school.	.92	.20
	We discuss things that appeared on T.V.		
5 Friction (15 items)	Some of the pupils quarrel with each other.	.96	.18
	I get distracted in the classroom		

Continuing motivation

Continuing motivation was measured with three separate variables which will be called CM1, CM2 and CM3. CM1 served as a measure of continuing motivation for two task areas, history and geography. The pupils were asked to imagine a situation after school in which they were completely free to do what they wanted, and to give a preference order for eleven activities, presented in Table 2.

Table 2. Activities of a continuing motivation measure for history and geography

---

1. Playing indoors or outdoors.
2. Reading, comics for instance.
3. Watching T.V.
4. Doing homework.
5. Doing odd jobs (for instance, cleaning up your room, or doing some shopping).
6. Reading a book on history.
7. Doing sports, but not in a club (for instance on the street).
8. Taking a walk or hiking.
9. Occupying yourself with animals.
10. Going to your club.
11. Reading a book on geography.

This measure was based on interviews with pupils. In these interviews most pupils expressed their dislike for two activities, doing homework and doing odd jobs (4 and 5). CM1 was analyzed using the Smacof3 program (Heiser & De Leeuw 1979) for metric unfolding. A plot of the activities in the first two dimensions is presented in Figure 1.

The second dimension of the solution of the unfolding problem serves as our basic measure of CM1. This dimension contrasts preferences for social, playful activities with individual, task-related activities. It appeared that the preference for the two task areas, history (6) and geography (11), was closely related to the disliked activities (4 and 5). The region marked in the figure contains a high concentration of pupils. Thus, a majority of the pupils prefer social activities in their free time. Although the sample was not randomly drawn, we submit that these results are representative for the population, since they agree with common sense.

CM2 and CM3 were intended to measure continuing motivation for the subject-matter. CM2 was constructed by analogy with Maehr and Stallings (1972) and refers to the intention to continue working on the subject-matter after an interruption. CM3, in contrast, refers to activities related to the subject-matter already carried out. Both scales contained three items, presented in Table 3.

155

Figure 1. Plot of activities in preference space, first dimension horizontally, second dimension vertically

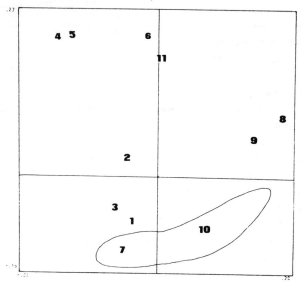

Note 1. The enclosed area contains a high concentration of pupils.
Note 2. Activities are listed in Table 2.

The scales approximated a Guttman scale. After optimal scaling of the items using the Homals program (Gifi 1981), the reliabilities of classroom mean scores for CM2 and CM3 were .90 and .89, respectively.

Achievement

Achievement on lessons in which no choice of subject to pupils was permitted, was measured by a test containing 12 three choice items. The items were a sample from a pool covering most of the lessons content. The reliability of this test is .77.

Table 3.   Content-specific continuing motivation measures

CM2

1. Would you like to know more about whales?
   1. No
   2. Don't know
   3. Yes, by reading in the textbook.
   4. Yes, by reading another book about whales.
   5. Yes, by watching a film about whales.
   If you have circled the number 3, 4 and/or 5, you can also answer
   next questions. If you circled the number 1 or 2 go straight on
   to the next page.

2. Would you do this when you have a free period at school?
   1. No.
   2. Don't know.
   3. Yes.

3. Would you do this after school?
   1. No.
   2. Don't know.
   3. Yes.

If you circled the number 3 with questions 2 or 3, then write your name
below and indicate when you would like to do this.

CM3

1. Have you thought about whales after school?
   a. Always.
   b. Often.
   c. Sometimes.
   d. Never.

2. Have you discussed whales with others after school?
   a. Always.
   b. Often.
   c. Sometimes.
   d. Never.

3. Have you read about whales after school?
   a. Always.
   b. Often.
   c. Sometimes.
   d. Never.

RESULTS

The analysis has been conducted using class means (n = 39). A full multi-level analysis will be presented elsewhere.
The predictability of CM1, CM2, and CM3 from the classroom climate variables will be investigated separately.
First we present results pertaining to the structure of the classroom climate and continuing motivation variables. Table 4 contains the correlations between the variables.

Table 4. Correlations between classroom climate, continuing motivation, and achievement (n = 39)

	Op	PI	Fr	Emp	Rel	CM1	CM2	CM3	Ach
Op	1	.58	.10	.66	.02	.30	-.03	.10	-.15
PI		1	-.41	.76	.31	.57	-.08	.14	-.14
Fr			1	-.19	-.79	-.01	-.19	-.05	-.26
Emp				1	.25	.33	-.11	-.01	-.05
Rel					1	-.09	0	-.17	.30
CM1						1	-.02	.21	-.27
CM2							1	.61	.48
CM3								1	.24
Ach									1

CM1 indeed appears to be correlated with the classroom climate variables *pleasure at school, empathy of teacher* and *openness/diversity in the classroom.* These results are largely consistent with the findings of Pascarella et al. (1981). Surprisingly, however, these classroom climate variables and CM1 are not correlated with the content-specific measures for continuing motivation, CM2 and CM3, nor with the achievement test. No substantial correlation exists between CM1 and the two measures of the quality of pupil interaction. In contrast, content-centered continuing motivation and relationships between pupils are correlated with achievement.
   To give a clearer impression of the structure, Figure 2 contains a plot of loadings on the first two ortho-oblique rotated principal components.

Figure 2. Plot of loadings of classroom climate and three continuing motivation measures on first (horizontally) and second (vertically) rotated component

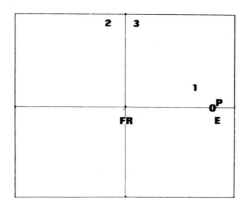

F = Friction, R = Relationship, O = Openness, P = Pleasure,
E = Empathy of teacher, 1 = CM1, 2 = CM2, 3 = CM3

The plot shows that *openness/diversity, pleasure in school, empathy of
teacher* and CM1 form a cluster almost orthogonal to the content-centered
continuing motivation measures.

Friction in the classroom and *relations between pupils* loaded substantially
on the third rotated component (.94 and -.93, respectively).

The first three principal components accounted for 79% of the total variance. The second and third rotated components correlate negatively (-.16).
The other correlations are effectively zero.

Next, the predictability of all continuing motivation measures from classroom climate variables, and the predictability of achievement from classroom
climate and continuing motivation measures will be discussed. The method
used was a stepwise multiple regression procedure. We prefer OLS estimation
of seperate equations instead of a simultaneous path analytic estimation procedure, because the OLS estimators are probably better (in the mean
squared error sense) in small samples and because this procedure suits better our questions. To reduce the influence of chance capitalization, a random

variable from a normal distribution was created. Variables were not retained in the regression equation if they entered after the random variable.

Table 5. Regression weights of stepwise selected variables for predicting continuing motivation (CM) and achievement (Ach) (n = 39)

	B	SB	.p
CM1		$R^2 = .40$	p < .0001
PI	.29	.06	.0001
Rel	-.24	.11	.04
Ach		$R^2 = .31$	p < .001
CM1	-.06	.03	.07
CM2	.004	.001	.001
Ach		$R^2 = .16$	p < .05
PI	-.03	.02	.11
Rel	.07	.03	.02

PI = pleasure
Rel = relationships
B   = regression weight
SD = standard error of regression weight
p   = descriptive significance level

Table 5 contains the results: adjusted R^2-values are .37, .27 and .11 respectively. Among the continuing motivation variables, only CM1 appeared to be predictable from classroom variables. However, *openness/diversity* and *empathy of teacher* do not enter the regression equation, possibly due to their correlation with *pleasure in school*. Achievement was predictable from continuing motivation as well as from classroom climate measures.

Although *relations between pupils* is not significantly correlated with CM1, it has a negative regression weight. This can be understood by noting that te weights must be interpreted conditionally: given a certain amount of pleasure in school, CM1 tends to be lower when *relations between pupils* is higher. This relation between CM1 and *relations between pupils* does not show in the correlation because of a certain "skewness" in the bivariate distribution of *pleasure in school* and *relations between pupils*. For example, low scores on *pleasure in school* together with high scores on *relations between pupils* result in a low score on CM1, while the reverse results in a high score on CM1. A high score on both variables results in an intermediate CM1 score. The fact that CM1 and CM2 are uncorrelated suggests that classes low on CM1 become relatively more continuously motivated than might be expected. The regression weights show that achievement scores are highest when these classes have high CM2 scores. A significant relation with regression weights of the same sign is also obtained when CM2 is replaced by CM3, but the squared multiple correlation is lower (.17).

The regression weights for the prediction of achievement from classroom climate suggest that a lower evaluation of "traditional education" and a higher quality of relations between pupils results in higher achievement. There is, however, no direct relationship between these variables and CM2 at the class level.

SUMMARY AND DISCUSSION

The results partly confirm the first hypothesis. Continuing motivation for history and geography (CM1) was indeed correlated with the classroom climate measures *openness/diversity, empathy of teacher* and *pleasure in school*. It had no direct relationship with the measures of quality of pupils' interaction, i.e. with *relations between pupils* and *friction in the classroom*. When the predictability from classroom climate was investigated using multiple regression, *relations between pupils* appeared to be negatively related to this continuing motivation measure, conditional on *pleasure in school*. The value of the squared multiple correlation, .40, was quite substantial. However, classroom climate was not related to the other two continuing motivation measures. The second hypothesis is also partly confirmed. CM1 had a negative, and CM2 a positive correlation with achievement. These two variables together produced a substantial squared multiple correlation with achievement (.31). Achievement was also predictable from a regression equation containing *pleasure in school* and *relations between pupils*, but the squared multiple correlation was not very high (.16).

The results indicate that continuing motivation may be influenced by the instructional process. This is inferred from the almost zero correlation between CM1 and CM2, and CM2 and classroom climate. Note, however, that this interpretation implies that CM1 and CM2 would be correlated, when CM2 asked about the same kind of motivation for a regular lesson. One might suggest that with regular lessons the same zero correlation would be obtained, because CM2 also asks for the motivation to watch a film. This was in fact a much chosen option, and watching television was an activity with a relatively high preference order in CM1. However, the relation of CM2 with achievement is not easily explained in this way. We therefore think that the instructional process indeed aroused continuing motivation.

Next, the question arises to what factors in the instructional process these outcomes may be attributed. As a *first factor* we suggest the that lessons are contiguous to the value areas of a large (see the high concentration area in Figure 1) number of pupils. A *second factor* probably is the purposively minimized extent of external evaluation (Lepper & Greene 1975). We suggest that a *third factor* may be the satisfaction of the pupils' personal and social needs during the lessons. This inference is based on the following results: 1. the regression weights of *pleasure in school* and *relations between pupils* for the prediction of CM1: given a certain amount of *pleasure in school*, individual and task-related activities are more often preferred when the quality of relations between pupils is lower. We interpret this choice as a negative one, arising from a lesser opportunity for satisfactory social interactions outside school. 2. the regression weights of CM1 and CM2 for predicting achievement.

However, this interpretation would be more convincing when the same kind of relationship had been obtained between CM2 and *pleasure in school* and *relations between pupils*, as between those classroom climate variables and achievement.

As for this relationship, we suggest that better relations between pupils have a favorable effect because the lessons require social activities of the pupils. Conditional to a certain quality of these relationships, however, a more negative evaluation of traditional education results in higher achievement, although not necessarily in higher continuing motivation.

The postulation of the third factor as influential should be viewed as a hypothesis, to be tested more thoroughly in future research. A better understanding of the present results might be obtained from a full multilevel analysis. However, if this hypothesis is confirmed, it would be an important result because those pupils constitute the majority of the population. The results of Pascarella et al. (1981), the apparent inconsistency between continuing motivation and achievement, can also be understood better. Traditional education seems not only to hinder the self-determination of pupils, but the inconsistency might also be attributed to the circumstance that a teacher-controlled classroom climate does not sufficiently meet the social needs of most pupils. Because of that, the continuing motivation to learn cannot concur with the motivation of the pupils for social interaction.

Hermans (1985) has demonstrated that two fundamental motives are present in value areas. The Z-motive relates to behavior directed towards competence; central to this motive is the acquirement of autonomy and self-determination. This motive may be compared with the motive to control, or the motive for mastery.

The A-motive is characterized as the readiness to undergo the influence of others and the environment. Hermans (1983) has argued that the A-motive is largely neglected in the educational context. In a reply to Hermans, Van Parreren (1983) has suggested that relative to the Z-motive, the A motive has a minor impact on learning in the case of younger pupils. We tentatively suggest that this may be only partly true. For many pupils the negligence of the A-motive may reduce the continuing motivation for learning, although not necessarily their achievement.

ACKNOWLEDGEMENT

This research was supported by grant 1050 from the Dutch Foundation for Educational Research, S.V.O.
The authors are indebted to Prof. Dr. F.K. Kieviet and Prof. Dr. H.J.M. Hermans for their helpful comments on earlier versions of this manuscript.

REFERENCES

Beem, A.L., & Brugman, D. (1983). *The effects of values development lessons on classroom behavior and pupils' outcomes as measured by questionnaires, and the relations between classroom behavior and those outcomes.* Leyden: University of Leyden, Leids Interdisciplinair Centrum voor Onderwijs Research.

Deci, E.L. (1975). *Intrinsic motivation.* New York: Plenum.

Gifi, A. (1981). *Non-linear multivariate analysis.* Leyden: University of Leyden, Faculty of Social Sciences, Department of Datatheory.

Heiser, W.J., & De Leeuw, J. (1979). *How to use SMACOF-III.* Leyden: University of Leyden, Faculty of Social Sciences, Department of Datatheory.

Hermans, H.J.M. (1976). *Values areas and their development.* Amsterdam: Swets & Zeitlinger.

Hermans, H.J.M. (1983). De halve persoonlijkheid van de onderwijspsychologie. In D. Dijkstra, A.C.M. Dudink & R.J. Takens (Eds.), *Psychologie en onderwijs* (pp. 185-193). Lisse: Swets & Zeitlinger.

Hermans, H.J.M. (1985). *De grondmotieven van het menselijk bestaan.* Lisse: Swets & Zeitlinger.

Howe, L., & Howe, M.M. (1975). *Personalizing education. Value clarification and beyond.* New York: Hart.

Johnson, D.W., & Johnson, R.T. (1979). Conflict in the classroom: controversy and learning. *Review of Educational Research, 49,* 51-69.

Kagan, J. (1972). Motives and Development. *Journal of Personality and Social Psychology, 22,* 51-66.

Kruglanski, A.W., & Klar, Y. (1985). Knowing what to do: on the epistemology of actions. In J. Kuhl & J. Beckman (Eds.), *Action control* (pp.41-60). Berlin, New York: Springer.

Lepper, M.R. (1983). Extrinsic reward and intrinsic motivation: implications for the classroom. In J.M. Levine & M.C. Wang (Eds.), *Teacher and student perceptions: implications for learning* (pp. 281-319). Hillsdale, N.J.: Lawrence Erlbaum.

Lepper, M.R., & Greene, D. (1975). Turning play into work: Effects of adult surveillance and extrinsic rewards on children's intrinsic motivation. *Journal of Personality and Social Psychology, 31,* 479-486.

Lowry, N., & Johnson, D.W. (1981). Effects of controversy on epistemic curiosity, achievement and attitudes. *The Journal of Social Psychology, 115,* 31-43.

Maehr, M.L. (1976). Continuing Motivation: An analysis of a seldom considered educational outcome. *Review of Educational Research, 46,* 443-462.

Maehr, M.L. (1984). Meaning and motivation: Toward a theory of personal investment. In R.E. Ames & C. Ames (Eds.), *Research on motivation in education. Vol. 1. Student motivation.* (pp. 115-144). New York, London: Academic Press.

Maehr, M.L., & Stallings, W.M. (1972). Freedom from external evaluation. *Child Development, 43,* 177-185.

Moos, R.H. (1979). Educational climates. In H.J. Walberg (Ed.), *Educational environments and effects* (pp. 79-100). Berkeley, CA: McCutchan.

Parreren, C.F. van (1983). Repliek op de coreferaten. In S. Dijkstra, A.C.M. Dudink & R.J. Takens (Eds.), *Psychologie en onderwijs* (pp. 209-217). Lisse: Swets & Zeitlinger.

Pascarella, E.T., Walberg, H.J., Junker, L.K., & Haertel, G.D. (1981). Continuing motivation in science for early and late adolescents. *American Educational Research Journal, 18,* 439-452.

Plas, P.L. van der (1981). *Waardenontwikkeling in het onderwijs.* 's Gravenhage: Stichting voor Onderzoek van het Onderwijs (with a summary in English).

Pope, M.L. (1982). Personal construction of formal knowledge. *Interchange, 13,* 3-14.

Smith, K., Johnson, D.W., & Johnson, R.T. (1981). Can conflict be constructive? Controversy versus concurrence seeking in learning groups. *Journal of Educational Psychology, 73,* 651-663.

Stahl, R.J. (1979). Developing values dilemmas for content-centered social studies instruction: theoretical construct and practical applications. *Theory and Research in Social Education, 7,* 50-75.

Stahl, R.J. (1981). Achieving values and content objectives simultaneously within subject matter-oriented social studies classrooms. *Social Education, 45,* 580-585.

Tjosvold, D., & Johnson, D.W. (1978). Controversy within a cooperative or competitive context and cognitive perspective-taking. *Contemporary Educational Psychology, 3,* 376-386.

SEX DIFFERENCES IN STUDENTS' ATTRIBUTION OF HOMEWORK EVALUATED AT SCHOOL

Nitha M.E. Neuwahl
Peter H.M. van den Bogaart

University of Leyden

SUMMARY

Two main topics in attribution research are situation specificity and sex differences. In the context of our research project on homework we conducted a study on students' attribution of homework evaluated at school. 339 students from 7 schools in secondary education (grades 1 to 4 of MAVO) participated. The data were gathered through newly developed questionnaires. The questions centered on foreign languages (English, French), mathematics, physics and geography. Students were asked to indicate their perceived efforts and their expectations of results, their perceived efforts and their attributions of success and failure.

Here we report the results of the 148 students from grade 2. These show that (1) the correlations between perceived ability, expectation of results and attribution to (dis)ability are high enough to construct a perceived ability index, (2) the perceived ability index is more positive for boys than for girls, (3) there is no clear difference in perceived effort between boys and girls, (4) differences between school subjects in perceived effort are greater for girls than for boys, and (5) the correlation between the attribution of success/failure to liking/disliking the school subject and perceived effort with regard to that school subject is greater for girls than for boys. The motivation for doing homework seems to be different across sexes.

INTRODUCTION

Since 1980 the section of developmental psychology of the Leyden University has been doing research into different aspects of homework (Neuwahl, Van den Bogaart & Van Veen 1981, 1983; Neuwahl & Van den Bogaart 1984, 1985). One conclusion from this research is, that many students in secondary education have difficulties with their homework, especially motivational difficulties and difficulties in concentrating their thoughts: homework is boring to them, they find it difficult to get started with homework and to continue homework for a long period of time, they are distracted while doing homework, etc. These difficulties influence students' school results and emotional well-being. Our theorizing about homework difficulties and our search for possibilities to diminish homework difficulties have resulted in research into a large number of variables. These variables concern the ways teachers and students handle homework. On the basis of the results of this research we expect task motivation to be a very important concept in understanding homework difficulties. Attribution theoretical models used in educational psychological research - especially the model of motivation as a self-reinforcing system (Heckhausen 1975; Alberts & Bergen 1983) and the attribution theoretical model for teachers' and pupils' behavior (Bar-Tal 1982) - offer good possibilities to interpret results of research into students' task motivation. Therefore, we have based this study of homework motivation on those attribution-theoretical models.

One fundamental assumption of attribution theories is, that task motivation is not primarily dependent on objective abilities, "... but first of all on the subjective experiences that are crystallized in relatively stable task dependent cognitions" (Bergen & Alberts 1983, p. 203). Important task dependent cognitions are perceived ability, expectation of results, perceived effort and the nature of causal attributions of success and failure. Attribution theory distinguishes between success orientation and failure orientation. These orientations are characterized by a specific pattern of task dependent cognitions. Characteristics of success orientation are realistic expectations of results and highly positive perceived abilities.

Being successful is primarily attributed to ability and effort. Failing is primarily attributed to lack of effort, task difficulty and bad luck. Characteristics of failure orientation are setting extremely high or extremely low goals and perceived inability. Being successful is primarily attributed to low task difficulty and luck. Failing is primarily attributed to inability. Success orientation and failure orientation are self-reinforcing systems. It is possible, therefore, to distinguish between success oriented and failure oriented persons.

The question to what extent task motivation can be generalized across situations has occupied many researchers. One difficulty in this matter is that the concept 'situation' is not clearly defined. A study by Peters (1983) shows that homework can be conceived of as a specific situation. Together with, among other things, school tests it belongs to a cluster of situations that inform students about their progress at school. It is possible to differentiate homework further into more specific situations, e.g. different kinds of homework tasks: memorizing, problem solving, essay writing, etc. Bergen and Alberts (1983) differentiate between task motivation for different school subjects. The differentiation between foreign languages, mathematical subjects (physics, chemistry, etc.) and other subjects (geography, history, etc.) is deeply rooted in the Dutch educational system and plays an important role in the way students perceive their education. This is one of the reasons why we have chosen to study homework motivation for English, French, mathematics, physics and geography. By examining the correlations between these school subjects with regard to different concepts of the attribution theory, an indication can be acquired of the degree in which homework motivation is school subject specific. We expect these correlations to be low.

Differences between girls (women) and boys (men) are consistently found in research concerning task motivation. Attribution research shows, that boys in relation to girls are more success oriented. Girls in relation to boys are more failure oriented and show more effort. These differences are partly school subject specific (Bergen & Alberts 1983; Kiewied, Van den Dungen & Bergen 1982). Based on these results our hypotheses concerning sex differences in homework motivation are (see Table 1): Boys in relation to girls have more positive expectations of results, have higher perceived abilities, attribute successes more to ability and attribute failures less to inability. Girls in relation to boys have higher perceived efforts, attribute success more to stable effort and to external causes. They attribute failure less to lack of stable effort. These differences are absent or reversed for foreign languages and more significant for mathematics and physics.

Table 1. Hypotheses concerning sex differences in homework motivation

Concept	All five school subjects	English French	Mathematics Physics
Expectations of results	boys > girls	boys ≤ girls	boys >> girls
Perceived ability	boys > girls	boys ≤ girls	boys >> girls
Attribution of success to ability	boys > girls	boys ≤ girls	boys >> girls
Attribution of failure to inability	boys < girls	boys ≥ girls	boys << girls
Perceived effort	boys < girls	boys ≥ girls	boys << girls
Attribution of success to stable effort	boys < girls	boys ≥ girls	boys << girls
Attribution of failure to lack of stable effort	boys > girls	boys ≤ girls	boys >> girls
Attribution of success to external causes	boys < girls	boys ≥ girls	boys << girls

METHOD

Three hundred and thirty-nine students from seven schools in secondary education (grades 1 to 4 of MAVO) participated. The schools were located in the 'Randstad' (the cities Amsterdam, Utrecht and Rotterdam and the area enclosed by these cities). In the first grade of MAVO, physics is not a school subject. In the third and fourth grade of MAVO, students are allowed to select a limited number of elective school subjects. In our sample only a few boys selected French and only a few girls selected physics. In the second grade all students in our study had all five subjects included. For these reasons, we will here report the results of the 89 girls and the 59 boys in second grade. Almost all those students were 13 of 14 years old.

170

Table 2. Concepts grouped under 'Perceived Ability Index': Pearson's product-moment correlations between school subjects (N=148)

School subjects	Perceived ability				
	English	French	Mathematics	Physics	Geography
English	---	.28	-.11	-.06	.04
French		---	.12	-.05	.00
Mathematics			---	.10	.08
Physics				---	.29
Geography					---

School subjects	Expectations of results				
	English	French	Mathematics	Physics	Geography
English	---	.42	.01	-.03	.01
French		---	.10	-.07	-.00
Mathematics			---	.28	.14
Physics				---	.30
Geography					---

School subjects	Attribution of success to ability				
	English	French	Mathematics	Physics	Geography
English	---	.14	-.06	-.12	.01
French		---	.01	-.07	.01
Mathematics			---	.11	.12
Physics				---	.26
Geography					---

School subjects	Attribution of failure to inability				
	English	French	Mathematics	Physics	Geography
English	---	.13	-.15	.03	.13
French		---	-.07	.02	.02
Mathematics			---	.13	.07
Physics				---	.27
Geography					---

Based on the studies of Bar-Tal and Guttmann (1981), Alberts and Bergen (1983), Roede (1983) and Neuwahl, Van den Bogaart and Van Veen (1983) a questionnaire was developed. The items of the questionnaire measure concepts of the the attribution theory for English, French, mathematics, physics and geography. For each school subject the students rated their perceived abilities, their expectations of results (school report marks) and their perceived efforts while doing homework, on a five-point scale. They indicated for each school subject the causes to which they attributed successes and failures of homework evaluated at school. For each of seven possible causes they rated on a five-point scale the amount of agreement with it being a real cause. The seven possible causes are: ability in the school subject, stable effort and variable effort while doing homework, difficulty of the homework task, study environment at home, attractiveness of the school subject and mood. Because of the interactionistic and situation specific nature of the self-reinforcing system of task motivation it is difficult to use classical measures of reliability. There are, however, indications for the validity of the theory. The correlations between perceived ability, expectation of results, attribution of success to ability and attribution of failure to inability are an important indication. In this study these correlations are high: almost all of them were greater than 0.60, the mean being 0.71. This means, that it is possible to construct a perceived ability index.

The questionnaire was filled in during school hours. In all classes the students being present filled in the questionnaire. The teacher was not present or was asked not to interfere. The anonymity of the students was guaranteed. Almost all students filled out the questionnaire in less than 40 minutes.

The data have been analyzed by a computer. Standard software of SPSS-X was used. Statisticsl measures used are Pearson's product-moment correlation and the t-test or differences between two means.

RESULTS

In Table 2 the correlations between the five school subjects with respect to the concepts grouped under 'perceived ability index' are given.

In Table 3 the correlations between the five school subjects with respect to perceived effort, attribution of success to stable effort and attribution of failure to lack of stable effort are given.

Table 3. Perceived effort, attribution of success to stable effort and attribution of failure to lack of stable effort. Pearson's product-moment correlations between school subjects (N=148)

| School subjects | Perceived effort | | | | |
	English	French	Mathematics	Physics	Geography
English	---	.31	.19	.20	.37
French		---	.16	.12	.33
Mathematics			---	.28	.19
Physics				---	.33
Geography					---

| School subjects | Attribution of success to stable effort | | | | |
	English	French	Mathematics	Physics	Geography
English	---	.15	-.04	.14	.31
French		---	-.06	.14	.19
Mathematics			---	.16	.27
Physics				---	.27
Geography					---

| School subjects | Attribution of failure to lack of stable effort | | | | |
	English	French	Mathematics	Physics	Geography
English	---	.27	.34	.33	.34
French		---	.10	.10	.08
Mathematics			---	.40	.44
Physics				---	.50
Geography					---

Tables 2 and 3 show, that - although there are some substantial correlations - homework motivation in general is different for these school subjects. Thus it seems legitimate to use school subjects as a unity for studying homework motivation.

We now come to a description of the results with respect to our hypotheses concerning sex differences in homework motivation. We expected, that the concepts grouped under 'perceived ability index' are more positive for boys than for girls. As Table 4 shows, all significant differences and non-significant tendencies are in the expected direction. Differentiating between school subjects it can be seen, that for physics and geography 7 differences out of 8 are significant at a 0.01 level. For English there are neither significant differences nor non-significant tendencies. For French and mathematics there are some non-significant tendencies, but just one significant difference (p<0.05). This means, that our expectations concerning school subject specific sex differences in homework motivation are only partly confirmed.

Results concerning our expectations that girls in relation to boys have higher efforts, attribute success more to stable effort and attribute failure less to lack of stable effort, are presented in Table 5. Contrary to our expectations we found only two significant differences between girls and boys in these respects, only one of them pointing in the expected direction.

Results concerning our expectations that girls in relation to boys attribute their success more to external causes are presented in Table 6. Contrary to our expectations we found only a few significant differences between girls and boys in this respect. These differences are related to the attribution of success to the attractiveness of the homework task, none of them pointing in the expected direction.

DISCUSSION

From the time research in achievement motivation started (McClelland et al. 1953), a distinction has been made between the intensity aspect and the extensity aspect of the achievement motive. In theory construction as well as in test construction time after time the question arose: to what extent is the achievement motive - or more in general the task motive - a generalized personality trait? For a review see: De Bruyn, Alberts and Peters (1979). The results of a study by Alberts and Bergen (1983) and of our study show that it is important to differentiate between school subjects. The question can be posed whether further differentiation of situations (e.g. different kinds of tasks per school subject) is necessary. In our opinion the question of how many and which situations must be differentiated, should be answered by two criteria: (1) motivation differs sufficiently between the situations and (2) the situations are relevant for every day's school practice (see Boekaerts 1983, p. 97). The differentiation in school subjects meets both criteria. So in our opinion the differentiation of homework in school subjects contributes to the ecological validity of our study.

Table 4. Sex differences in concepts concerning perceived ability for five school subjects (N Boys = 59, N Girls = 89)

Concepts	Sex	School Subjects English Mean SD	French Mean SD	Mathematics Mean SD	Physics Mean SD	Geography Mean SD
Perceived[1] ability	Boys	2.67 .89	2.81 1.07	3.07 .98	2.64 .78	2.51 .82
	Girls	2.64 .94	3.09 1.04	3.22 1.07	3.20 1.03	2.89 .87
		t = .21	t = -1.56	t = -.87	t = -3.74	t = -2.69
		n.s.	n.s.	n.s.	$p < .001$	$p < .01$
Expection[2] of results	Boys	1.97 1.11	1.98 1.06	2.27 1.14	1.83 .85	1.90 .89
	Girls	1.81 1.02	2.20 1.20	2.54 1.21	2.46 1.07	2.15 .94
		t = .87	t = -1.18	t = -1.37	t = -3.97	t = -1.63
		n.s.	n.s.	n.s.	$p < .001$	n.s.
Attribution[3] of success to ability	Boys	2.44 1.13	2.59 1.15	2.76 1.17	2.49 1.01	2.44 1.01
	Girls	2.32 1.17	3.00 1.28	3.02 1.33	3.20 1.29	2.98 1.12
		t = .63	t = -2.00	t = -1.25	t = -3.75	t = -3.04
		n.s.	$p < .05$	n.s.	$p < .001$	$p < .005$
Attribution[3] of failure to inability	Boys	3.59 1.30	3.36 1.40	3.19 1.34	3.54 1.25	3.59 1.09
	Girls	3.74 1.26	2.98 1.33	2.93 1.45	2.69 1.36	2.94 1.23
		t = -.67	t = 1.64	t = 1.10	t = 3.90	t = 3.32
		n.s.	n.s.	n.s.	$p < .001$	$p < .005$

Note: Scores range from 1-5.
1 High scores indicate low perceived abilities, low scores indicate high perceived abilities.
2 High scores indicate expectations of bad results, low scores indicate expectations of good results.
3 High scores indicate that the attribution is not the cause, low scores indicate that the attribution is the cause.

Table 5. Sex differences in perceived effort concerning attribution of success to stable effort and attribution of failure to lack of stable effort for five school subjects (N Boys = 59, N girls = 89)

Concepts	Sex	School Subjects English Mean SD	French Mean SD	Mathematics Mean SD	Physics Mean SD	Geography Mean SD
Perceived[1] effort	Boys	2.22 .77	2.34 1.11	2.31 1.06	2.44 .99	2.36 .98
	Girls	2.10 .81	2.36 1.11	2.19 1.03	2.59 1.11	2.16 .89
		$t = -.90$	$t = -.13$	$t = .67$	$t = -.83$	$t = 1.25$
		n.s.	n.s.	n.s.	n.s.	n.s.
Attribution[2] of success to stable effort	Boys	1.92 .75	2.19 1.09	2.41 1.19	2.53 1.15	2.32 1.01
	Girls	1.79 .80	2.23 1.24	2.02 1.03	2.38 1.23	2.31 1.03
		$t = -.99$	$t = -.21$	$t = 2.02$	$t = .72$	$t = -.04$
		n.s.	n.s.	$p < .05$	n.s.	n.s.
Attribution[2] of failure to lack of stable effort	Boys	3.83 1.18	3.88 1.13	3.76 1.25	3.76 1.26	3.81 1.07
	Girls	4.32 .92	3.98 1.08	4.08 1.05	3.80 1.09	3.90 .97
		$t = -2.68$	$t = -.51$	$t = -1.62$	$t = -.17$	$t = -.51$
		$p < .01$	n.s.	n.s.	n.s.	n.s.

Note. Scores range from 1 - 5.
1 High scores indicate low perceived effort, low scores indicate high perceived effort.
2 High scores indicate that the attribution is not the cause, low scores indicate that the attribution is the cause.

Table 6. Sex differences in attribution of success to external causes for five school subjects (N Boys = 59, N Girls = 89)

Concepts	Sex	School Subjects English Mean SD	French Mean SD	Mathematics Mean SD	Physics Mean SD	Geography Mean SD
Attribution of success to low task difficulty	Boys	2.22 1.18	2.56 1.47	2.59 1.32	2.44 1.25	2.42 1.21
	Girls	2.24 1.26	2.45 1.21	2.34 1.20	2.39 1.13	2.28 1.40
		$t = -.08$	$t = -.45$	$t = 1.20$	$t = .27$	$t = .72$
		n.s.	n.s.	n.s.	n.s.	n.s.
Attribution of success to study environment	Boys	2.07 1.39	1.98 1.36	1.88 1.30	1.92 1.26	1.93 1.40
	Girls	2.00 1.39	2.01 1.33	2.09 1.42	2.15 1.46	2.02 1.44
		$t = .29$	$t = -.13$	$t = -.92$	$t = -1.02$	$t = -.38$
		n.s.	n.s.	n.s.	n.s.	n.s.
Attribution of success to attractiveness of the homework task	Boys	2.49 1.43	2.97 1.54	2.75 1.33	2.54 1.29	2.51 1.28
	Girls	1.99 1.25	3.13 1.62	2.84 1.54	3.25 1.54	2.97 1.40
		$t = 2.20$	$t = -.60$	$t = -.42$	$t = -3.01$	$t = -2.05$
		$p < .05$	n.s.	n.s.	$p < .005$	$p < .05$

Note. Scores range from 1 - 5.
High scores indicate that the attribution is not the cause, low scores indicate that the attribution is the cause.

In motivation research the question how to conceive girls' task motive has often been posed. Research focussed on task dependent cognitions shows again and again that girls compared to boys have lower expectations of results and lower perceived abilities. In line with this is the fact that girls compared with boys, attribute their successes less to ability and attribute their failures more to inability (Alberts & Bergen 1983). These differences were also found in our study. In two respects the results of our study differ from the results of other studies: We did not find differences between boys and girls regarding perceived effort nor differences regarding attribution of success to external factors. For these unexpected results we can only give tentative explanations. Further research is needed.

Kiewied, Van den Dungen and Bergen (1982) state, that "... girls work at every task with the same effort" (p. 40). The results of our study contradict this statement: girls in relation to boys differentiate *more* between tasks (i.e. school subjects). Like Kiewied, Van den Dungen and Bergen we assume that girls show effort on the basis of other criteria than boys do. From their study of the relevant literature they conclude that girls are more than boys motivated by the affiliation motive. From our study we have the impression that also some intrinsic aspects, like attractiveness of the task, play a more prominent role for girls than for boys.

REFERENCES

Alberts, R.V.J., & Bergen, Th.C.M. (1983). Enige aspecten van situatie-specifieke motiefmetingen en hun bruikbaarheid in de onderwijspraktijk. In Th.M.C. Bergen & E. Roede (Eds.), *Motivatie gemeten?* Harlingen: Flevodruk.

Bar-Tal, D. (1982). The effects of teacher's behavior and pupils' attributions: a review. In C. Antaki & C. Brewer (Eds.), *Attributions and psychological change.* New York: Academic Press.

Bar-Tal, D., & Guttmann, J. (1981). A comparison of teachers', pupils' and parents' attributions regarding pupils' academic achievement. *British Journal of Educational Psychology, 51,* 301-311.

Bergen, Th.C.M., & ALberts, R.V.J. (1983). Sexe-verschillen en situatie-specifieke motiefmetingen. In Th.C.M. Bergen & E. Roede (Eds), *Motivatie gemeten?* Harlingen: FLevodruk.

Boekaerts, M. (1983). Motivatie en onderwijs: Theorieën en modellen op een rij gezet. In S. Dijkstra, A.C.M. Dudink & R.J. Takens (Eds.), *Psychologie en onderwijs*. Lisse: Swets & Zeitlinger.

Bruyn, E.E.J. de, Alberts, R.V.J., & Peters, V.A.M. (1979). Prestatie-motivatie-theorie en meetmethoden. In E.E.J. de Bruyn (Ed.), *Ontwikkelingen in het onderzoek naar prestatiemotivatie*. Lisse: Swets & Zeitlinger.

Heckhausen, H. (1975). Fear of failure as a self-reinforcing system. In I.G. Sarason & C.D. Spielberger (Eds.), *Stress and anxiety. Volume 2*. Washington: Hemisphere.

Kiewied, A.M., Van den Dungen, P.G.M., & Bergen, Th.C.M. (1982). *Motivatie in het voortgezet onderwijs. Deelrapport 6*. Nijmegen: Katholieke Universiteit.

McClelland, D.C., Atkinson, J.W., Clark, R.A., & Lowell, E.L. (1953). *The achievement motive*. New York: Appleton.

Neuwahl, N.M.E., Van den Bogaart, P.H.M., & Van Veen, A.F.D. (1981). *Concentratiemoeilijkheden bij het maken van huiswerk. Interimrapport 1*. Leiden: Rijksuniversiteit.

Neuwahl, N.M.E., Van den Bogaart, P.H.M., & Van Veen, A.F.D. (1983). *Concentratiemoeilijkheden bij het maken van huiswerk. Interimrapport 3*. Leiden: Rijksuniversiteit.

Neuwahl, N.M.E., & Van den Bogaart, P.H.M. (1984). Enkele onderwijspsychologische aspecten van huiswerk. *Pedagogische Studien, 61*, 7/8, 296-303.

Neuwahl, N.M.E., & Van den Bogaart, P.H.M. (1985). Huiswerk. *School, 12*, 5, 27-43 and 48-49.

Peters, V.A.M. (1983). De rol van de situatie in het meten van motivatie: een klassificatie en dimensionalisering van schoolse taaksituaties. In Th.C.M. Bergen & E. Roede (Eds.), *Motivatie gemeten?* Harlingen: Flevodruk.

Roede, E. (1983). Operationalisatieproblemen bij het meten van motiverende factoren in het onderwijs. In Th.M.C. Bergen & E. Roede (Eds.), *Motivatie gemeten?* Harlingen: Flevodruk.

PARENTAL EXPECTATIONS AND THE DEVELOPMENT
OF ACHIEVEMENT MOTIVATION

Clemens Trudewind
Thorsten Brünger
Karin Krieger

Ruhr University of Bochum

SUMMARY

The relevance of parents' aspirations and expectations of the child's proficiency at school for the development of achievement motivation and the origins of its interindividual differences is still an open question because in most of the studies referring to this problem the expectations and aspirations were only assessed after the children had visited school for some years and the parents had received information about their school performance and achievement behavior. In our "Bochum Longitudinal Investigation of the Ecological Determinants of the Development of Achievement Motivation" (Trudewind 1982) we measured these variables before the children started school. These variables turn out to be bad predictors for children's achievement motivation in the fourth grade. On the other hand, we were able to show that, for children who missed their parents' standards of excellence by far, different courses of the development of achievement motivation come about depending on the relation between the expectations and aspirations of their parents. By analizing some ecological variables and parental causal attributions we could specify the interdependent conditions which even favour the development of a success-oriented achievement motivation of children who receive bad school grades.

INTRODUCTION

The development of standards of excellence is one of the most important processes in the genesis of achievement motivation and the origin of interindividual differences within this behavior system (cf. Trudewind 1976, 1982). This process runs in several interdependent subprocesses. The discovery and differentiation of criteria for the assessment of the grade of the outcome of activities is followed by the discovery and differentiation of frames of reference which makes an evaluation of one's own ability possible.

These developmental changes may be accounted in a cognitive-structural developmental framework (Halisch & Halisch 1980; Nicholls & Müller 1984; Ruble et al. 1980) Parallel to this a development takes place in which certain degrees of excellence acquire the character of standards of excellence, and a personal commitment to these standards arises. Conditions of socialization as for instance parental sanctions, independence training and the setting of high standards of excellence in the early and middle childhood are supposed to influence this process (Trudewind 1975; Harter 1978). McClelland et al. (1953) assume the height and amount of parental achievement requirements assume to be the most important determinants of the strength of children's achievement motivation (cf. Winterbottom 1958; McClelland 1958; Rosen & D'Andrade 1959).

Hermans et al. (1972) showed that parents of success-oriented children had relatively high expectations of their children's performance. These expectations and the parents' ambitions for the child's career at school and in profession are good predictors for the child's marks, his or her intelligence and achievement motivation as it is shown in ecologically oriented research (e.g. Dave 1963; Wolf 1964; Marjoribanks 1972; Trudewind 1975). Contrary to the positive effects of parental achievement expectations found in these studies high levels of aspirations and high evaluations of scholastic performance are also held responsible for children's school anxiety and low self-esteem (Jacobs & Strittmatter 1979; Schneewind et al. 1983; Jopt & Engelbert-Holze 1984). All these studies have in common that the parental expectations and aspirations were only assessed after the children had visited school for some years and the parents had received information about their school performance. Besides they had the opportunity of observing their children's efforts. So the parental expectations are influenced by this information and are confounded with the consequences of good or bad school performances.

Therefore, in order to clarify the relations between parental expectations and aspirations and children's school performances on the one hand and the children's development of achievement motivation on the other hand it is necessary to measure the parents' variables before the children enter school.

In our "Bochum Longitudinal Investigation of the Ecological Determinants of the Development of Achievement Motivation" we measured these variables before the children started school, at the end of the first grade and in the middle of the fourth grade. In the following we should like to describe some patterns of relationship between the parents' expectations and aspirations, the children's school performances and their development of the achievement motive over the years of elementary school. But parental expectations and aspirations represent just a small subset of variables involved in the genesis of achievement motivation and included in our longitudinal study. The intention of these longitudinal study is to declare the ecological determinants responsible for the growth of interindividual differences in the achievement motive. For this study we took an ecological-taxonomical approach described by the following characteristics:

1. The development of interindividual differences in the achievement motive during elementary school should be explained as a function of the characteristics constituting child's life-space and of the kind of his experience in achievement-related situations. Therefore, we have to determine the amount of challenges and the opportunity structures to achievement-related behavior in the child's environment. Furthermore, it is necessary to assess the amount of success- and failure-experiences.

2. A specific feature of the ecological approach is its field-orientation. The variables which are taken into account to explain the differences in the motive represent the naturalistic environmental conditions of the individual. They are not conceptualized as broad and generalized parental child-rearing attitudes, but the concrete conditions of daily life are used in order to operationalize the specific variables.

3. The ecological approach tries to take into account the totality of the relevant environmental conditions in a holistic view. The primary goal of this multivariate approach is to unveil the network of empirical interactions between these variables. We start out from different effect of the same environmental variable on the genesis of achievement motivation for different subgroups of children depending on the constellation of other environmental variables. So, unveiling these patterns of interactions by means of linear regression analyses for the whole group is not an appropriate strategy; the explained variance of a single variable in the whole group offers little information about their importance for the development of the motive. Rather, this importance emerges from the manifold interactions with other variables, which are explainable in a consistent and systematic manner, often only after the inspection of the whole pattern of results (see Trudewind 1975, 1978, 1982).

4. To consider environmental characteristics as many as possible one needs a classification system which allows to combine these features according to a theoretical point of view. This classification system has to be or-

dered hierarchically to receive scores characterizing increasing segments of the environment. These taxonomic variables represent the psychological aspects of the concrete physical and social environmental characteristics.

Trudewind (1975) defined such a taxonomy of conditions responsible for the development of achievement motivation and proved its relevance in a cross-sectional study. A modified version of this taxonomy builds up the fundament of the referred "Bochumer Longitudinal Study". The taxonomy was divided hierarchically according to (a) major dimensions, (b) clusters of variables, (c) variables, and (d) characteristics. A higher order category summarizes the corresponding elements of the next subordinate level. At the lowest level, concrete physical, social, geographical, and psychological characteristics of the environment are distinguished. At the next level, environmental characteristics are integrated according to their intensity into psychological variables. At the next higher level, variable clusters are formed from these variables. Variable clusters combined the variables of the same environmental segment. At the highest level, major dimensions are composed of several clusters of variables. Three major dimensions were derived from the conceptualization of the achievement motive as a system of self-reinforcement, and we tried to divide the variety of relevant environmental characteristics into these major dimensions. The first of the major dimensions of the taxonomy consists of 11 variables describing the intellectual and achievement-related stimulation potential of the child's environment. The second dimension characterizes in 10 variables the degree of parental achievement pressure on the child and - separated from that - in three variables the parental efforts, interest and expectations regarding the child's proficiency at school. The third dimension consists of six variables designed to measure the cumulative experience of success and failure relating to school work and non-scholastic achievement.

In the following we summarize the major dimensions, the variable clusters and the variables with which we try to describe the relevant environmental conditions at the three observation periods in our longitudinal study:

A.   Intellectual and achievement-related stimulation potential

1. Scope of experience
   1. Freedom of movement in and near the home.
   2. Earliness of child-centered independence training.
   3. Variability and instability of the living space by journeys and removals

4. Frequencies and incentive potential of trips and excursions.

2. Stimulation from the equipment in the home
   1. Stimulation from toys and art materials.
   2. Stimulation form pets, art, crafts, hobbies, and duties in household.
   3. Stimulation from books, magazins, radio, and records.
   4. Favorable or unfavorable conditions for playing and learning: availability of learning aids.

3. Stimulation from social contacts
   1. Variety of social contacts.
   2. Frequency and quality of parent-child interactions.

4. Intensity of speech training

B.   Degree of parental achievement pressure

1. Parental aspirations for the child's proficiency at school
   1. Parental standards for the child's grades in the annual school certificate and their ambitions for his school-career.
   2. Degree of dissatisfaction with the child's scholastic achievement.

2. Parental activities to make the child achieve "well" at school
   1. Intensity of intended and factually performed control of the child's homework.
   2. Intensity of intended and factually offered help with homework assignments.
   3. Special efforts to improve the child's achievement at school.

3. Parental sanctions
   1. Extent of material reinforcement for good achievements at school.
   2. Extent of physical-emotional reinforcement for good achievement at school.
   3. Extent of material punishment for poor achievements at school.
   4. Extent of physical or emotional punishment for poor achievements at school.

4. Earliness of training skills to unburden the parents
   Parental indications regarding the child's self-perception of ability
   1. Special efforts to accelerate the child's development in the
      pre-school years.
   2. Parental interest in the child's school life.
   3. Parental expectations for the child's scholastic achievement.

C. Cumulative success and failure experiences
   1. Rank on general intelligence.
   2. Rank on nonverbal intelligence.
   3. Perceived ability with respect to scholastic achievement.
   4. Experiences of success and failure in comparison with siblings
      and peers
   5. Physical handicaps.
   6. Special experiences of success and failure.

The patterns of relationships between these ecological variables and the
change of achievement motivation during the years of elementary school will
be published elsewhere in a systematic manner (Trudewind, in preparation).
In the present report we examined the ecological variables ordered in the
taxonomy as well as some attributions of the parents and their children in
order to find out differences corresponding to differences in the parents'
expectations and aspirations. For a special subgroup we want to analyse
which ecological and attributional variables mediate the discovered relations
between the parents' variables and the change in the children's achievement
motivation.

THE COURSE OF THE STUDY

The course of the study is represented in Figure 1. The longitudinal
study spanned four years - from the beginning to the end of the elementary
education of one cohort of children entering school.[1] During this time, characteristics of the home environment were measured. The parents were first
administered a questionnaire when their child initially entered school. The

---

[1]   The longitudinal study was funded by the "Deutsche Forschungsgemeins-
      chaft" (Az. Tr 125).

questionnaire consisted of 128 content areas and a total of 354 items. The questionnaire included inquiries about characteristics of the stimulation potential at home existing during the child's preschool years, parental ambitions for their children's scholastic education, parental achievement expectations, and other aspects of the parents' present and prospective independence and achievement training. In addition, questions about their children's previous success and failure experiences and the parents' causal attributions about their children's prospective school achievements were included. On the first day of school, about 75 percent of the parents, who had volunteered for the investigation, returned the completed questionnaire (i.e., 3465 questionnaires).

At the end of the first year, all parents who had completed the first questionnaire were given a second one. The second questionnaire contained 122 items in 52 areas related to the parents' achievement training during the previous year, their reactions to the grade reports in the first evaluation, and their current achievement expectations, achievement requirements, and ambitions for their child's scholastic education. In addition, questions were asked about some aspects of the stimulation atmosphere at home and the parents' causal attributions about their child's achievements at school. About 60 percent of the parents who received the new questionnaire, (i.e., 2080 parents) completed this second on (i.e., 2080 questionnaires).

A third questionnaire was administered in the middle of the fourth grade. About the same percentage (60 percent) of parents returned this completed questionnaire. In this last questionnaire, 377 items in 116 areas were included. The questions dealt with parental causal attributions, the present incentive atmosphere at home, parental achievement pressure, and the cumulative success and failure experiences of the child.

Figure 1. The course of the study

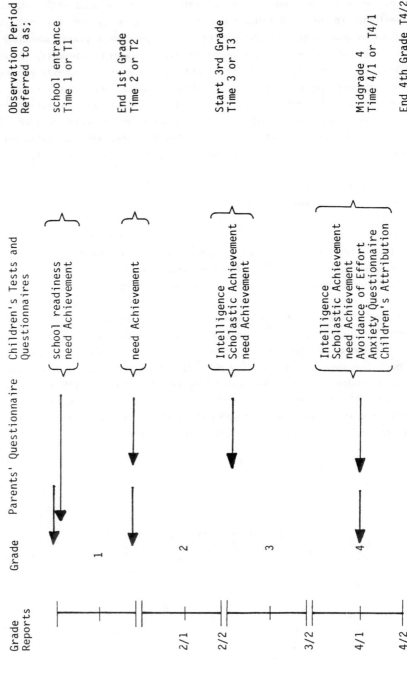

186

The information of the questionnaires about the environmental character-istics are used to operationalize each of the variables in the corresponding taxonomy. For scaling purposes, a key for weighting environmental charac-teristics was developed for each variable (Trudewind & Geppert 1982; Krie-ger, Geppert & Trudewind 1983). The raw scores of the variables were computed as the sum of the weighted characteristics. The standardized vari-ables were combined to form a composite score for each cluster and for each of the major dimensions in the taxonomy.

Parental expectations of school proficiency were operationalized by the question: "What grades in math and spelling do you believe your child to be capable of at the end of the fourth year?" Accordingly the minimal level of aspiration was assessed by the question: "What grades in math and spelling would just satisfy you at the end of the fourth year?" The grades ranged from 1 (= the best mark) to 6 (= the poorest mark).

Children's tests and questionnaires administered at the various observa-tion periods are represented in the third column of Figure 1.

Schmalt's (1976) achievement motivation grid was used to measure the lev-el of achievement motivation in our children in the middle of the fourth grade. This semi-projective procedure cannot be group administered with children who are less than nine years old. Our own instrument was developed to measure interindividual differences in the achievement motive of the chil-dren when they entered school and when they were in the second grade. The "Leistungsmotivationstest für Kinder" ("Achievement Motivation Test for Children"; LMTK, Trudewind et al. 1975) consists of 22 items measuring the level of children's success oriented willingness toward learning and achieve-ment versus their tendency to expect and fear failures in their school achievement. The test can be administered to groups of children that are un-able to read and write. This instrument was used to test the children at the beginning and the end of the first grade and the beginning of the third grade. In the fourth grade, two additional measurement instruments, which assess in detail the willingness to learn at school, were included: the "An-strengungsvermeidungstest" ("Avoidance of Effort Test"; AVT, Rollett & Bartram 1977) and the "Angstfragebogen für Schüler" ("Anxiety Question-naire for Students"; AFS, Wieczerkowski et al. 1974). Rollett and Bartram (1977) define avoidance of effort as "the tendency to avoid exertion in cer-tain areas" (p. 4; translation by the author). This construct is an important supplement of the construct of achievement motivation. The AFS contains four subscales. Three of them are relevant to our study. The first subscale, "Test Anxiety", measures the level of anxiety and psychological impairment encountered by students in test situations. The second subscale, "Manifest Anxiety", measures the enduring level of anxiety. The third subscale, "Dislike for School", measures a general attitude towards school. In addition, children were administered school readiness tests at the beginning of the first grade, and intelligence and scholastic achievement tests were given at the beginning of the third and in the middle of the fourth grade. The collected grade reports are represented in the first column of Figure 1.

RESULTS AND DISCUSSION

Relations between parental expectations and motive development in the whole group

Our first step to clarify the relationships between the parental expectations and levels of aspirations at time 1 and the children's achievement motivation was a correlational one. For the 1002 subjects for whom complete data were available we found no correlations between these variables and the children's need achievement-scores at the various points of measurement. We found significant correlations, however, between the grades in the first term reports of the second grade and the scores for need achievement as well as those for avoidance of effort, test anxiety and dislike for school in the middle of the fourth year.

Parental expectations and aspirations assessed before school entrance turn out to be bad predictors for children's motivation in the fourth grade. That does not mean, however, that they are unimportant for the development of achievement motivation and the origin of its interindividual differences. As explained previously, the meaning of a single ecological variable depends on the specific constellation of the other variables. Therefore, it must be assumed, that the *relations* between parents' expectations, their minimal level of aspiration and the grades actually received by the children are indeed important for the development of interindividual differences in the achievement motive.

To examine this hypothesis we have formed two new variables. The first variable called "Deviation from Parents' Achievement Standards" is operationalized by the difference between the parents' minimal level of aspiration before school entrance and the average marks in math and spelling received by the children in the fourth year. According to the distribution of these difference-scores the sample could be divided into three groups. The average marks of the subjects in the first group missed their parents' minimal level of aspiration by more than 0.5 grade units. The second group achieved and the third surpassed the minimal level of aspiration by more than 0.5 grade units.

The second variable called "The Parents' Range of Tolerance of Children's Performance" is operationalized by the difference between the parents' expectations and their minimal level of aspiration. According to the distribution of these differences the sample could be divided into two groups. In the group with a broad range of tolerance the minimal level of aspiration lies one or more grade units below the expectations. In the group with a small range of tolerance (low difference-group) the difference is less than one grade unit.

Figure 2. Mean hope of success at school entrance and in the middle of 4th grade of children missing, achieving or surpassing their parents' minimal level of aspiration as a function of their parents' range of tolerance of children's performance (n = 1002)

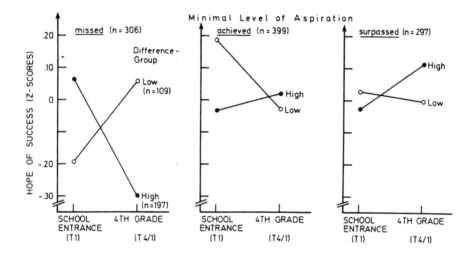

With these two variables as independent factors and the standardized need achievement scores at T1 and T4/1 as dependent variables we conducted a 3 x 2 x 2 ANOVA with repeated measures on the last factor. The most interesting results were found for the "hope of success"-score. The means of the standardized hope of success-scores are to be seen in Figure 2.

The analysis of variance yielded a significant main effect for the "Deviation from Parents' Achievement Standards" ($F(2; 996) = 3.05$; $p<.05$) and a highly significant 3-factorial (Deviation x Range of Tolerance x Hope of Success) interaction ($F(2; 996) = 8.75$; $p<.0001$). The analyses of variance separately conducted for the different levels of the factor "Deviation from

189

Parents' Achievement Standards" show that the interaction Group x Observation period for the ones who surpassed is not significant, while the interaction for the ones who achieved was marginally significant (F(1; 397) = 3.80; p<.053) and the interaction for the ones who missed was highly significant (F(1; 304) = 13.06; p<.0004).

Parental expectations and ecological variables for children missing their parents' minimal level on aspiration
At the first glance the decrease of hope of success in the four years of elementary school with the children in the low difference group who achieved their parents' minimal standards can be explained easily. These parents exercise a higher degree of achievement pressure on their children to make them accomplish the goals. So the children's efforts are more externally controlled which in the long run may lead to a decrease of the intrinsic component of the achievement motivation. This general explanation is questionable when the change of motivation is considered with the children who by far miss their parents' achievement standards. In this group especially the children of parents with a low range of tolerance show increasing hope of success. Contrary to that the hope of success with the children whose parents have a broad range of tolerance decreases gravely.

For these two groups the parents' expectations and minimal level of aspiration as well as the report grades at the end of the fourth grade are compared to one another in Figure 3. In both groups the children miss their parents' minimal standards on an average by approximately one grade unit. In spite of that the children of the low difference-group show a relatively high degree of hope of success. These children - notwithstanding objectively bad grades - keep or improve their achievement motivation in the course of elementary school. It seems to be of great theoretical and practical importance to find out what conditions produce these different courses of development. The first hypothesis which we examined says that the achievement training of parents with different ranges of tolerance differ from each other. The aspects of the achievement training recorded at three different times in the questionnaires are scaled in the variables of the dimension of our taxonomy characterizing the degree of achievement pressure.

They offer an empirical base for an examination of this hypothesis. For both groups combined we found in a series of two-factorial (Tolerance Group x Degree of Achievement Pressure-Variables) ANOVAs with repeated measures on the last factor we have tried to find out, in which domains of the achievement training the two groups of parents differ. For both groups we found a significant increase from the first to the fourth grade in the following variables:

a) Degree of dissatisfaction with the child's scholastic achievement
   $(F(1; 272) = 7.16; p< .008)$.
b) Intensity of control of the child's homework
   $(F(2; 544) = 7.72; p<.0005)$.
c) Amount of help with homework
   $(F(2; 544) = 23.45; p<.0000)$.
d) Parental interest in the child' school life
   $(F(2; 544) = 8.59; p<.0002)$.

Figure 3. Means of parents' expectation and minimal level of aspiration and
children's marks (n = 306)

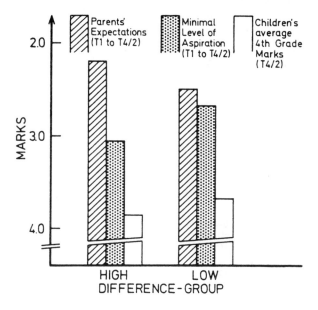

To our own surprise we found no differences between the two groups.
But we did find differences in the variable in which we had scaled the parents' level of aspiration and their ambition for a higher education. Though
the two groups of parents reduce their level of aspiration continually during
the three periods of observation $(F(2; 544) = 35.48; p<.0000)$ the low difference-group showed a constantly higher level of aspiration than the high difference-group $(F(1; 272) = 10.23; p<.002)$.

The scaled variables of achievement pressure alone cannot explain the differential course of the children's development of achievement motivation (see
also Trudewind & Husarek 1979). The higher level of aspirations and ambi-

191

tions of the parents with a small range of tolerance as well does not specify the conditions under which the high achievement standards of the parents favorably influence the development of motivation.

The second hypothesis which we examined states that the children of the low difference-group can compensate their failure in scholastic achievement by more experiences of success in non-scholastic domains than the children of the high difference-group. Therefore, in the course of elementary school the cumulative experience of success should be greater for the low-difference-group.

To examine this hypothesis we conducted a 2 x 2 (Tolerance Group x Cumulative Success Experience) ANOVA with the last factor as repeated measure. The means are to be seen in Figure 4.

Figure 4.   Mean cumulative success experience at school entrance (T1) and in the middle of the fourth year (T4/1) as a function of parents' range of tolerance (n = 306)

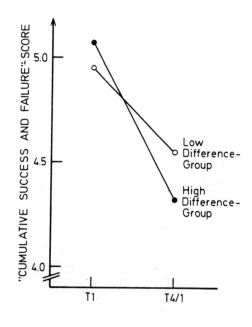

It shows that for both groups, during the elementary school time, the experiences of success decrease with regard to our whole sample $(F(1; 304) = 417.73; p<.000)$. But, nevertheless, the low difference-group has more experiences of success at the end of elementary school time than the high difference-group. The Interaction Group x Observation Period is highly significant $(F(1; 304) = 9.01; p<.003)$. As, however, the amount of cumulative experiences of success for the low difference-group still lies far below the whole sample (Mean: 5.00) this variable alone cannot explain this group's favorable course of the development of motivation.

That is why we also examined the variables of the first major dimension of our taxonomy. Among the variables which measure the level of intellectual and achievement-related stimulation potential in the child's environment we found remarkable differences between the two groups. The amount of stimulation from equipment in the home changed significantly for both difference-groups during elementary school time.

In Figure 5 are represented the means of the two groups at the beginning of school time (T1) and in the middle of the fourth year (T4/1).

Figure 5. Mean stimulation from equipment in the home as a function of parents' range of tolerance and observation period (n = 306)

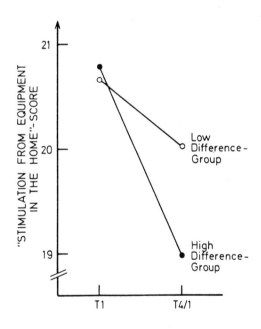

In both groups the "stimulation from the equipment in the home" decreases ($F(1; 304) = 17.21$; $p<.0000$). But the loss of stimulation in this domain is much greater for the high difference-group (Interaction Group x Observation Period: $F(1; 304) = 4.15$; $p<.05$) than for the low difference-group.

This may be a possible explanation for the different development of achievement motivation in both groups. The parents of the children with a small range of tolerance are not discouraged by the unexpectedly bad marks of their children. They try more intensively to advance the intellectual development and the achievement motivation of their children by providing toys, art materials, books, learning material and by arranging favorable conditions for playing and learning at home. They support hobbies and ask more frequently for household duties. So these children get more opportunities for achievement-related transactions which they can carry out according to their own standards of excellence. This again may prevent these children from developing a generalized concept of less ability as a consequence of their failures at school.

Attributional variables
You might go further and ask why the parents with a small range of tolerance try to advance their children in this way and how they achieve that the positive experiences at home are not invalidated by the failure experience at school. The answer may be found in the parents' causal attributions for the children's school performances. Therefore, we have compared the two groups concerning these variables. In the parents questionnaires at Time 1 we had asked the parents to scale how important they thought the given causal factors for their children's school performances to be. At Times 2 and 4/1 these questions were repeated but now separately for the satisfying and the dissatisfying performances.

It showed that at beginning of school time the parents with a broad range of tolerance attribute a greater importance to the intelligence and ability of their children than the parents of the other group ($t(233) = 1.84$; $p<.07$). In all other causal factors no significant differences were found between the two groups. In the middle of the fourth year (T4/1) the parents of the high difference-group attribute satisfying performances more to the factor "luck" ($t(300) = 2.45$; $p<.002$). Failures at school are attributed in a higher degree by the same parents to missing intelligence and ability ($t(298) = 1.95$; $p<.10$), to lacking effort ($t(298) = 1.81$; $p<.07$) and little interest of the child ($t(300) = 2.67$; $p<.008$). Combining the scores of these three concepts to only one score that characterizes in what amount the parents make the child himself or herself responsible for his or her bad performances (cf. Trudewind & Salk 1979), important differences between the two groups are to be seen (see Figure 6). Parents with a broad range of tolerance put the responsibility for the bad performances increasingly on their children themselves (Interaction Group x Observation Period: $F(1; 304) = 7.99$; $p<.005$). At the end of the first year (T2) parents with a small range of tolerance attribute scholastic success in a higher degree to their own help than the other parents ($t(304) = 1.84$; $p<.07$). In the same manner they attribute the failures in a higher degree to the child's relations to the teacher than the other group ($t(249) = 1.71$; $p<.09$).

Figure 6.   Mean child-centered attribution as a function of parents' range of tolerance and observation period (n = 306)

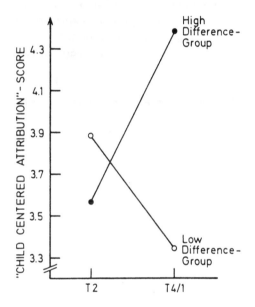

These parental attributions correspond partly with the children's attributions in the fourth year. Children of the low difference-group attribute their scholastic success more to their interest in the subject than the children in the high difference-group ($t(296) = 2.54$; $p<.02$). Contrary to them the children in the high difference-group attribute their failures at school, just like their parents, more to lacking abilities ($t(241) = 1.92$; $p<.057$).

Concomitant intellectual development

Finally, one more result may be shown which shows that the clarification of the conditions under which the pupils of the elementary school in spite of bad marks can develop a success-oriented achievement motivation, is also of practical importance. We have examined whether the differences in the development of motivation between the two groups and the accompanying differences in the providing and using of stimulating equipments have any different effects on the development of the intelligence. A 2 x 2 (Group x Intelligence) ANOVA with repeated measure at the last factor brought out a marginally significant Interaction Group x Observation Period ($F(1; 279) = 3.06$; $p<.09$). Figure 7 illustrates the course of the development of intelligence.

The means in both groups are lower than the one of the whole sample but a more favorable career in the secondary school may be expected for the children whose parents show a small range of tolerance of their children's performance if these parents keep up their successful strategies of achievement training.

Figure 7. Mean intelligence as a function of parents' range of tolerance (n = 306)

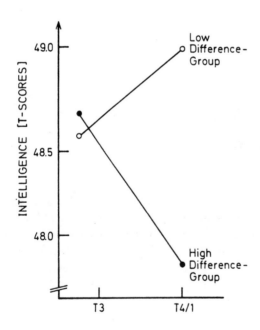

CONCLUDING REMARKS

Parental expectations and levels of aspiration which are measured before the child starts school are in our study bad predictors of the child's achievement motivation at the end of the fourth year. On the other hand the minimal level of aspiration related to the received marks of the children and the expectations relative to the minimal level of aspiration proved to be essential variables for the origin of interindividual differences in the children's achievement motivation during elementary school time. We could make evident that for children who by far missed the parental minimal achievement standards a favorable achievement motivation developed if there are only small differences between parental expectations and minimal level of aspiration at school entrance contrary to those children whose parents show great differences between these two variables. The interdependency of three groups of variables seems to be responsible for the differences in the development of achievement motivation in these two groups. Parents of the high difference-group attach greater importance to the child's intelligence in relation to school performance already before he or she starts school. As a consequence they attribute the unexpected failure of their children more and more to their lacking ability, missing efforts and small interest at school. The parents of the low difference-group, however, try to advance the children's abilities by providing a more stimulating environment. Accordingly, as the children use these opportunities they can make experience of success in the non-scholastic domain. These experiences of success allow the children to take over their parents' favorable attributions and so to inhibit the generalization of the consequences of the failures at school.

ACKNOWLEDGEMENT

The authors are grateful to Charlotte Lange for her help in translation.

REFERENCES

Dave, R.H. (1963). *The identification and measurement of environmental process variables that are related to educational achievement*. Unpublished doctoral dissertation, University of Chicago.

Halisch, C. & Halisch, F. (1980). Kognitive Voraussetzungen frühkindlicher Selbstbewertungsreaktionen nach Erfolg und Misserfolg. *Zeitschrift fur Entwicklungspsychologie und Padagogische Psychologie, 12,* 193-212.

Harter, S. (1978). Effectance motivation reconsidered. Toward a developmental model. *Human development, 21,* 34-64.

Hermans, H.J., Ter-Laak, J.J. & Maes, P.C. (1972). Achievement motivation and fear of failure in family and school. *Developmental Psychology, 6,* 520-528.

Jacobs, B., & Strittmatter, P. (1979). *Der schulangstliche Schuler.* München: Urban & Schwarzenberg.

Jopt, U.-J., & Engelbert-Holze, A. (1984). Elterliche Wertschätzung schulerischer Tüchtigkeit: Ein Beitrag zur Erziehungsstilforschun. *Zeitschrift fur Empirische Paedagogik und Padagogische Psychologie, 8,* 119-142.

Krieger, K., Geppert, U., & Trudewind, C. (1983). *Dokumentation der Programmierung des Verrechnungsschlussels und Datei-Erstellung fur die Variablen der Taxonomien der hauslichen Umwel* (1974, 1975, 1978 und Gesamt-Taxonomie). Arbeitspapier 14-3 zum DFG-Projekt "Leistungsmotivgenese". Psychologisches Institut der Ruhr-Universität Bochum.

McClelland, D.C. (1958). The importance of early learning in the formation of motives. In J.W. Atkinson (Ed.), *Motives in fantasy, action, and society* (pp. 437-452). Princeton, N.J.: Van Nostrand.

McClelland, D.C., Atkinson, J.W., Clark, R.A., & Lowell, E.L. (1953). *The achievement motive.* New York: Appleton-Century-Crofts.

Marjoribanks, K. (1972). Environment, social class, and mental abilities. *Journal of Educational Psychology, 63,* 103-109.

Nicholls, J.G., & Müller, A.T. (1984). Development and its discontents: The differentiation of the concept of ability. In J.G. Nicholls (Ed.), *The development of achievement motivation* (pp. 185-218). Greenwich, CN: JAI Press.

Rollett, B., & Bartram, M. (1977). *Anstrengungsvermeidungstest.* Braunschweig: Westermann.

Rosen, B.C., & D'Andrade, R. (1959). The psychological origins of achievement motivation. *Sociometry, 22,* 185-218.

Ruble, D.N., Boggiano, A.K., Feldman, N.S., & Loebl, J.H. (1980). A developmental analysis of the role of social comparison in selfevaluation. *Developmental Psycholgy, 16*, 105-115.

Schmalt, H.-D. (1976). *Das LM-Gitter.* Göttingen: Hogrefe.

Schneewind, K.A., Beckmann, M., & Engfer, A. (1983). *Eltern und Kinder.* Stuttgart: Klett.

Trudewind, C. (1975). *Hausliche Umwelt und Motivenentwicklung.* Göttingen: Hogrefe.

Trudewind, C. (1976). Die Entwicklung des Leistungsmotivs. In H.-D. Schmalt, & W.-U. Meyer (Eds.), *Leistungsmotivation und Verhalten* (pp. 193-219). Stuttgart: Klett.

Trudewind, C. (1978). Probleme einer ökologischen Orientierung in der Entwicklungspsychologie. In C.F. Graumann (Hrsg.), *Okologische Perspektiven in der Psychologie.* Bern: Huber, p. 33-48.

Trudewind, C. (1982). The development of achievement motivation and individual differences: Ecological determinants. In W.W. Hartup (Ed.), *Review of Child Development Research, Vol. 6* (pp. 669-703). Chicago: University of Chicago Press.

Trudewind, C., & Geppert, U. (1982). *Verrechnungsschlussel zur Skalierung der leistungsmotivgenetisch relevanten Bedingungen der hauslichen Umwelt* (Gesamttaxonomie). Arbeitspapier 11-1 zum DFG Projekt "Leistungsmotivgenese". Psychologisches Institut der Ruhr-Universität Bochum.

Trudewind, C., & Husarek, B. (1979). Mutter-Kind-Interaktion bei der Hausaufgabenanfertigung und die Leistungsmotivenentwicklung im Grundschulalter - Analyse einer ökologischen Schlüsselsituation. In H. Walter, & R. Oerter (Eds.), *Okologie und Entwicklung* (pp. 229-246). Donauwörth: Auer.

Trudewind, C., Jennessen, H., Geppert, U., & Mendack, D. (1975). *Entwicklung eines Gruppentests zur Erfassung der Lern- und Leistungsmotivation bei Schulanfangern (LMTK).* Arbeitsbericht 1 zum DFG-Projekt "Leistungsmotivgenese". Psychologisches Institut der Ruhr-Universität Bochum.

Trudewind, C., & Salk, J. (1979). Elterliche Ursachenerklärungen für kindliche Schulleistungen. In L. Eckensberger (Ed.), *Bericht uber den 31. Kongress der Deutschen Gesellschaft fur Psychologie* (pp. 50-54). Glöttingen: Hogrefe.

Wieczerkowski, W., Nickel, H., Janowski, A., Fittkau, B., & Rauer, W. (1974). *Angstfragebogen fur Schuler (AFS).* Braunschweig: Westermann.

Winterbottom, M. (1958). The relation of need for achievement to learning experiences in independence and mastery. In J.W. Atkinson (Ed.), *Mo-*

tives in fantasy, action, and society (pp. 453-478).   Princeton, N.J.:
Van Nostrand.

Wolf, R.M. (1964). *The identification and measurement of environmental process variables related to intelligence.* Unpublished doctoral dissertation,
University of Chicago.

THE CHANGEABILITY OF STUDENTS' ACHIEVEMENT MOTIVATION BY TEACHERS

Theo C.M. Bergen
René V.J. Alberts

University of Nijmegen

SUMMARY

The purpose of this study is to examine whether students' achievement motivation for their tasks at school could be enhanced under the present structural circumstances.

An important assumption is that there are sufficiently significant differences in motivation at micro level under the present macro- and meso-structural circumstances. A second major assumption is that these differences in motivation could well be explained in terms of achievement motivation.

A survey was made of the literature concerning attempts at influencing students' achievement motivation. Distinctions were made in target groups and in the theoretical orientations. This survey shows that: Relatively short training programs in terms of duration based on the conception of the achievement motive as a self-reinforcing motive system can be effective. The effects of such programs have more impact if teachers are able to integrate their experiences into their lessons over a relatively long period of time. These considerations led to the development of the Nijmegen achievement motivation training program for teachers.

A field-experimental intervention study showed inconsistent effects on the motive system of the experimental groups. The discussion will be focused on the feasibility of enhancing motivation within the present setting of the school.

INTRODUCTION

In reading educational publications it strikes one that one of the main problems teachers are faced with in carrying out their jobs is the low motivation of large groups of students for their tasks at school. Many teachers see this low motivation as a problem to which they hardly have an adequate answer. The teachers' complaints are mainly directed at the unconcentrated way their students work, their low interest in homework, their lack of interest in the subject matter, and their annoying behavior in class. These complaints from the practice of teaching, which are often referred to as students' motivation problems, cannot, conceptually speaking, be simply labeled as such. It was decided to start by conceptually clarifying the term 'motivation', and, after that, examine, by way of an intervention study, whether students' achievement motivation for their task at school could be enhanced under the present structural conditions. An important assumption made is that under the present macro- and mesostructural circumstances there are sufficiently significant differences in students' motivation at micro level. A second major assumption is that these differences in motivation can well be explained in terms of achievement.

Achievement motivation as a self-reinforcing system

Cognitive processes have been playing an increasingly important part in recent developments of the achievement motivation theory. Heckhausen (1974, 1975) has managed to integrate the behavioral correlates of the achievements and fear of failure motive and the more cognitive attributional processes into a conception of the motive as a self-reinforcing system.

By this conception, fear of failure person will lead to choose for extremely high or low goals. By making such a choice the attribution of the result is already preprogrammed. A failure will be ascribed to the high degree of difficulty. Success will be seen as a result of a low degree of difficulty. The result is determined by external factors in both cases, and the person will not reconsider his self-concept. If success is caused by external factors it will not, in principle, give much pride or satisfaction and as such it will not enhance the degree of attractiveness of this kind of tasks. The fear of failure student confirms his low concept of his own competence in this way, and the attraction for this kind of tasks will decrease. The conception of the achievement motive as a self-reinforcing system accounts for avoidance motivated students not developing success motivation and maintaining a low self-concept in spite of experiences of success.

In the motivation literature several motivation training programs within the framework of education are described, and the effects these programs have on teachers and their students (McClelland 1973; Krug 1976; Bergen 1979). McClelland's motivation program is the oldest and best-known training program, the more recently developed programs do not only take strategies from this program but parts as well. Alschuler's program (1973) and that of McClelland and Steele (1972) are mainly based on McClelland's motivation theory and they are primarily directed at the students. DeCharms' (1976) motivation program takes several parts of the program of McClelland, but it has a different theoretical orientation. DeCharms emphasizes students' personal causation on their achievements and he tries to achieve this by training students to be "origins". The teachers are trained to realize a working climate in their classrooms within the students are able to experience themselves as "origins" of their own results. Krug and Hanel's (1976) motivation training program is conceptually based on Heckhausen's self reinforcing system in task situations (1974, 1975). The training Krug and Hanel developed is directed at the students. A survey made of the literature concerning the various attempts at influencing students' achievement motivation shows that:

- training programs relatively short in terms of duration and based on the conception of the motive as a self-reinforcing system can be effective (cf. Krug & Hanel 1976);
- the effects of such training programs have more impact if teachers are able to integrate (cf. deCharms 1976) their experiences into their lessons for a lengthy period of time.

As a result of these considerations a motivation training program for teachers was developed, based on the conception of the motive as a self-reinforcing system (Bergen 1979). It was the objective of this program to provide teachers with knowledge of and insight into the achievement motivation theory, which could then be translated into teaching skills required to enhance students' achievement motivation. For a change in the motivation of the avoidance motivated students, these students should, according to Krug and Hanel (1976):

- be shown how to set realistic goals in accordance with their own competence;
- enhance their concept of own competence by way of a more favourable attributional process;
- come to experience a more positive self-reinforcement causing an increase in the attraction of achievement orientated behavior.

If the directives formulated by Krug and Hanel are to be put into practice by teachers, the teachers should be trained in teaching skills closely related to the components of the self-reinforcing system. In Heckhausen's conception the motive is seen as a cyclic system, within which a number of motive components are to be discerned. These central components are: self-concept of one's own competence, goal setting behavior, the way result is attributed (attributional prejudice as well), the affective experience and the success expectancy.

Rheinberg (1980) has managed to integrate the different teaching skills related to each component of the motive system into a teaching style directed at employing individual reference norms. A teacher using individual reference norms mainly evaluates a student's achievement in relation to the earlier level of achievement of the same student. A teacher using social reference norms on the other hand will evaluate a student's result mainly in relation to the achievement of his class-mates. In the practice of teaching these evaluation norms of teachers are of great importance to the students' motivation, for they are connected with a number of teachers' behaviors related to the components of the self-reinforcing system. We shall briefly look into the matter of goalsetting behavior, attribution of results, evaluation of results, and expectations of future results successively.

Goalsetting behavior:
A teacher evaluating his students on the basis of social reference norms will, above all, look at the differences between the students. To be able to evaluate the achievements on the basis of a social reference norm the teacher will have to set the same, or at least comparable, tasks to all students. Rheinberg's (1977) survey shows that teachers making more use of an individual reference norm are prepared to individualize to a larger extent than their colleagues with a more social reference norm.

Attribution of results:
If a teacher using a social reference norm has to explain his students' achievements, he will mention causes why one student's achievement is better than the achievement of another student. Teachers using a social reference norm to a large extent attribute these differences to stable student characteristics, such as aptitude and social class. Teachers using an individual reference norm, on the other hand, will be especially inclined to state why a certain student's achievement is better or worse than his previous achievement. Because they are, strictly speaking, posing a different question they will also point to different factors to explain this result. Preferably they will explain the variation in a student's achievement with variable factors, such as the student's interest and effort for instance. From an attribution-theoretical point of view it is essential that the teacher will not attribute the student's failure to stable factors and uncontrollable factors.

Moreover, if failure is attributed to low ability it will work as a threat to the student's self-esteem in relation to his class-mates. In this case negative effects of attributions to ability cannot be precluded (cf. Halisch 1976).

Evaluation of results:
Teachers using a social reference norm will mainly attune their evaluations to the rank-order of the students' achievements. This may lead to a situation in which the teacher doesn't value so much the differences in effort but much more the differences in the students' competence, rewarding the gifted student and punishing the less gifted one. Teachers using an individual reference norm will attune their evaluation much more to the progress or fall off the individual student has made. This last aspect is more informative to the student's self-reinforcement. In addition, a difference in reference norm will correlate with the frequency of reward or punishment in the classroom situation. Roughly speaking, the use of a social reference norm will lead to the same number of positive as well as negative evaluations. On the other hand, the use of the individual reference norm will, in an effective classroom situation, lead to positive evaluation more often than to a negative one.

Expectations of future results:
Finally, the use of individual or social reference norms also has important effects on the expectations teachers have with respect to their students these expectations are closely related to the way in which they explain their student's results. When teachers are of the opinion that their students' results are caused by stable factors, they will have stable expectations of their students as well.
Rheinberg shows that teachers using a social reference norm are more inclined to have stable expectations. On the other hand, teachers with an individual reference norm are more inclined to think that the development of the students' achievements cannot be predicted a long time in advance and they ground their expectations mainly on the most recent achievements. For this reason they are less likely to be influenced by expectancy effects.

Rheinberg (1976) expects as an educational system using individual reference norms to lead to a success oriented motive system for students in the long run, and to make the development of an avoidance orientated motive system for students less likely. In doing so he draws attention to the important similarities between Krug and Hanel's (1976) training program and an educational system using individual reference norms. The central concepts form the self-reinforcing system on which Krug and Hanel's training is based and which are influenced in mutual connection, will be influenced in a similar way by an educational praxis in which individual reference norms are used.

Because of these similarities such an educational praxis can be considered to be a 'natural' motivation training program for students.

In line with the above mentioned theoretical insights with regard to the conception of the motive as a self-reinforcing system, we expect two effects of the training program:
- An increase in the hope of success motive (approach motivation).
- A decrease in the fear of failure motive (avoidance motivation).

A brief description of the Nijmegen training program for teachers

The target group of the Nijmegen training program is formed by teachers and students of a class in the first and second year of secondary education (students aged about 13). In practice this means that about twelve teachers teaching the same class will be voluntarily engaged in stimulating their students' achievement motivation together with a few members of the study project during four months. One of the important starting points of the program is that teachers should themselves be taught to help students who have developed an avoidance orientated motive system, to enhance their motivation and influence their motive system. One condition that has to be met is that teachers should have sufficient insight into the theoretical concepts underlying the motivation process and that they will be able to realize that teaching behavior is essential to stimulate students' motivation.

Roughly speaking, the program can be subdivided in two parts. First, a teacher's training of 3 to 5 days to acquire knowledge of and insight into those concepts playing a part in task motives, and translate this knowledge and these insights into teaching skills functioning in instruction-situations. Secondly, a 12 week application period to facilitate the transfer of the teaching skills newly acquired in the training situation to the everyday classroom situations.

Scheme I gives an outline of the Nijmegen training program for teachers.

Scheme I : Schematic outline of the Nijmegen program with regard to the target group, the concepts, the techniques, and the objective of the Nijmegen training program.

1. *Target group and training organization:*
   - teachers and students.
   - students aged 12-14 years.
   - teachers active with secondary education voluntarily integrate the trained behaviors in their lessons. Teachers' supervision is directed at students who are most qualified to be supervised according to the test results and the teachers' judgements.

206

- a training of 3 to 5 days and a 12 week application period in the classroom to apply what they have been taught.
- students are trained by their teachers.

2. *Concepts on which is trained:*
   - setting realistic goals in accordance with their own competence.
   - making attributional prejudices more adequate after success and failure.
   - making the affective assessment more favourable after success and fail-
     ure.
   - increasing the perceived concept of own ability for future tasks.

3. *Techniques and methods used in the training:*
   - double-bottomed method (the training team's behavior serves as a model
     for the teacher's behavior in class).
   - self reflection on one's own task behavior.
   - learning by experience.
   - observations of teaching behavior.
   - micro teaching.
   - supervision.

4. *Important materials used during the training:*
   - theoretical information (literature to be studied).
   - gain experiences through entry-test, ring-toss game and block stocking
     game.
   - integration between knowledge and experience.
   - carry out lessons.
   - discuss the lessons registrated in class (in the application period).
   - design strategies and tasks to supervise students in task-situations.

5. *Training objective:*
   - translate the knowledge of and insight into the concepts of cognitive
     processes playing a part in task motivation into skills which will en-
     hance the students' task motivation in classroom situations.

A brief description of the instruments for measuring motivation

Two newly developed instruments were used in order to assess the effects
of the training program. These instruments were Bergen's (1981) Situation
Specific Anxiety Test (SSAT) and Smits' (1982) Test of Cognitive Motivation
(TCM). These situation-reaction questionnaires are based on the conception
of motivation as a self-reinforcing system, on which also the training program is based.

The situation specific test (SSAT) has been developed to investigate more
thouroughly the fear of failure motive of pupils during lessons. Characteristics like standard of evaluation and probability of success are related to

207

items about (1) self concept of own ability (OA), (2) evaluation anxiety which consists of two components namely the worry component referring to expectancies, self-evaluations and other evaluations and the emotionality component referring to psycho-physiological phenomena (EA), (3) Avoidance tendency which consists of two aspects referring to consequences of evaluation-anxiety on the intentional level of behavior namely the sense of personal control and the instrumental activities in order to escape the evaluation situation (Av.M). The 14 class situations of the SSAT are represented by pictures with a description in order to get a more thorough and realistic experience for the pupils. For each of the 14 situations items are formulated which operationalize the self concept of own ability (OA), evaluation anxiety (EA) and avoidance motivation (Av.M). The reliability of the SSAT is very satisfactory. The internal consistencies of the SSAT expressed in Cronbach's Alpha are for OA .78, for EA .93 and for Av.M .84. The stability coefficient after 14 weeks is respectively .80, .84 and .81. The correlations between OA and EA and OA and Av.M are respectively -.42 and -.51, between EA and Av.M .34.

The test of cognitive motivation (TCM) has been developed to investigate the interaction between value dispositions, the so called motives and motive relevant aspects of the perceived situations. The measurement takes into account the self concept of own competence (SC), causal attributional preferences for success and failure and approach motivation (Ap.M) like performance standards and risk preference, generalized expectancies of success or failure, intensity and persistence of goal directed activities. These differential motive constructs, which represent sources of individual differences are situated in ten different achievement situations from the domain of the school, the sport and the hobby world. In this study we used two concepts of the TCM, namely self concept of own competence (SC) and approach motivation (Ap.M).

The stability of both concepts is satisfactory. The stability coefficients after 16 weeks are .62 for SC and .74 for Ap.M. The author doesn't report internal consistencies because the situations of the TCM are taken from different situation domains. The correlation between SC and Ap.M is .32.

The correlations between the three concepts of the SSAT and the two concepts of the TCM are presented in Table 1.

Table 1. Product-moment correlations between the self-concept of own ability (OA), Evaluation anxiety (EA), Avoidance Motivation (Av.M)
of the SSAT and self-concept of own competence (SC), Approach
Motivation (Ap.M) of the TCM (n = 104)

SSAT	TCM SC	Ap.M
OA	.34	.34
EA	-.39	-.29
Av.M	-.11	-.42

The relations are in the expected direction and can be interpreted in a
theoretically meaningful way. Remarkable is the moderate negative relationship between Av.M and Ap.M. We can state that both instruments meet the
classical psychometric criteria to a sufficient degree. Within the framework of
this article we cannot go in further detail on the structure and the scoring
procedures of both instruments, but confine ourselves to a reference to Bergen (1981) and Smits (1982).

METHOD

The program was carried out at three different schools. At each school
the results of the experimental class were compared with the results of a
parallel class from the same school, functioning as control class. At the first
and second school only the teachers' program was carried out. At the third
school this teachers' program was supported by a students' training program
comparable with Krug and Hanel's (1976) program. All the students involved
in the experiment took the two motivation measuring instruments (SSAT and
TCM), both before and after the program.

Table 2. Means, standard deviations and F value of the variables SC (selfconcept of own competence), OA (own ability), Ap.M (Approach Motivation), EA (Evaluation Anxiety), Av.M (Avoidance Motivation) for each of the three schools.

Variables		Pretest										Posttest									
		SC1		OA		Ap.M1		EA		Av.M		SC		OA		Ap.M		EA		Av.M	
	n	M	SD	M	SD	M	SD	M	SD	M	SD	M	SD	M	SD	M	SD	M	SD	M	SD
School 1																					
Exp. (23)		2.54	1.70	44.30	9.14	16.09	4.70	40.78	12.00	22.33	8.41	4.67	2.1	44.09	6.29	17.44	5.60	39.83	16.40	21.80	8.39
Contr.(19)		3.71	2.0	42.26	3.46	14.71	4.20	42.32	16.10	25.45	7.96	3.18	2.1	43.42	2.78	14.37	5.10	43.58	17.70	25.00	9.04
F												7.90**		< 1		3.62		< 1		< 1	
School 2																					
Exp. (28)		2.52	1.75	34.64	3.41	9.63	3.38	31.29	9.62	18.25	5.54	2.16	1.55	34.21	4.59	8.98	3.05	30.32	11.00	19.45	6.78
Contr.(28)		2.30	1.21	34.86	3.78	9.36	3.48	30.02	8.78	18.59	5.90	2.45	1.16	33.68	4.68	8.18	3.09	23.50	8.26	19.71	6.29
F												1.04		< 1		1.34		4.10*		1.00	
School 3																					
Exp. (24)		2.98	1.94	36.38	3.98	11.88	3.39	24.42	8.24	15.17	4.70	2.92	1.80	35.00	3.99	10.15	3.20	27.76	10.75	16.83	4.59
Contr.(27)		2.83	1.82	34.14	5.09	9.65	3.04	24.30	10.73	17.80	7.42	2.41	1.76	34.12	5.49	9.22	3.13	23.46	10.91	16.79	8.47
F												< 1		< 1		< 1		3.59		2.62	

1 For school 2 and 3 a short version of the TCM was used.
F = F test for difference between Exp. and Contr. on the posttest with the pretest as covariate.

* p < .05
** p < .01

RESULTS

The results of the training program are given in Table 2 for the three schools. A comparison has been made between the experimental class and control class for each school. The test is an analysis of covariance on the scores of the post-test with the pre-test scores as a covariate. The results are not consistent for the three training programs. At the first school the experimental class differs in a significant way on the score for a positive self concept of own competence and the rest of the results shows a tendency in the expected direction. At the second school the experimental class reaches a significant effect in diminishing evaluation anxiety. The other components are only partly showing a tendency in the expected direction. No significant effects are to be established at the third school. Contrary to the expectations the results are tending into the opposite direction. This is the more remarkable as the teachers' program was supported by a students' program in this intervention. This intervention had been expected to have the greatest impact on the students' motivation system. The overall results we have in these three interventions are disappointing. We shall discuss three possible explanations, namely the restrictions of a field study, the question of the sensitivity of the measurements and the ecological validity of the approach.

DISCUSSION

1) The restriction of a field experimental design.

Quite often it is not possible to manipulate all relevant variables in a field study as described above. It is only possible to do some kind of check after the study has been finished.

Teachers play an important part in the method we have chosen. Before theoretically understandable effects are to be expected, a number of conditions will have to be met first. The effect of the training programs depends strongly on the teachers' willingness to apply the newly learned skills during the whole period of supervision after the training. The questionnaires thatthe students filled in on the behavior of their teachers, show that significant differences appeared with regard to only a few teachers in comparison with their colleagues from the control class. The ascertainment that only a few teachers change their teaching behavior in the students' perception, makes it more plausible to expect subject-specific effects than effects on the general motivation structure as measured with the SSAT and TCM.

2) The sensitivity of the measurements.

The SSAT and TCM have to meet the paradoxical demand that they must register that which has a certain stability over time and situations, while at the same time they have to be sufficiently sensitive to be able to reflect (small) changes in the operationalized constructs. A good measuring instrument should meet the sensitivity criterion according to McClelland (1971). This criterion requires a measure to fluctuate or register changes proportionally to a change in the behavior of which the measure is supposed to be the index. As to TCM and SSAT, we are of the opinion that the sensitivity criterion has not been solved conclusively. So the question remains to which extent the absence of results regarding the SSAT and TCM may be a result of the insufficient sensitivity of the measuring instrument.

3) The ecological validity of the approach.

An important explanation for thelack of effects might perhaps be sought in the low ecological validity of the approach chosen. Bergen (1983) has attributed the low effect of intervention-research to a controversy immanent in the present function of secondary education, which is in principle unsolvable within the present educational system. This controversy refers to different conceptions on the function education has in society.

Above all, the allocation and selection function of education is of importance in this context. The norms teachers employ when evaluating their students' results, result from the allocation taking place on the basis of the selection function. In all situations within the educational system in which students have to be evaluated, teachers mainly use a social evaluation norm to carry out this allocation adequately. Examples of such situations are, among other things, final exams and demands relating to end-of-year tests. These evaluation situations are organized in such a way that by using a social evaluation norm the allocation and selection function of the educational system can be exercised as fairly as possible for the students. As a matter of course, the students as well often direct their attention to the social evaluation norm and attune their own efforts to it. Teachers' motivating behavior emphasizing an individual evaluation norm hardly stands a chance if the allocation and selection function of the educational system is left unhindered. Teachers wishing to employ an individual evaluation norm in their teaching all the same, get themselves into an awkward predicament as the demands the theory makes do not harmonize with the demands from the broader structure of the educational system.

Meyer (1980) shows that teachers' behavior based on an individual reference norm may even lead to negative effects in students employing a social
reference norm. Therefore the disappointing results could be explained in
the insufficient space and therefore low chance of success the chosen approach has within the present educational system. This means that teachers
will only be able to realize a successfully motivating teaching behavior under
the approach chosen, if radical measures are taken with regard to the selection and allocation function of our present educational system. Boekaerts
(1983a, 1983b) gives suggestions for another strategy to improve the ecological validity of motivation study in education. Boekaerts (1983a) has given a
few critical comments on achievement motivation models. The various models
are mainly directed at explaining the complex of behaviors in so far as it
leads to a certain achievement (or result). Study based on these models mainly restricts itself to situations in which students have to achieve. Other motivational processes (such as power-motivation and social motivation among
other things) and environmental factors are not being involved in the students' perception of the situation. Boekaerts (1983b) proposed to improve
the ecological validity by setting up a class-orientated motivation study under a more comprisingly conceptual framework. In expanding this framework
justice can be done in a better way to the complexity and specificity of the
classroom situation and the individual differences in learning behavior. This
approach has one drawback, namely that the study of motivational processes
during the lessons will become considerably more complex, as several motives
will have to be integrated. It is our opinion that the demand for ecologically
valid class orientated lessons is asking very much of the present intervention
research. But by choosing the long way it will eventually give more insight
into the way in which students are functioning in real classroom situations
and how their motivation process is to be enhanced.

CONCLUSION

Since McClelland's (1973) publication 'What is the effect of achievement
motivation training in the schools' which shows that their is only a slight effect of motivation training in the schools and that consistent effects with
school achievements were never found, there have not been many changes.
The study described above confirms once again that it is extremely difficult
to prove within the actual setting of the school that the students' motive system has changed under the influence of a training program. The successful

attempts by deCharms (1976) and Krug and Hanel (1976), who did demonstrably improve the students' motive structure by means of their training programs, seem to be much more an exception to a rule than a proof that we should continue in the direction they have indicated. The assumption that under the present macro and meso structural circumstances teachers can influence the motive system of failure orientated students, is too optimistic. This means that the requests from educational workers to motivation researchers to help them reduce their students' motivation problems cannot be adequately met with the present development of theory.

REFERENCES

Alschuler, A.S. (1973). *Developing achievement motivation in adolescents.* Englewood Cliffs, N.J.: Educational Technology Inc.

Bergen, Th.C.M. (1979). De veranderbaarheid van taakgebonden motieven in onderwijsleersituaties. In E.E.J. de Bruyn (Ed.), *Ontwikkelingen in het onderzoek naar prestatiemotivatie: theorie, meetmethode en toepassing in het onderwijs.*Lisse: Swets & Zeitlinger.

Bergen, Th.C.M. (1981). *Evaluatie-angst en vermijdingstendens. Een onderzoek naar de orientatie van leerlingen om mislukkingen te vermijden in taaksituaties tijdens de les.* Academisch proefschrift. S.V.O.-reeks 47. 's-Gravenhage: Staatsuitgeverij.

Bergen, Th.C.M. (1983). Motiverend lesgedrag van docenten in het algemeen voortgezet onderwijs. Een realistisch model? In A.M.P. Knoers & J.J.R.M. Corten (Eds.), *Ontwikkelingen in het Nederlandse onderwijs. Aspecten van kwaliteit en beleid.*Mededelingen nr. 11. Vakgroep Interdisciplinaire Onderwijskunde, Katholieke Universiteit Nijmegen.

Boekaerts, M. (1983a). Enige kanttekeningen bij het interactionistisch motivatiemodel. In Th.C.M. Bergen & E. Roede, *Motivatie gemeten?* Harlingen: Flevodruk.

Boekaerts, M. (1983b). Motivatie en onderwijs: theorieën en modellen op een rij gezet. In S. Dijkstra, A.C.M. Dudink & R.J. Takens (Eds.), *Psychologie en onderwijs.* Lisse: Swets & Zeitlinger.

DeCharms, R. (1976). *Enhancing motivation: change in the classroom.* New York: Irvington.

Halisch, F. (1976). Die Selbstregulation leistungsbezogenen Verhaltens: das Leistungsmotiv als Selbstbekräftigungsystem. In H.-D. Schmalt & W.-U. Meyer (Eds.), *Leistungsmotivation und Verhalten.* Stuttgart: Klett.

214

Heckhausen, H. (1974). Bessere Lernmotivation und neue Lernziele. In F.E. Weiner, C.F. Graumann, H. Heckhausen, M. Hofer u.a., *Funk-Kolleg Pädagogische Psychologie I*. Frankfurt am Main: Fischer.

Heckhausen, H. (1975). Fear of failure as a selfreinforcing motive system. In I.G. Sarason & C.D. Spielberger (Eds.), *Stress and anxiety (Vol. 2)*. Washington, D.C.: Hemisphere.

Krug, S. (1976a). Förderung und Änderung des Leistungsmotivs: theoretische Grundlagen und deren Anwendung. In H.-D. Schmalt & W.-U. Meyer (Eds.), *Leistungsmotivation und Verhalten*. Stuttgart: Klett.

Krug, S., & Hanel, J. (1976). Motivänderung: Erprobung eines theoriegeleiteten Trainingsprogrammas. *Zeitschrift für Entwicklungspsychologie und Pädagogische Psychologie, 8,*274-287.

McClelland, D.C. (1971). *Assessing human motivation*. New York: General Learning Press.

McClelland, D.C., & Steele, R.S. (1972). *Motivation workshops*. New York: General Learning Press.

McClelland, D.C. (1973). What is the effect of achievement motivation training in the schools, In A.S. Alschuler (Ed.), *Developing achievement motivation in adolescents*. Englewood Cliffs, N.J.: Educational Technology Inc.

Meyer, W.-U. (1980). *Effects of evaluative and helping behavior on perceived ability and affect*. Paper presented at the conference "Attributional approaches to Human Motivation", University of Bielefeld.

Rheinberg, F. (1980). *Leistungsbewertung und Lernmotivation*. Göttingen: Hogrefe.

Rheinberg, F., Luhrmann, J.V., & Wagner, H. (1977). Bezugsnorm-Orientierung von Schülern der 5. bis 13. Klasse bei der Leistungsbeurteilung. *Zeitschrift für Entwicklungspsychologie und Pädagogische Psychologie, 9,* 90-93.

Smits, B.W.G.M. (1982). *Motivatie en meetmethode*. Academisch proefschrift. Lisse: Swets & Zeitlinger.

PART IV

ACADEMIC ACHIEVEMENT AND MOTIVATION

PROBLEM-BASED LEARNING AND INTRINSIC MOTIVATION

Maurice L. de Volder
Henk G. Schmidt
Jos H.C. Moust
Willem S. de Grave

University of Limburg

INTRODUCTION

In current research on intrinsic motivation two themes can be distinguished. The first focuses on the effect of extrinsic rewards on intrinsic motivation (Deci 1971; Lepper & Greene 1975; Morgan 1984). The second deals with the relationships between instructional methods, intrinsic motivation and achievement (Bloom 1976; Johnson & Johnson 1979; Steinkamp & Maehr 1983). Our paper can be situated in the second line of research.

A serious obstacle in reviewing the literature on intrinsic motivation, is the fact that different terms are in use referring to more or less the same phenomenon. Intrinsic or continuing or cognitive motivation, subject-related affect or attitude or interest, epistemic curiosity: when looking at the various measures no clear demarcation can be found. Deci (1975, p. 23) defines intrinsically motivated activities as ones for which there is no apparent reward except the activity itself. The activities appear to be ends in themselves rather than means to an end: they bring about certain kinds of internal states which are found rewarding. In a more educational context, Fransson (1977) defined intrinsic motivation as a state where the relevance (perceived value) for the learner of the content of the learning material is the main reason for learning. The learning content can be rather specific, such as: the Battle of Gettysburg, or rather general e.g.: history. When knowledge in general is positively valued, terms such as epistemic curiosity and cognitive motivation are used.

It is interesting to note that without specification the term intrinsic motivation is not very informative. There exists no intrinsic motive like one speaks of an achievement motive or power motive. When someone informs us that person A is intrinsically motivated, this may mean that person A is interested in geography or Playboy, or anything else for that matter. Although the term 'interest' with a specification (e.g. interest in history, or in the Civil War) would be a very accurate and sufficient substitute for all other terms, we too will use the other terms as they have become such popular labels in psychological publications.

When summarizing various large-scale studies, Bloom (1976) found an average correlation of about .31 (about .10 higher when corrected for attenuation) between affect toward a school subject and achievement in that subject. Correlations were slightly lower in the primary school period and for literature and reading, while correlations were slightly higher in the high school period and for science, mathematics and second language. Bloom also reports a number of small, experimental, and school-based studies contrasting mastery learning approaches with more conventional approaches. Interest in a learning task, at the beginning of that task, and achievement at the end of the task correlated about .30 (.38 after correction for unreliability). It was also found that in the mastery groups interest in the subject tends to increase, while in the control groups interest tends to remain the same or even decline. Bloom concluded that achievement and affect are interrelated or that one influences the other in a kind of spiral effect. Thus, high achievement (or more exactly: perceived high achievement) increases positive affect.

According to Bloom, the evidence reported in concurrent, predictive, longitudinal and experimental studies is consistent in suggesting that affect is a causal link in determining learning and in accounting for educational achievement. In Bloom's view, affect helps to determine the extent to which the learner will put forth the necessary effort to learn a specific learning task, i.e. how hard (intensity) and how long (persistence) the learning will be. Bloom proposes that subject-related affect should be altered (i.e., increased) by implementing teaching, curriculum and grading policies in the school which stress high ratios of success experiences to failure experiences.

Johnson and Johnson (1979) report that there is evidence that epistemic curiosity can also be sparked by other means than success experiences. Controversy among students or between the students and the teacher can be used to create conceptual conflict and epistemic curiosity within students. Controversy exists when one person's ideas, information, conclusions, theories or opinions are incompatible with those of another person, and the two seek to reach an agreement.

Conceptual conflict has high arousal potential, motivating attempts to resolve it by seeking new information or by trying to reorganize the knowledge one already has. The greater the disagreement among students or between the teacher and the students, the more frequently the disagreement occurs, the greater the number of people disagreeing with a student's position, the more competitive the context of the controversy, and the more affronted the

218

student feels, the greater the conceptual conflict the student will experience (Johnson & Johnson 1979).

Smith, Johnson and Johnson (1981) compared controversy, concurrence seeking and individualistic learning. All three types of learning begin with students categorizing and organizing their present information and experience so that a personal conclusion is derived. In individualistic learning the student becomes fixed and satisfied with the information he has. Within concurrence seeking, there is a suppression of different conclusions, an emphasis on quick compromise, and lack of disagreement. New information that may challenge the conclusions is avoided. In controversy the students realize that others have a different conclusion, become uncertain about the correctness of their own conclusion, and actively search for more information. Students actively represent their position and reasoning to the opposition, thereby engaging in considerable cognitive rehearsal of their position and its rationale. In their search for a more adequate cognitive perspective, students listen to and attempt to understand conclusions and rationale of other students. The results of Smith, Johnson and Johnson (1981) indicate that controversy, compared with concurrence seeking and individualistic study, promotes higher achievement and retention as well as continuing motivation.

Controversy learning is strikingly similar to an instructional method called problem-based learning, which is increasingly used in health professions education (Schmidt & De Volder 1984). Students are confronted with a problem, i.e. a real-life phenomenon (e.g.: a case of A.I.D.S. after a blood transfusion) in need of some kind of explanation. The task of the students is to formulate possible explanations, then to search additional information, and finally to discuss the different viewpoints and try to understand the underlying mechanisms of the phenomenon studied. Problems are supposed to make the students "hungry for knowledge" (Barrows 1984, p. 24). So far, however, research evidence is lacking for this assumption.

While it has been shown that intrinsic motivation can be generated by educational methods such as mastery learning and controversy learning, it is less clear whether there is a causal link from intrinsic motivation to school achievement. As described earlier, Bloom (1976) concludes that affect influences achievement. Steinkamp and Maehr (1983), however, suggest that it is primarily the acquisition of proficiency that leads to positive attitudes: one is most likely to feel positively toward science as one actualizes one's ability through science achievement. The conclusions of Steinkamp and Maehr are based on the following pattern of correlations. Mean correlations between achievement and cognitive ability in science are significantly positive for high school boys ($r=.36$) and girls ($r=.32$). The relationship between achievement and science-related affect is small but significant: for males the mean correlation is .19 and for females .18. Although it would seem that students with the ability to do science would like science, in which case data on cognitive ability and science would be strongly related, the synthesized studies showed that the expected relationship does not exist for boys or for girls (r=.07 and .02, respectively). Confronting Bloom with Steinkamp and Maehr, it seems safe to conclude that controversy exists with respect to the causal nature of the relationships between ability, affect and achievement.

METHOD

Our research focuses on two questions: First, can intrinsic motivation be generated by the problem-based learning method; and second: which causal relationships exist between ability, motivation and achievement?

Subjects

Subjects were 69 female and 15 male first-year students from four schools of allied health. The average age was 18,6 years with a standard deviation of 13 months.

Procedure

Subjects from each school were randomly assigned to the experimental or the control condition. In the experimental (problem-based learning) condition, seven groups of about six students were formed. In each of these groups a male experimenter was present. He briefly explained the problem-based learning method by means of a written example consisting of a plant releasing oxygen in a bright environment but not in a dark environment. In a hand-out of one and a half pages, the phenomenon was analysed from a few viewpoints and a number of more or less elaborated explanations were offered. The experimenter actively involved subjects to check their understanding of the way they were to proceed with the next problem. He emphasized that they were to brainstorm about possible explanations for the problem and to analyse the explanations offered by discussing them with each other. This briefing took five to ten minutes. The experimenter then announced that the problem-analysis discussion should not take longer than fifteen minutes, and the problem was given in writing. It read: "A red blood cell is placed in pure water. Under the microscope we can see it swells very quickly and finally bursts. Another blood cell is placed in salt water and begins to shrink." When subjects have finished reading the problem, the dis-

220

cussion starts. The experimenter acted as discussion leader: asking questions, paraphrasing answers and summarizing. It was essential that, while leading the discussion, he did not provide new information. This was verified by audiotaping the discussion.

In the control condition, four groups of about 11 subjects were formed. Subjects in these groups were instructed to write down - individually - everything they remembered about osmosis within fifteen minutes. After the experimental and control episode, all subjects received a sheet with the following question: "I am interested in knowing more about osmosis." They were asked to indicate their opinion on a five-point scale from "not at all" (point 1) to "very much" (point 5). Then, all subjects were given a text of six pages on the topic of osmosis. The text contained no formulas, tables, figures, or other didactic features in order to avoid interference between conditions and text features. Subjects were instructed to study the text during 15 minutes. After 15 minutes of text study, subjects were told how the experiment would carry on. Since no time limits were set for the next phases, each subject was allowed to raise his hand after completion of a phase and to proceed with the next phase. When this was clear to the subjects, they received a booklet (the free-recall test) with three blank pages and a front page with the following instruction: "Write down everything you remember about the text on osmosis. Write sentences and do not use a telegram style or drawings." When the subjects felt they did not remember anything more than they had already written down, they were give a second booklet. The second booklet contained a completion test consisting of 44 items related to the text on osmosis. Some examples of items are: "Diffusion proceeds quicker when molecules are .... (answer: smaller), and: "When two concentrations possess the same maximum osmotic pressure, they are called .... (answer: isotonic). Alpha reliability of the completion test was calculated at .73.

Inter-rater reliability for counting the number of correctly recalled propositions, calculated for a number of randomly selected free recall protocols, was 90% and higher.

In addition, the biology grade received in the final examinations of the last year of secondary education (i.c. approximately 6 months before our experiment) was recorded from the school files.

Means and standard deviations of all variables are shown in Table 1. Pearson intercorrelations between all variables are shown in Table 2.

Table 1.   Means and standard deviations of the following variables: previous achievement in biology (Biology), intrinsic motivation (Motivation), free recall (Recall) and test achievement (Test) (n = 84)

	Mean	S.D.
Biology	6.50	0.85
Motivation	2.80	0.77
Recall	55.02	34.72
Test	31.15	4.12

Table 2.   Pearson correlations between previous achievement in biology (Biology), experimental (code 1) versus control (code 0) condition (Condition), intrinsic motivation (Motivation), free recall (Recall) and test achievement (Test) (n = 84)

	1	2	3	4	5
1. Biology	1	.14	.13	.04	.23
2. Condition		1	.24	.01	.11
3. Motivation			1	.12	.15
4. Recall				1	.07
5. Test					1

A t-test for independent samples (experimental versus control group) was carried out on the data obtained from the question on interest in osmosis.

In the experimental group the mean interest score (2.98) was significantly higher (t=2.23, df=82, p=0.03, two-tailed) than in the control group (mean score of 2.61).

Structural relations between the research variable were analysed with multiple regression techniques (Kenny 1979). In the first multiple regression, intrinsic motivation served as criterion, and two predictors were used. The experimental condition was scored "one" versus the control condition "zero". This dummy variable (problem based learning versus individual activation of prior knowledge) served as first predictor. The second predictor was biology grade. In the second multiple regression, the completion test score was used as criterion, and intrinsic motivation, the experimental versus control condition and biology grade served as predictors.

In the third multiple regression, the free recall score was used as criterion, and the same predictors were used as in regression number two.

No structural relations were hypothesized between the completion test and free recall, or between biology grade and the experimental versus control condition. Therefore, only simple Pearson-correlations were calculated for these relationships. Regression results are shown in figure 1.

DISCUSSION

The results supported the hypothesis that problem-based learning enhances intrinsic motivation or subject-related interest when compared to individual activation or prior knowledge. According to Johnson and Johnson (1979) interest in a certain subject is a function of the need for knowledge or epistemic curiosity that has been aroused by the conceptual conflict or controversy experienced during group discussion. We feel, however, that this is only one possible explanation, referred to as the need for knowledge explanation in Murray's (1964) terminology. Another possible source of avowed interest (in casu in osmosis) could be the need for achievement which has been aroused by confronting students with a problem to be solved, thus letting them compete with a personal standard of excellence in problem solving (Atkinson 1964). Finally, the need for affiliation could also play a role. Studies on cooperative learning (Slavin 1983) have shown that working with other students gratifies social needs and enhances interest in the subject the group is working on.

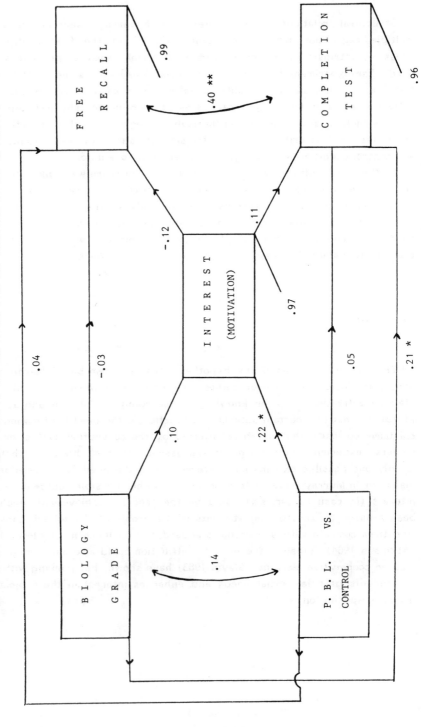

Figure 1: Path coefficients (beta-weights) between biology grade, problem-based learning (P.B.L.) versus control condition, interest in osmosis, free recall, and completion test. Coefficients with an asterisk are significant at the 10% level; with two asterisks at the 1% level.

In our view, these different explanations indicate the difficulty of operationalizing the theoretical concept of intrinsic motivation as defined by Deci (1975). The most often used operationalization, namely letting subjects indicate their interest in or preference for a certain activity, leaves doubts about the intrinsic or extrinsic nature of the motivation involved. Let us illustrate this point referring to the three motivational explorations mentioned earlier. When interest in osmosis is a function of a generalized need to know, one could accept the conclusion that no apparent external reward is present except the activity itself of getting to know more about something. In the case of interest arisen in cooperative groups and thus based on the gratification of social needs, it could be safely argued that the social contacts constitute an external reward. Interest sparked by the achievement motive lies somewhere in between: although theoretically the standard of excellence is internal, in practice it is often dependent on the norms put forward by a group or authority figure, and thus the reward of reaching the standard of excellence becomes externally mediated.

Looking again at the definition of intrinsic motivation, it must be noted that nothing is said about the way intrinsic motivation comes about, but only about the effect of intrinsic motivation: intrinsic motivation is the causal, driving force behind certain activities. This leaves three questions. We have already addressed the first, namely: since there is no such thing as an intrinsic motive, can intrinsic motivation be defined in terms of the general need for knowledge eventually narrowed to more specific topics? As the need for knowledge satisfies the Deci definition, contrary to the needs for achievement and affiliation, as we have argued earlier, in our view the answer to this first question should be affirmative (but only, of course, with respect to intrinsic motivation for school subjects).

The second question is: how can intrinsic motivation, thus interpreted, be purely measured? We tried to do this by focusing on the knowledge aspect (I am interested in *knowing* more about osmosis), but it is in our view fundamentally impossible to maintain that this interest is purely epistemic and to exclude the possibility that this interest could also be related to the achievement and affiliation motives.

This is obvious in our experiment, but also when interest is measured in a non-experimental study, it is unclear whether interest is purely epistemic or based upon the expectations of the respondents to be able to satisfy their social or achievement needs, or even other needs. To paraphrase an old saying: intrinsic motivation is in the eye of the experimenter.

The third question is: which activities are meant in the definition of intrinsic motivation? Or put differently: if interest is a pure measure of intrinsic motivation, which activities are influenced by this interest? In our experiment, we used two activities: free recall of the text on osmosis and achievement on a completion test on osmosis. In retrospect, we doubt that these two variables are well chosen as dependent variables, influenced by intrinsic motivation interpreted as purely epistemic.[1] Curiosity leads to information gathering (e.g.: reading a book, viewing a movie, talking to a professor) and thus only indirectly and eventually to higher achievement. Free and cued recall tests do not satisfy a curiosity need, but rather an achievement need, and perhaps a score of other needs.

A better dependent variable would be time spent on studying the text on osmosis. We opted for an equal allotment of study time, because we primarily focused on the amount (intensity) of the motivation generated and not so much on the persistence resulting from this motivation. And also because, given a certain time for study, the amount of *intrinsic* motivation should have an effect upon the amount of energy spent while studying and thus upon the recall measures. In the design phase, we based this assumption on the results reported in the reviewed literature. Now, we think it is time to be more careful with the term intrinsic motivation, and we for our part view interest not only as intrinsic but as intrinsic and/or extrinsic.

More or less unwittingly, we have arrived at the second part of the discussion, focusing on the relationships between previous biology grade, problem-based learning, (intrinsic?) motivation, and subsequent achievement on free and cued recall tests. The results showed that achievement is not significantly influenced directly by problem-based learning or indirectly through the intervening variable of interest (from now on, we will omit the term "intrinsic motivation" and refer to the interest measure instead). Traditionally, the first explanation to be put forward, is sloppy research. There are contra-indications for this interpretation, however.

First, some of the involved variables do show significant relationships, indicating that these variables are not totally unreliable. Secondly, post-experimental inspections of the procedure (audio-taped discussions) did not reveal any alarming mishaps. Thirdly, where possible, reliabilities were calculated and proved to be satisfactory (see the paragraph on procedure).

Why, then, was interest not related to achievement? Although achievement is multi-determined, one would expect a small but significant relationship with interest. Its absence can have two causes. First, it is possible that the constraints of our experimental situation hindered the motivational processes normally at work. In regular school work, interest in a certain

---

[1]   It should be clear by now, of course, that we do not favor this purely epistemic interpretation of the interest measure.

subject can lead to a variety of extra activities leading to higher achievement.

In our two-hour experiment, we controlled all that. Also, a one-time only experiment has a very limited impact: we were able to arouse interest, but for how long and with how many consequences for effort-costly and multi-determined measures of achievement?

The second reason says just the opposite: in general interest simply does not influence achievement. Steinkamp and Maehr (1981) advocate this idea. No real explanation is offered, so we assume the parsimony hypothesis is invoked here, saying that the simplest solution is to be preferred, which is: there is no causal link. However, Steinkamp and Maehr also conclude that interest is a function of previous achievement. Our results showed no significant relationship between biology grade and interest in osmosis. Perhaps the difference in level of generality (biology versus osmosis) is a factor. But in our view, this is also an indication that the first explanation is probably the right one: it is unwarranted to have too high expectations from a limited experiment.

In conclusion, the controversy still remains, perhaps arousing interest, and perhaps even stimulating more research activities.

ACKNOWLEDGEMENT

With thanks to Bert Kerkhofs for his assistance in data collection and analysis.

REFERENCES

Atkinson, J.W. (1964). *An introduction to motivation.* New York: Van Nostrand.

Barrows, H.S. (1984). A specific problem-based, self-directed learning method designed to teach medical problem-solving skills, and enhance knowledge retention and recall. In: H.G. Schmidt & M.L. De Volder (eds.), *Tutorials in problem-based learning.* Assen: Van Gorcum.

Bloom, B.J. (1976). *Human characteristics and school learning.* New York: McGraw Hill.

Deci, E.L. (1971). Effects of externally mediated rewards on intrinsic motivation. *Journal of Personality and Social Psychology, 18,*, 105-115.

Deci, E.L. (1975). *Intrinsic motivation*. New York: Plenum

Fransson, A. (1977). On qualitative differences in learning: IV-effects of intrinsic motivation and extrinsic test anxiety on process and outcome. *British Journal of educational Psychology, 47*, 244-257.

Johnson, D.W. & Johnson, R.T. (1979). Conflict in the classroom: Controversy and learning. *Review of Educational Research, 49*, 51-70.

Kenny, D.A. (1979). *Correlation and causality*. New York: Wiley.

Lepper, M.R. & Greene, D. (1975). Turning play into work: Effects of adult surveillance and extrinsic rewards on children's intrinsic motivation. *Journal of Personality and Social Psychology, 31*, 479-486.

Morgan, M. (1984). Reward-induced decrements and increments in intrinsic motivation. *Review of Educational Research, 54*, 5-30.

Murray, E.J. (1964). *Motivation and Emotion*. Englewoord CLiffs, N.J.: Prentice-Hall

Schmidt, H.G. & De Volder, M.L. (eds.) (1984). *Tutorials in problem-based learning*. Assen: Van Gorcum.

Slavin, R.F (1983). *Cooperative learning*. New York: Longman.

Smith, K., Johnson, D.W. & Johnson, R.T. (1981). Can conflict be constructive? Controversy versus concurrence seeking in learning groups. *Journal of Educational Psychology, 73*, 651-663.

Steinkamp, M.J. & Maehr, M.L. (1983). Affect, ability, and science achievement: a quantitative synthesis of correlational research. *Review of Educational Research, 53*, 369-396.

THE MEASUREMENT OF STATE AND TRAIT MOTIVATIONAL
ORIENTATION: REFINING OUR MEASURES

Monique Boekaerts

University of Nijmegen

INTRODUCTION

Many authors (Mischel 1969, 1977; Magnusson & Endler 1977; Cronbach & Snow 1977) have defended the view that the main source of behavioral variation is to be found in the interaction between person variables and environmental variables. Mischel (1968) reviewed a number of studies in which a person's behavior was predicted on the basis of either psychometric tests (traditional personality tests) or self-reports of relevant past behavior and self-predictions. He came to the conclusion that the latter form of assessment was superior in predicting a person's performance. Stagner (1976) challenged this conclusion and presented a number of studies in which trait measures prove to be as effective or even more effective than situation-specific predictions. At present the nature of the relationship between measures of relatively stable learner characteristics (based on the relative consistency of behavior hypothesis) and measures of specific behavior-in-situations (behavioral specificity hypothesis) is still obscure. For example, in the field of motivation it is difficult to know the extent to which available achievement motivation tests can predict the learner's action tendency for a specific (type of) learning activity and the extent to which they instead reflect his general orientation to engage in school tasks.

I have argued recently (Boekaerts 1985, 1986a) that the person-environment interactional perspective from which research on achievement motivation is undertaken (Atkinson 1957; Atkinson & Feather 1966; Heckhausen 1980) is heavily biased: The environment variable is almost exclusively defined and measured in terms of task difficulty; whereas the person variable is defined in terms of the cognitions and affects about success and failure in relation to task difficulty.

Although the task dimensions incorporated in the models on achievement motivation may be highly relevant and specific to the selected experimental situations, they may be less salient in everyday learning situations. Other task dimensions such as e.g. its perceived utility, the teacher's perceived utility and its attractiveness may play a more important role in the learner's appraisal of classroom tasks. The point I want to make is that research on achievement motivation has provided us with pertinent leads about the incentive value of tasks with varying degrees of difficulty and about the relationships that exist between motive strength and the probability of success. They have, however, left us ignorant about the differential effect of environmental variables or of various aspects of the learning situation on the so called 'motives'. Thus, the question: 'How relevant are success and failure oriented cognitions, as measured by existing achievement motivation tests to task-specific action tendency'? still needs to be answered.

It is a common sense observation that some learners are more motivated than others to do school tasks. It has equally been noted that the degree of effort that a learner wants to put into a learning task may differ considerably across learning tasks and across school subjects. In order to explore these relationships one should ideally make longitudinal recordings of pupils' learning endeavors for various school subjects. For in the course of his learning history a learner gets acquainted with different types of learning tasks which gives rise to different learning experiences. He may for example experience anxiety and task avoidance during some types of learning activities, and develop task commitment and responsibility for learning for other learning tasks. Some of these cognitions and feelings may remain highly task-specific (see Boekaerts 1985, 1986a,b,c) while others may be transferred to all school subjects, to some school subjects or to specific learning tasks (e.g. anxiety may be transferred to all arithmetic tasks). The degree of generalization of these cognitions and feelings may be directly proportional to the perceived similarity (functional equivalence) of the tasks.

In the same vein it could be argued, that individuals who take part in laboratory experiments perceive all experimental tasks as functionally equivalent. Whether a subject succeeds or fails is relatively unimportant to him: he is helping the experimenter and in doing so has committed himself to execute a task. Under these highly specific (learning) conditions subjects may perceive and appraise the (learning) task and its context on the basis of a trans-situational expectancy effect (i.e. feelings and cognitions generalized to most experimental situations are elicited). The behavior studied under these restricted conditions may be different from the pupils' normal, or habitual behavior. More specifically, learning tasks which are consequential in nature (i.e. which are part of the everyday school curriculum) may give rise to a richer set of appraisal processes, and as such result in *situation-specific* action tendencies.

The question that needs to be answered in this respect thus can be phrased as follows: 'Is the learner's action tendency, defined as his willingness and intention to spend processing resources on the task *domain-specific* (or subject-matter oriented); or is it to a large extent based on the general motivational orientation of the learner'? In order to answer this question a distinction should be made between (1) a pupil's General Motivational Orientation (GMO) to do school tasks, (2) his Task-Specific Motivational Orientation (TSMO) and (3) his Situation Specific Action Tendency (SiSAT). The first construct represents the learner's baseline level of motivation. A learner's GMO has been affected by multiple sources of generalized anxiety, task avoidance, success expectancy, perceived competence etc. It may give rise to a trans-situational expectancy effect for many school tasks and is measured by traditional achievement motivation tests. The second construct, TSMO, refers to the outcome of a set of appraisal processes at the moment a learner is confronted with a learning activity. It should be assessed by a special motivation questionnaire such as described by Boekaerts (1985, 1986a). Finally, SiSAT, refers to the learner's task commitment; to his willingness and intention to put effort into the task. It should be measured during the actual learning task, or at least just before or immediately after the execution of the task.

The present study is an attempt to disentangle the effects of GMO and TSMO on action tendency. Three frequently encountered learning activities were selected in order to answer the following research questions: (1) What is the effect of GMO measures on SiSAT? (2) Does the type of learning activity modify these relationships? (3) What is the effect of TSMO measures on SiSAT? and (4) Are measures of GMO better predictors of a person's SiSAT than the teacher's ratings of a pupil's motivation?

METHOD

Subjects
The subjects were 241 sixth-grade pupils drawn from ten Flemish schools. They ranged from 10 yrs/11 months to 12 yrs/6 months. Because this study focussed on motivational processes whereby situation-specific appraisal processes would be measured, the pupils' teachers were asked to use standardized introductory statements and to keep the pupils uninformed as to the exact nature of the study.

Measures and procedure

In order to obtain information about the pupil's *General Motivational Orientation* (GMO) three tests were selected. The first test we used was the Achievement Motivation Questionnaire for Children (PMT-K) constructed by Hermans (1967). This is a 89-item questionnaire measuring the pupil's need achievement (Ach); inhibiting anxiety, or negative threat of failure (Fmin); facilitating anxiety, or positive threat of failure (Fplus) and his social desirability (SD). The second questionnaire was the Situation-Specific Anxiety Test (SSAT) constructed by Bergen (1981) on the basis of Heckhausen's achievement motivation theory. This questionnaire presents the pupil with fourteen classroom situations and provides three subscale scores, viz. the pupil's Own Competence judgment (OC); his score on the Anxiety Index (AnxI) and on the Avoidance Index (AvI). The third measure of GMO was the Telic Dominance Scale for children (Boekaerts and Hendriksen, in preparation). This is a 27-item questionnaire which was adapted and extended from the Telic Dominance Scale for adults constructed by Murgatroyd, Rushton, Apter and Ray (1978). It measures the degree to which a pupil recognizes an imposed, relevant or unavoidable goal; accepts responsibility for it and plans ahead to accomplish it (TEL). In addition to these tests we collected the teacher's ratings of the pupil's motivation (TMOT) and his rating of the pupil's skill with respect to the respective learning tasks (Tsc). Teachers were asked to give their ratings on a five point scale prior to the actual testing sessions.

Three learning activities were scheduled as part of the normal school curriculum, viz. an arithmetic task, a reading comprehension task and a drawing task. They were presented to the pupils during the normal scheduled time by their classroom teacher and were not singled out as extra curricular tasks or tests. The only difference with regular classroom activities was that the pupils had to fill in a motivation questionnaire immediately prior and after the learning activity.

The pupils Situation-Specific Action Tendency (SiSAT) was assessed by means of five questions asked at on-set and off-set of the respective learning tasks. Pupils gave an indication on a five point scale of their task commitment and their willingness to put in some effort. In order to assess their *Task-Specific Motivational Orientation* (TSMO) we asked them to fill in a questionnaire immediately prior to and after the learning task. This questionnaire consisted of a number of five-point-scales pertaining to seven dimensions of the learning tasks and resulted in the pupil's Self-Efficacy Judgment (Seff); his Personal Utility Judgment (PU); his Success Expectancy (SE); his Teacher Perceived Utility Judgment (TPU); his Peer Success Expectancy Judgment (PSE); his Attractiveness Judgment (Att) and his Perceived Difficulty Judgment (PDiff) of the respective tasks. Finally the pupil's score (PSc) on the respective tasks was computed.

RESULTS AND DISCUSSION

First order correlations

A graphic representation of the Pearson Product-moment correlations between the variables used in this study can be found in Figures 1-4. Figure 1 shows the correlations for the arithmetic task; Figure 2 for the reading comprehension task; Figure 3 for the drawing task and Figure 4 for the aggregated data. In order to answer the question 'To what extent are GMO measures correlated with SiSAT?' and the additional question; 'Does the type of learning activity modify this relationship?' the correlations between pairs of variables will be analysed.

As is evident from the graphical representation of the *GMO-with-SiSAT* relations in Figures 1-4, some of the GMO measures correlate moderately high with SiSAT. The substantial negative relationship between the Avoidance Index (AvI) and SiSAT occurs in every learning activity, suggesting that lower levels of task avoidance are associated with higher levels of SiSAT irrespective of the task. In the collapsed data moderately high correlations are also noted for OC (.40), ACH (.45) and TEL (.44). Hence, higher levels of perceived own competence, achievement motivation and telic dominance seem to be associated with higher levels of SiSAT. However, the size of the correlations between these GMO measures and SiSAT seem to be affected by the type of learning activity. Finally, it is interesting to note that the association between SiSAT and the positive and negative threat of failure subscale of the PMT-K is less substantial. This observation is especially relevant if one compares the correlations between AnxI-with-SiSAT and AnxI-with-PSC.

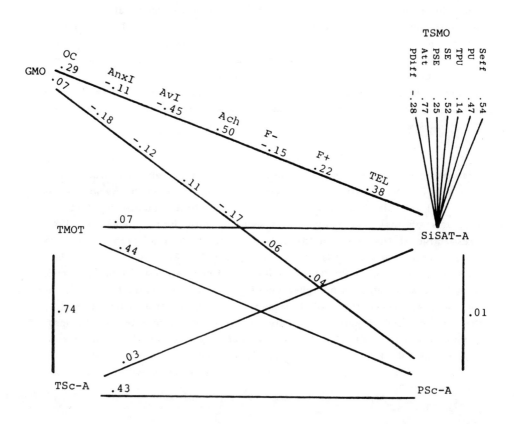

Figure 1. Graphic representation of Pearson product-moment correlations for the *arithmetic* task

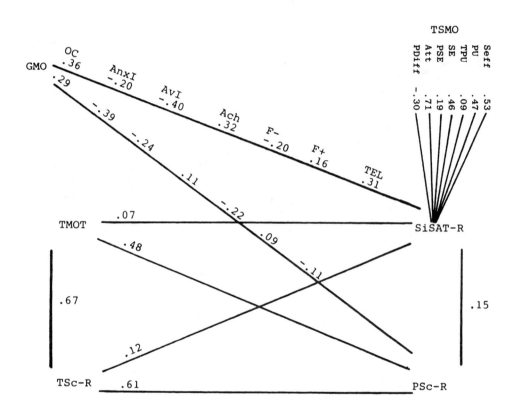

Figure 2. Graphic representation of Pearson product-moment correlations for the *reading* task

235

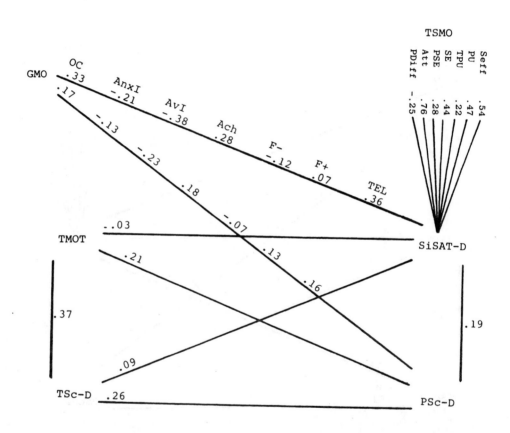

Figure 3. Graphic representation of Pearson product-moment correlations for the *drawing* task

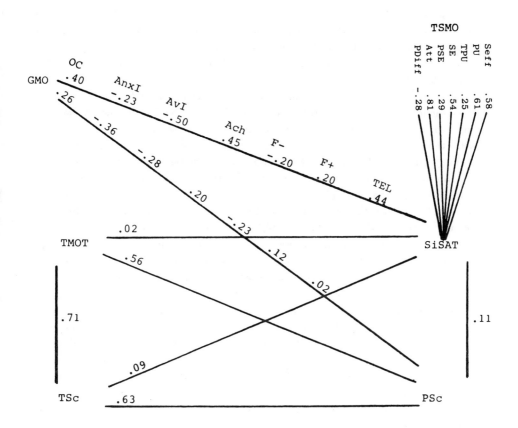

Figure 4. Graphic representation of Pearson product-moment correlations for
the *aggregated data* (all three tasks)

In order to answer the question: 'To what extent are TSMO measures correlated with SiSAT?' the *TSMO-with-SiSAT* correlations were inspected. As can be seen from Figures 1-4, the correlation between SiSAT and most appraisal processes is quite substantial. This suggests that higher levels of Si-SAT are associated with higher levels of perceived attractiveness of the learning activity (.77; .71; .76; .81); with perceived self-efficacy in relation to the task (.54; .53; .54; .58); with perceived success expectancy (.52; .46; .44; .54); and with perceived utility of the learning task (.47; .47; .47; .61). Whether the teacher finds the learning activity relevant seems to have a negligible association with SiSAT in either the arithmetic task or the reading task (.14; .09). Finally, a weak - though significant - association exists between SiSAT and the perceived difficulty level of the task (-.28; -.30; -.25; -.28) and between SiSAT and peer success expectation (.25; .19; .28; .29).

In order to answer the question: 'Is GMO a better predictor of SiSAT than the teacher's motivation rating?' the *TMOT-with-SiSAT* correlations was inspected. Intuitively one would expect that primary school teachers who work with their pupils all day have a good idea of their motivation to do school tasks. One would expect TMOT and SiSAT to be highly correlated. Inspection of Figures 1-4 tells us however that the correlation between TMOT and SiSAT is non-existing (.07; .07; .03; .02), implying that the teachers were not able to rate their pupil's 'motivation' accurately. However, the moderately high correlation between TMOT and PSC (.44; .48; .21; .56) seems to suggest that the teachers based their motivation rating on their perception of the pupil's skill to do these school tasks. This assumption gains support from the rather high correlation between TMOT and TCS which can be seen in the arithmetic task and in the reading task (.74; .67).

We also want to mention that the relationship between measures of GMO and learning outcome (Psc) is small. It is striking that the association between Psc and the learner's perception of his own competence (.29); his overall anxiety (-.39); his task avoidance (-.24) and his fear of failure (-.22) is strongest in the reading task, suggesting that higher levels of reading comprehension skill are associated with higher levels of perceived competence; but, also with *lower levels* of task avoidance, inhibiting anxiety and fear of failure.

Let us finally turn to the relation between *SiSAT-with-PSC*. When collapsed across learning activities the correlation of SiSAT-with-PSC is .11. When data are categorized by learning activity, more pronounced patterns become apparent. The non-existent correlation for the arithmetic task (.01) contrasts with the weak relationship for the reading task (.19). But, despite these noted differences, an important conclusion to be drawn from these data is that the influence of SiSAT on PSC is small: Most GMO measures have a more pronounced relation with SiSAT than with learning outcome except for the Anxl. Inhibiting anxiety, as measured by the SSAT has a more pronounced effect on the learner's reading comprehension score (learning outcome) than on his SiSAT for the reading task (-.39 versus -.20), and the same pattern is noted - though less strongly - in the arithmetic task (-.18; -.11).

A number of interesting points emerged from Figures 1-4. First, it is worth noting that in general the correlations between TSMO and SiSAT are larger than those between GMO and SiSAT. The correlation between some individual pairs are surprisingly large. For example, the consistent high correlation between the pupil's attractiveness judgement and his SiSAT, seems to indicate that for twelve-year old pupils the attractiveness of a task is an important task dimension. Or, to put it more concretely, it seems that pupils are more committed to a learning task and are more willing to spend some effort on a task when they find it attractive. Secondly, it should be observed that GMO measures correlate to a different extent with the pupil's SiSAT for different learning tasks. On analysing the collapsed data in Figure 4, one may jump to the conclusion that GMO measures - especially the OC and Avl subscales of the SSAT, the Ach subscale of the PMTK and the Telic Dominance Scale - can give us a good indication of a pupil's situation specific action tendency. However, when these correlations are compared and contrasted with the domain-specific correlations in Figures 1-3, a somewhat different picture emerges. For only the Avl seems to have a relatively stable association with SiSAT across the three different learning situations (-.45; -.40; -.38; -.50). This stable negative correlation may be interpreted as a *trans-situational expectancy effect*. Put differently, the Avl subscale of the SSAT elicits generalized feelings of task avoidance which are negatively related to the learner's task commitment and his willingness and intention to put effort into a learning activity. This moderately high negative relation does not seem to be affected by the type of learning activity.

The slightly weaker relationship that holds between SiSAT and three other measures of GMO (OC; Ach; TEL) does seem to be modified by the type of learning activity (e.g. *Ach*-with-SiSAT .50; .32; .28). The weaker relationship found in the reading and drawing task may be due to the fact that learning activities vary in the degree to which they elicit cognitions and feelings that are similar to the ones elicited by the items of the PMT-K. The arithmetic task may have elicited cognitions and feelings which were more achievement oriented than those elicited by the other learning activities (functional equivalence of tasks).

In this respect it is also informative to contrast *OC* as a measure expressing the pupil's overall competence judgement with *Seff* expressing an on-line self-efficacy judgement. For the arithmetic task OC-with SiSAT is .29 and Seff-with-SiSAT is .54. For the reading task these correlations are .36 and .53 and for the drawing task .33 and .54. Whether or not disparities of this magnitude are of practical importance remains a moot point.

Multiple Regression Analyses

In order to overcome the limitations associated with zero-order correlations and to get a better indication of the strength of the relationship between the various predictor variables and the criterion variable SiSAT it was decided to carry out a series of stepwise multiple regression analyses (Hull & Nie 1981). Because the pattern of relationships between GMO measures and both SiSAT and Psc were not the same across learning activities, there is reason to believe that different GMO measures will be differently effective in accounting for the variance in SiSAT.

In a first set of analyses, GMO and TSMO measures both served as predictors. The results of these four stepwise multiple regression analyses are printed in Table 1. As can be seen, all SiSAT's were best predicted by the pupil's attractiveness judgment (43.2%; 45.9%; 39.2% and 63.7%). The second variable which entered the regression equation was different in each case. On the basis of the first-order correlations we had expected the Avoidance Index to play a dominant role. This was not the case. In the arithmetic task two GMO predictors entered the equation: The Ach score explained nearly 6% of the variance and the Anxl 3%. In the aggregated data Ach entered as a fourth step, explaining 1% of the variance. It is interesting to note that peer success expectation (PSE) plays an important role in the drawing task (also in the aggregated data).

On the basis of these data it may be concluded that a large part of the variance in SiSAT is accounted for by situation-specific appraisal processes (TSMO measures). At least it seems that for the reading task and for the drawing task the pupils' task commitment and their willingness to spend effort on the task is determined to a large extent (47.3% - 47.7%) by situation-specific perception and interpretation processed. Especially the attractiveness of the task; its perceived relevance and for the drawing task its difficulty level and the degree to which other learners will be successful, plays an important role.

Table 1. Stepwise multiple regression analyses predicting SiSAT from GMO and TSMO measures and from GMO measures

Predictors	SiSAT-ARITHMETIC						SiSAT-READING						SiSAT-DRAWING						SiSAT-AGGREGATED					
	GMO + TSMO			GMO			GMO + TSMO			GMO			GMO + TSMO			GMO			GMO + TSMO			GMO		
	S	R²	BETA	S	R²	BETA	S	R²	BETA	S	R²	BETA	S	R²	BETA	S	R²	BETA	S	R²	BETA	S	R²	BETA
Attractiveness (Att)	1	43.2	.65				1	45.9	.67				1	39.2	.62				1	63.7	.79			
Personal Utility (PU)	4	54.0	.18										3	46.1	.21				2	67.6	.23			
Peer Success Exp (PSE)													2	43.2	.20				3	69.3	.13			
Self-efficacy (Self)							2	47.3	.17															
Perceived Difficulty (PDi)													4	47.4	.14				5	71.0	.10			
Avoidance Index (AvI)				2	27.6	-.24				1	17.3	-.23				1	13.1	-.36				1	25.1	-.50
Anxiety Index (AnxI)	3	51.7	.19	3	30.7	.20																		
Own Competence (OC)										2	20.5	.20				4	23.8	.19				3	33.7	.16
Achievement Motiv. (Ach)	2	48.6	.25	1	24.2	.49													4	70.2	.10			
Inhibiting Anxiety (F-)																								
Telic Total (TEL)										3	48.2	.18				2	18.3	.25				2	31.6	.28
Teacher Mot. Rating				4	32.4	.14										3	21.2	-.17				4	35.4	-.14

Note: S = Step in multiple regression equation

241

It should be noted, however, that the intercorrelations among some GMO and TSMO predictors were moderately high. This implies that very few predictors could enter the multiple regression equations. When the TSMO measures were deleted from the multiple regression analyses (see Table 1) the predictive power of GMO measures becomes apparent. The amount of variance explained by GMO measures varies for the three criterium variables. In the case of the arithmetic task the variance explained is 32.2%; in the reading task 48.2%; in the drawing task 23.8% and in the aggregated data 35.4%. Thus, the elimination of the TSMO measures from the regression equation brings about a sizeable decrease in the variance explained in the arithmetic task (54.0% - 32.4%); in the drawing task (47.7% - 23.8%) and in the aggregated data (71.0% - 35.4%). In the reading task the percentages of explained variance are virtually the same. It is interesting to observe that Seff enters as a second step when GMO and TSMO predictors are used, and that the OC judgment enters as a second step when the GMO predictor set is used. Nevertheless, OC accounts for very little SiSAT variability (3%) whereas the telic dominance score accounts for an extra 28% as a third step.

When close attention is paid to the predictive power of the various predictors, it becomes evident that the eminent role played by the avoidance index in the first-order correlations and also when an exclusive GMO predictor is used, disappears when the TSMO measures are introduced. It is worth noting in this respect, that negative beta's are produced.

We may conclude, then, that the amount of variance associated with TSMO measures is greater than that associated with GMO measures. What is more, any shared variance among TSMO and GMO measures appears to be totally subsumed by the TSMO variables. This seems reasonable, since after all GMO variables are trait measures whereas TSMO measures are state measures. Nevertheless, the predictive value of GMO measures is far from valueless. There seems to be a domain-specific or subject-matter oriented effect of arithmetic tasks; own competence and telic dominance in reading tasks and telic dominance in drawing tasks. Further research with extreme groups on these measures, would be useful here.

CONCLUSION

This research provides evidence that at least within the 12 year old age range, the pupil's attractiveness judgment is an important predictor of his

SiSAT and that measures of GMO have a *domain-specific effect*. The results of the present study suggest that caution is appropriate when using GMO measures as predictors for a pupil's SiSAT. There are indications that motivation is a less unitary construct than researchers have believed so far. Certain pupil characteristics such as the 'tendency to avoid tasks (AvI)'; 'the tendency to be anxious (AnxI; F-); 'the tendency to judge oneself as competent (OC)'; and the tendency to be telically dominant interact with learning situations in a *unique way*.

For example, the tendency to avoid tasks and to reject responsibility for learning (as measures by the AvI of the SSAT) is an important personality characteristic that interacts with other person characteristics so as to determine the learner's baseline level of motivation for a *domain* of learning tasks. In a learning environment where arithmetic or math's tasks should be performed the avoidance motive may interact with (supress) the achievement motive; in a learning context where reading assignments are given the avoidance motive may interact with (supress) the own competence judgement and telic dominance and in a context where drawing activities are performed the avoidance motive may interact with (supress) telic dominance. The net result of such interaction processes may be the pupil's *domain-specific* or *subject-matter oriented* motivation profile which in turn interacts with situational cues and produces a learned bias in the appraisal processes.

What this study tells us is that in order to predict a learner's SiSAT for a range of learning situations, it is necessary to take account of a learner's *profile* of learner characteristics for that domain of learning tasks. Assessing his motivation in one type of learning situation is not enough to predict his SiSAT for all learning situations. That teachers do not seem to be able to differentiate between the pupil's motivation and his skill to perform a task, indicates the dominance of *cognitive* variables in their way of perceiving pupil (intended) behavior; but, more importantly it tells us something about the complexity of the issue. And, the greater importance of some GMO measures (learner characteristics) for some types of learning activities helps discredit the notion that overall motivation as measured by GMO measures is an adequate basis for predicting a pupil's SiSAT.

REFERENCES

Atkinson, J.W. (1957). Motivational determinants of risk-taking behavior. *Psychological Review, 64*, 359-372.

Atkinson, J.W., & Feather, N.T. (Eds.) (1966). *A theory of achievement motivation*. New York: Wiley.

Bergen, Th.C.M. (1981). *Evaluatie-angst en vermijdingstendens. Een onderzoek naar de orientatie van leerlingen om mislukking te vermijden in taaksituaties tijdens de les*. 's-Gravenhage: Staatsuitgeverij.

Boekaerts, M. (1985). Some new developments in the study of motivational processes in a classroom context. In G. D'Ydewalle (Ed.), *Cognition, Information Processing, and Motivation*. Vol. 3, XXIII International Congres of Psychology. Amsterdam: North Holland.

Boekaerts, M. (1986a). Situation-specific judgements of elements of the task-situation complex versus overall measures of motivational orientation. In E. de Corte, H. Lodewijks, R. Parmentier & P. Span (Eds.), *Learning and instruction*.

Boekaerts, M. (1986b). Motivation in theories of learning. *International Journal of Educational Research, 1*.

Boekaerts, M. (1986c). Telic dominance and learning behaviour. In R. Gupta & P. Coxhead (Eds.), *Cultural diversity and learning efficiency: Recent developments in assessment*. London: MacMillan.

Boekaerts, M., & Hendriksen, J. (in prep.). *A telic dominance scale for primary school pupils*.

Cronbach, L.J., & Snow, R.E. (1977). *Aptitudes and Instructional methods: a handbook for research on interactions*. New York: Irvington Pub. Inc.

Heckhausen, H. (1980). *Motivation und Handeln*. Berlin: Springer.

Hermans, H.J.M. (1967). *Motivatie en prestatie*. Lisse: Swets & Zeitlinger.

Hull, C.H., & Nie, N.H. (1981). *SPSS update 7-9. New Procedures and Facilities for Releases 7-9*. New York: McGraw-Hill Book Company.

Magnusson, D., & Endler, N.S. (1977). The interaction of person and situation. In D. Magnusson & N.S. Endler (Eds.), *Personality at the crossroads: current issues in interactional psychology*. Hillsdale, N.J.: Erlbaum.

Mischel, W. (1968). *Personality and assessment*. New York: Wiley.

Mischel, W. (1969). Continuity and change in personality, *American Psychologist, 24*, 1012-1018.

Mischel, W. (1977). The interaction of person and situation. In D. Magnusson & N.S. Endler (Eds.), *Personality at the crossroads: current issues in interactional psychology*. Hillsdale, N.J.: Erlbaum.

Murgatroyd, S., Rushton, C., Apter, M., & Ray, C. (1978). The development of the telic dominance scale, *Journal of Personality Assessment, 42*, (5), 519-528.

Stagner, R. (1976). Traits are relevant: theoretical analysis and empirical evidence. In N.S. Endler & D. Magnusson (Eds.), *Interactional psychology and personality*. Washington, D.C.: Hemisphere Publ.

EVALUATION OF LEARNING ACHIEVEMENT AND THE INTERACTIVE MULTILEVEL DEVELOPMENT OF SCHOOL SUBJECT MOTIVATION AND ACHIEVEMENT

Ton Mooij

University of Nijmegen

ABSTRACT

In this article attention is directed at the development of a pupil's school subject achievement in the course of a schoolyear in het framework of multi-level theorizing refers to two interactive motivational theories. In the first one the effects of a pupil's schoolmarks on his school subject motivation and school subject achievement are integrated within a causal model at the pupil level. In the second one the interlevel effects between those pupil level concepts and evaluation modes at the teaching situation level are the topic of concern. Both theoretical approaches are tested empirically with the aid of longitudinal data resulting from a research project granted by the Dutch Foundation for Educational Research (SVO-project 0483).

INTRODUCTION

White (1959, p. 297) uses the concept of *competence* to indicate: "(...) an organism's capacity to interact effectively with its environment". He also speaks about *competence motivation:* "The behavior (...) is not random behavior produced by a general overflow of energy. It is directed, selective, and persistent, and it is continued not because it serves primary drives, which indeed it cannot serve until it is almost perfected, but because it satisfies an intrinsic need to deal with the environment" (p. 318). This competence concept is further extended by Harter (for example Harter 1982a, 1982b). She pays special attention to developmental and socializational aspects of competence. Competence or mastery behavior can be carried out because of the affective consequences like pleasure, joy, and pride over competence in doing certain actions, which is reflected in 'intrinsic moti-vation dimensions', like independent mastery attempts, challenge seeking and curiosity (Harter 1981, p. 22). In this case the *process* of doing makes it possible for a person's self-esteem to be stimulated. However, when the at-tention is concentrated on the *product* of a person's actions this product can be approved or disapproved, which has consequences for the person's sense of competence (see Harter 1981, p. 5-8). Product-dependency of a person's actions leads to extrinsic motivation of these actions; in the teaching situ-ation for example: preference for easy work, being oriented towards getting grades and dependency on the teacher (p. 23).

Harter states much more explicitly than White that intrinsic mastery moti-vation functions as a domain specific process in which the sequence ac-tion-effect-affect can be distinguished. She embeds this sequence in a model (Harter 1981) in which the effect of evaluation by other people and the in-ternalization of cognitive-informational structures are also incorporated.

Comparable motivational aspects are also essential in Heckhausen's cogni-tive model of achievement motivation (see Heckhausen 1977, p. 287; 1980, p. 621). The kernel of Heckhausen's model is formed by four elements: the situ-ation, a person's action, the outcome of this action and the consequence of this outcome. One of the consequences of a certain outcome refers to the *self-evaluation* of a person (Heckhausen 1980, p. 571). With easy or difficult tasks an outcome will be attributed externally to the difficulty level of the task, but when a task has a mean difficulty level an outcome will be attri-buted internally, to one's own ability of effort. In Heckhausen's theorizing the concept of self-evaluation has a crucial function: as a person anticipates the probability of a certain outcome and the possible effect of the outcome for his self-evaluation, the expected outcome and effect influence the occurrence of the action in a certain situation. In other words: self-evaluation guides or 'motivates' a person's actions (see also De Bruyn 1979; Bergen 1981; Boekaerts 1984).

A person's achievement motivation naturally refers to a certain object or part of a person's environment. With respect tot education-relevant proc-esses the educational system is the most important environment. Within this system different hierarchical levels can be distinguished, which may be used in multi-level theorizing on pupil motivation and pupil achievement (cf. Mooij 1984). In this article the multi-level theorizing will be directed towards the construction and checking of two rivalling views on the influence of the eval-uation of learning achievement on the interactive development of pupil moti-vation and pupil achievement. In the first view only pupil-level variables are thought to be relevant in this development, while in the second view pupil-level variables and teaching situation level variables are assumed to play a role. The *goal* of this article is as follows:

1. to construct a *tentative pupil level model* on the effects of the evaluation of learning achievement on the development of a pupil's motivation and achievement within a school subject;

2. to work out a *first formulation of an interlevel theory* in which evaluation variables at the teaching situation level are assumed to influence the development of a pupil's motivation and achievement within a school subject;

3. to check the pupil level and interlevel theoretical approach empirically, and to compare their results. The data and facilities used to check the theorizing were supplied by a research project granted by the Dutch Foundation for Educational Research (SVO-project 0483).

MULTILEVEL THEORIZING ON SCHOOL SUBJECT MOTIVATION

An interactive pupil level process

When a pupil is being confronted with a school subject for the first time he will feel curiosity and will like to know what is going on. In Harter's terms: the pupil is intrinsically motivated. This will also be reflected in the intensity and concentration of the pupil's learning actions. The pupil will experience pleasure in *doing* the learning actions: the learning process is motivating because it is new. The pupil's feelings and actions - in other words, the pupil's *orientation* - towards the school subject will initially be positive and school subject directed.

During the schoolyear, however, especially the pupil's *product* in the school subject is evaluated. This product is usually expressed in the pupil's school subject mark. A pupil therefore comes to perceive his school subject mark as the most important effect of his own learning actions in the school subject (see also Licht 1982, p. 209-210). A pupil getting a low or 'insufficient' school subject mark will perceive the effect of his learning actions low or too low. This will elicit a rather negative affect: the pupil's feeling of *competence* with respect to these learning actions will then be low. On the other hand, a pupil getting a high mark will perceive a high effect of his learning actions. This will lead to a positive affect and to a rather high feeling of competence concerning these learning actions. The competence influences the next learning actions, while the next school subject mark again constitutes the effect, etc.

In the long run, then, it is hypothesized that an *interaction* exists between - on the one hand - a pupil's school subject marks and - on the other hand - the pupil's school subject orientation, school subject competence, and school subject achievement. This hypothesis will be worked out into a longitudinal causal model on the development of school subject motivation and school subject achievement in the course of a schoolyear. The model is based on the interactive theorizing with respect to the action-effect-affect sequence, but instead of trying to grasp this as a short-term process an exploratory extension of it is proposed here. The model is directed at the potential influences of a pupil's school subject marks (effects) on his school subject orientation, competence and achievement during a schoolyear, while controlling for the initial states of the latter three variables.

In the initial model a pupil's school subject orientation (ssor) and school subject competence (ssc) at the end of a schoolyear are each influenced by his school subject achievement (ssach) at that time. Those three variables, however, are each influenced by the pupil's school subject marks (ssmark) he received in the course of the schoolyear, and also by the respective initial values on the three variables at the start of the school year. It is expected that the pupil's school subject marks are affected by his initial ssach. Finally, this initial ssach is hypothesized to be influenced by background variables concerning the earlier school career (being held back in elementary education) and more socializational variables (father's occupation, and sex). Those background variables seem of relevance in long-term schooling processes (Tesser, 1984).

The above considerations constitute a model based on the action-effect-affect sequence, in fact a longitudinal structural model (Jöreskog 1979; Jöreskog & Sörbom 1977). Because the interactive action-effect-affect sequence may be domain specific, this model will be tested separately for two school subjects: dutch language and mathematics/arithmetics.

An interactive interlevel process

Usually, a pupil is a member of a class or specific group of pupils learning in the same teaching situation. A teaching situation is defined here as a situation in which a group of pupils is being instructed to realize a more or less circumscribed learning goal in a certain way.

At the teaching situation, level the pupil's learning achievement can be evaluated in different ways. First, this can be done comparatively, which means that the pupils' learning results are compared with each other; and on the basis of this comparison high achieving pupils get 'high' schoolmarks and low-achieving pupils get 'low' schoolmarks. Another way to evaluate achievement is evaluation along an absolute criterium, a certain norm based on learning content, or along an individual criterium, for example the degree in which a pupil is working, or the degree in which a pupil is making progress: (see also Rheinberg 1980).

In teaching situations characterized by comparative evaluation of learning achievement, all pupils have to be at about the same level of knowledge or skill. In those teaching situations the normal curve is implicitly used to determine pupils' achievement: usually most pupils achieve about the same, some pupils do very well compared with the other ones and some pupils do very badly compared with the other pupils. The schoolmarks are given parallel to this distribution. Thus comparative evaluation of learning achievement necessarily leads to a 'failure' of some pupils in the teaching situation. This failure does not occur in teaching situations where pupils' achievement is evaluated in an individual or an absolute way (cf. Rheinberg 1980, and the field experiments of Van Oudhoven 1983).

Usually, the pupils within a class will differ in their initial school subject achievement. These differences will lead to different marks and to different individual effects and affects concerning the relevant learning actions. Moreover, the marks a pupil gets, are important because the other pupils will perceive the pupil's achievement. This 'public' aspect of a pupil's achievement promotes comparison processes among pupils: a pupil will compare his learning results with those of the other pupils. When he has relatively high results, the result will be attributed internally, to own competence or ability, because of its self-evaluative effects. For this reason the own school subject orientation and competence will be enhanced, which will motivate the pupil to carry out subsequent learning actions concerning this school subject, which on their turn will heighten the pupil's school subject achievement. However, when he has relatively low results, the own school subject orientation and competence will be threatened. This threat can be reduced partly by externally attributing the result to bad luck or the task's difficulty. Also, the pupil will be less motivated to carry out the subsequent learning actions. So, in the long run, the perception of his relative standing in the classroom will influence the pupil's development of the own school subject orientation, competence, and achievement. Such a comparison effect is known as the 'frog pond effect' (see Davis 1966/1967).

This comparison is supposed to be stimulated if the kind of evaluation of the pupils' achievement in the teaching situation is done comparatively. On the other hand, this effect should be either missing or tempered in teaching situations where this evaluation is carried out in an individual way. So, from a multilevel point of view, a relationship is hypothesized to develop between the kind of evaluation in the teaching situation and the development in a pupil's school subject orientation, school subject competence and school subject achievement: in a teaching situation where this evaluation is carried out comparatively the pupils will - in the course of time - differ more on those concepts than in teaching situations where this evaluation is done individually. At the teaching situation level it can then be expected that, when pupils' learning achievement is evaluated on a comparative basis, a greater dispersion on those variables will be present when this evaluation is individually based.

METHOD

The research design requires longitudinal data at the pupil level and teaching situation level. The pupil data have to be gathered at the start and end of a schoolyear, while part of the teaching situation data (on the pupils' teaching situations) can be collected in the course of this schoolyear. A second part of the teaching situation variables consists of aggregated pupil level data. The data collection started in 1981 with all first-year pupils of 39 classes of 10 secondary schools, in which different educational types for relatively low-achieving pupils are represented: junior vocational education (lto), intermediate general education (mavo) and individual vocational education (ito). In 1981 the just starting pupils filled in a questionnaire containing background items and school subject motivational items. They also completed tests on achievement in the school subjects Dutch language and mathematics/arithmetics. At the end of the schoolyear the data collection with respect to the school subject motivational items and achievement tests was repeated. Moreover, information on each pupil's report marks was collected from the school administrations.

The teaching situation data were gathered in two ways. First, by asking the school subject teacher to complete a teacher questionnaire with four items on his evaluation mode of the achievement results within each specific class-specific aggregated pupil level data. Secondly, the teaching situation data consist in class-specific aggregated pupil data.

The operationalization and the procedures in creating acceptable scale scores at the *pupil level* are as follows (the names of the variables as used in the analysis and presentation of the data are indicated between brackets):
held back (= held back) was operationalized in question form: How many times were you held back in elementary school, (coded: 0 times = 0, 1 or more times = 1).

father's occupation (= fathoc) was asked by different questions (see Van Westerlaak et al. 1975a, 1975b) and coded in a scale with six ordered categories: higher occupation (6), secondary employee (5), small self-employed (4), lower employee (3), skilled labourer (2), unskilled labourer (1).

(initial) school subject achievement (= inssach and ssach): pupil's school subject achievement in Dutch language and mathematics/arithmetics was measured by using a standardized school achievement test used in a Dutch national cohort research (Smulders 1979). Each test was subjected to a Rasch scale analysis in order to construct a Rasch homogeneous scale (see Mooij, forthcoming). In the analyses the sum of the items included in a Rasch scale is used; this sum correlates .99 with the Rasch scale score.

(initial) school subject orientation (inssor and and ssor): the following three items were chosen as indicators of this construct: (1) do you pay attention to the learning content during the lesson? (2) do you work hard for this school subject? (3) are you interested in this school subject? Those items were coded as: (almost) never = 1, now and then = 2, most of the time = 3, always = 4.

(initial)school subject competence (inssc and ssc): three items were chosen here as measured variables: (1) do you sometimes have problems in this school subject? (2) do you meet troubles in this school subject? (3) is this school subject easy for you? The coding of the items is the same as with respect to (in)ssor. To get only one direction in the meaning of the items the code of the items 1 and 2 has been reflected.

school subject marks (ssmark): a pupil's school subject marks have been operationalized as the three report marks given during the schoolyear (at Christmas, Easter, and the schoolyear's end). The marks were collected from the school administrations of the 10 schools participating in the research.

The above mentioned variables will be included in explorative analyses using the Lisrel VI program. The initial model used is the longitudinal model as developed previously; the results of the analysis will be used to find a fitting model for each school subject.

The operationalization and measurement of the concepts at the *teaching situation level* is as follows. With respect to the kind of evaluation of pupils' learning achievement by the school subject teacher four different kinds of evaluation have been distinguished: comparative (evcomp), normative (evnorm), individual comparative (evinc), and individual effort-based (eveff). The formulation of the alternatives in the teacher questionnaire was:

a. Do you compare the pupils' tests among each other and do you give marks based on this comparison? (evcomp)

b. Do you determine a norm before holding a test and do you give marks based on this norm? (evnorm)

c. Do you compare a test result with the pupil's earlier results and do you give a mark based on this individual comparison? (evinc)

d. Do you take account of a pupil's effort when marking test papers? (e-veff)

Each question had to be answered dichotomously. The phi-coeffichients among the scores obtained are (n = 39):

Dutch language				mathematics/arithmetics		
	a	b	c		a	b	c
b	-.62			b	-.34		
c	.10	-.10		c	-.14	.05	
d	-.09	.09	.25	d	.47	-.08	.32

The pupils' heterogeneity in a certain variable within a class is indicated by the class' standard deviation on the variable. The transformation to determine this score is based on an equal weight of each pupil's score (cf. Hüttner 1985).

A final remark is that level-specific analyses should be controlled for contamination with variation at one or more higher levels (Finn 1974, pp. 78-83). This check has been carried out for all relevant analyses (see Mooij, forthcoming). It turned out that the results of uncorrected versus corrected analyses may differ considerably. With respect to the data in this article, however, the checking revealed no substantial differences; therefore, the results presented here are based on uncorrected analyses.

RESULTS

The interactive pupil level process

The explorative analyses using the Lisrel VI program (Jöreskog & Sörbom 1981, 1983) were carried out on the covariance structures of the data of respectively 602 pupils (Dutch language) and 588 pupils (mathematics/arithmetics). The original model has been changed in the course of the analyses on the basis of the results of intermediate school subject specific analyses' results. The final results of the analyses are given in figures 1 and

2. In those figures the structural coefficients are followed by their standard errors between brackets. Each model has an acceptable fit.

Some paths have been added to the initial model (as outlined in the section on Multilevel theorizing). First, a path has been inserted from inssc to inssor, and from ssc to ssor; going from competence to orientation is theoretically more plausible than a path the other way around. Also, more paths point towards ssmark: besides the lower than expected inssach-ssmark effect other effects have been integrated in the model: held back (negative), fathoc (only in Dutch language), inssor, and inssc). It thus seems that - at the pupil level - the school subject mark is a complex resultant of ability, achievement and motivational variables. In each model some specific paths had to be added. In Dutch language (Figure 1) it was necessary to introduce a relationship between the competence concept and the school subject mark given at Easter, possibly because this school mark indicates best the pupil's competence at the measurement time. In mathematics/arithmetics the relationships between the first two indicators of inssc respectively ssc are not needed. However, it seems that the third indicator of inssor also functions as an indicator of inssc, but this is not repeated with respect to the ssor-ssc relationship. The negative relationship between ssach and the Easter school subject mark probably means that the Easter mark underestimates the pupil's achievement, which may be done by the teacher to 'stimulate' the pupil's exertion in mathematics/arithmetics.

With respect to the initial pupil model the results are as follows. In both figures relatively important (possible) effects of ssmark on ssach and ssc exist, whereas the effect of ssmark on ssor is negligable. The effects of ssach on ssor and ssc respectively inssach on inssor and inssc do not seem worth while, except in mathematics/arithmetics at the start of the schoolyear. In Dutch language the exogeneous variable held back plays a more important role with respect to inssach and ssmark than in mathematics/arithmetics. Also, in Dutch language fathoc seems to exert some influence on ssmark whereas this is not the case in mathematics/arithmetics. In this last school subject an effect of sex on inssach is in accordance with the research findings of Tesser (1984).

Figure 1. Covariance structure (Dutch language), LISREL results for the final model

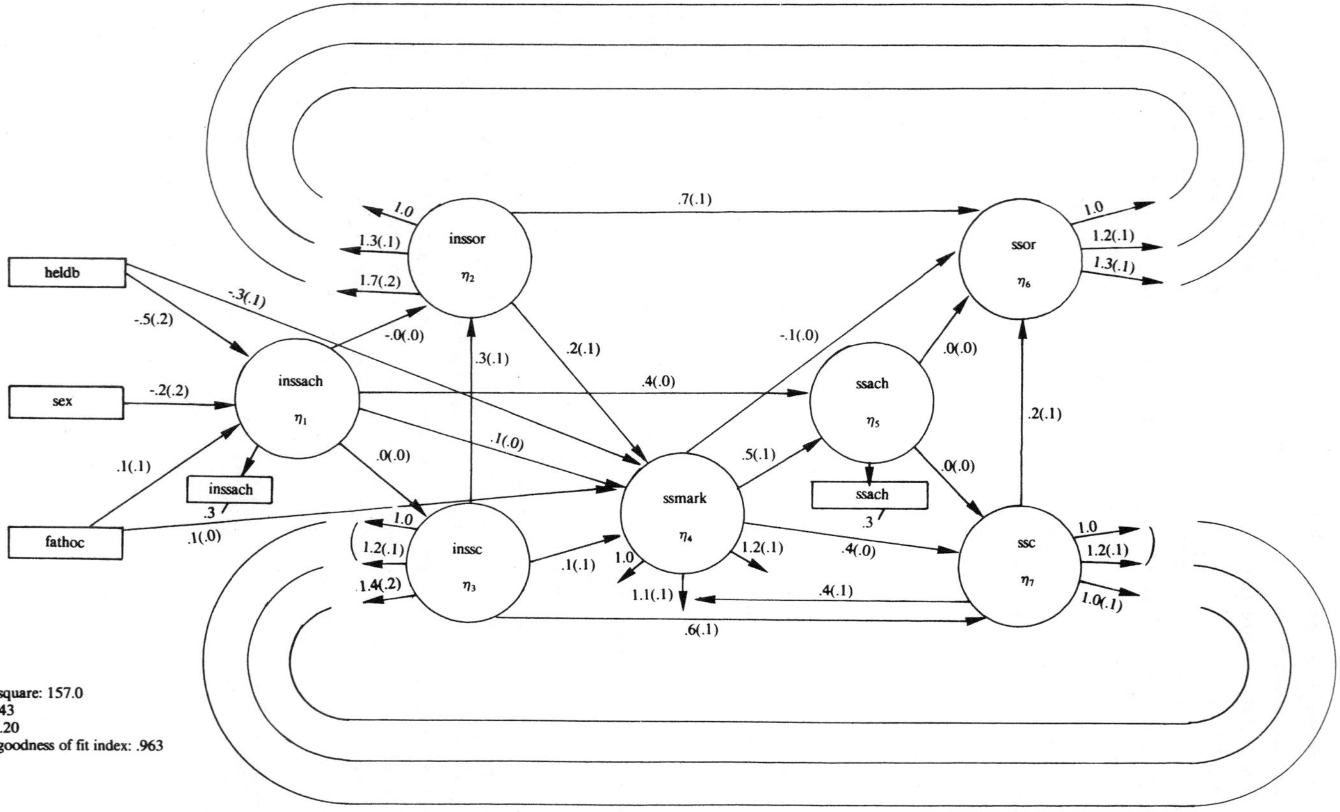

Chi-square: 157.0
df: 143
p = .20
adj. goodness of fit index: .963

Figure 2. Covariance structure (mathematics/arithmetics), LISREL results for the final model

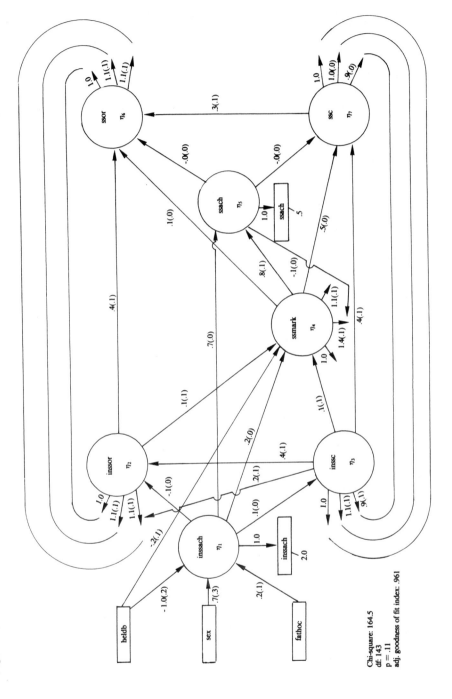

Chi-square: 164.5
df: 143
p = .11
adj. goodness of fit index: 961

257

All in all, those exploratory pupil level results point to the importance of the school subject mark for the development of a pupil's school subject competence and school subject achievement in the course of a schoolyear. The school subject mark itself seems based on a complex conglomerate of ability, achievement and motivational variables. The results do suggest that the pupil level theorizing might be improved by removing the relationships between (in)ssach and (in)ssor respectively (in)ssc. At the end of the schoolyear this might occur without too drastic consequences for the fit of the model. At the start of the schoolyear, however, this means that inssor and inssc and therefore also inssach are becoming exogeneous variables.

The conclusion based on the above findings in both school subjects is that a pupil's school subject mark directly influences the development of his school subject competence and school subject achievement, and indirectly - through the school subject competence - the development of his school subject orientation during the schoolyear. This conclusion lends support to the theorizing on the interactive pupil level process as outlined in the first part of this article.

The interactive interlevel process

It was hypothesized that an interactive interlevel process exists with respect to the development of a pupil's school subject orientation, school subject competence and school subject achievement. At the teaching situation level this process should result in a greater dispersion on those variables, if the evaluation of pupils' learning achievement is done comparatively instead of on an individual basis. To check this, the four kinds of teacher's evaluation and the pupils' heterogeneity in school subject marks in a class (to be able to compare the respective effects) are correlated with the pupils' within-class heterogeneity in school subject orientation, school subject competence and school subject achievement at the start and end of the first schoolyear. The results of those computations for 39 classes are presented in Table 1. The presentation is school subject specific.

Table 1. Pearson correlations between heterogeneity scores and teaching situation evaluation variables (by school subject; n classes = 39)

	ssor initial		ssc initial		ssach initial	
Dutch language						
evcomp	.00	.24	-.25	-.19	-.00	-.27
evnorm	-.05	-.37*	.17	-.05	.19	.06
evinc	.07	.20	-.16	.33*	.03	-.00
eveff	.01	-.09	.20	-.15	-.02	-.09
ssmark heterogeneity	.03	.19	-.04	.47**	.44**	.32*
Mathematics/arithmetics						
evcomp	.57**	-.20	.22	.13	-.03	.26
evnorm	-.06	.10	-.08	-.13	.42**	.05
evinc	.04	.14	.03	.04	-.05	-.17
eveff	.56**	-.02	.49**	.06	-.12	-.16
ssmark heterogeneity	-.15	.05	-.02	.04	-.16	.19

* $.01 \leq p \leq .05$ (two-sided)
** $p < .01$ (two-sided)

The information in Table 1 shows no support for the expected distribution or frog pound effects. In Dutch language an other finding is the increasing relationship between heterogeneity in school subject marks and heterogeneity in school subject competence, from -.04 to .47. (In the second schoolyear this result is consolidated) In mathematics/arithmetics the significant correlations at the start of the schoolyear are probably accidental, but the fact that they all disappear in the course of the schoolyear suggests that something is happening within the teaching situations. This 'something' might be a combined effect of the comparative and individual modes of evaluation.

DISCUSSION

In this paper two different theoretical approaches on the development of a pupil's school subject motivation and school subject achievement in the course of a schoolyear are presented. In the first one only pupil level variables are included in order to sketch the interactive effects of a pupil's school subject marks on his school subject orientation, school subject competence and school subject achievement. Structural analysis on the covariance matrix of longitudinal data in two school subjects (Dutch language, mathematics/arithmetics) revealed the existence of those effects on school subject competence and school subject achievement and - through competence - on the school subject orientation. It thus seems that the school subject mark stimulates the product-dependency of a pupil's actions in the teaching situation. Other data reveal that certain teaching situation characteristics do influence pupils' school subject orientation (on-task behavior): see Mooij, submitted.

In the second approach the interaction between the three pupil level variables and evaluation modes of pupils' learning achievement in the teaching situation are the topic of concern. In general, the results of the analyses do not support the theorizing. This may be caused partly by the fact that - in the educational practice - teachers use several contrasting criteria to evaluate pupils' achievement in the same teaching situation, which troubles a clear relationship between an evaluation mode and a pupil's mark, orientation, competence and achievement in a school subject. In such a case a pupil will only have his own school subject mark to estimate the own competence (see the increasing relationship between heterogeneity in school subject competence. If this reasoning is correct the research results of Rheinberg (1980) and Van Oudhoven (1983) might be based on the stringent use of only one evaluation criterium in the teaching situation. This situation is probably not like the common procedure used in educational practice.

The research results thus emphasize the importance of pupil level variables in case an educational process including pupil variables and teaching situation variables is being studied. It seems that individual level variables are probably most important in influencing a person's cognitions, feelings and behavior (cf. also Mooij 1980a, p. 307; 1980b, p. 165). However, the relevance of variables situated at other, higher, levels might increase if these variables do not interfere with each other.

REFERENCES

Bergen, T.C.M. (1981). *Evaluatie-angst en vermijdingstendens.* 's-Gravenhage: Staatsuitgeverij, SVO-reeks no. 47.

Boekaerts, M. (1984). *Some new developments in the study of motivational processes in a classroom context.* Paper presented at the symposium on motivation and information processing, Acapulco, 1984. Nijmegen, Katholieke Universiteit.

Bruyn, E.E.J. de (1979). Historische ontwikkelingen in de prestatiemotivatie-theorie. In E.E.J. de Bruyn (Ed.), *Ontwikkelingen in het onderzoek naar prestatiemotivatie* (pp. 5-28). Lisse: Swets & Zeitlinger.

Davis, J.A. (1966/1967). The campus as a frog pond: an application of the theory of relative deprivation to career decisions of college men. *American Journal of Sociology, 72,* 17-31.

Harter, S. (1981). The development of competence motivation in the mastery of cognitive and physical skills: is there still a place for joy? In G.C. Roberts & D.M. Landers (Eds.), *Psychology of motor behavior and sport 1980.* Champaign: Human Kinetics Publishers.

Harter, S. (1982a). The perceived competence scale for children. *Child Development, 53,* 87-97.

Harter, S. (1982b). A developmental perspective on some parameters of self-regulation in children. In P. Karoly & F.H. Kanfer (Eds.), *Selfmanagement and behavior change: from theory to practice.* Oxford: Permagon Press.

Heckhausen, H. (1977). Achievement motivation and its constructs: a cognitive model. *Motivation and Emotion, 1, 4,* 238-329.

Heckhausen, H. (1980). *Motivation und Handeln: Lehrbuch der Motivationspsychologie.* Berlin: Springer.

Jöreskog, K.G. (1979). Statistical estimation of structural models in longitudinal-developmental investigations. In J.R. Nesselroade & P.B. Baltes (Eds.), *Longitudinal research in the study of behavior and development* (pp. 303-351). New York: Academic Press.

Jöreskog, K.G., & Sörbom, D. (1977). Statistical models and methods analysis of longitudinal data. In D.J. Aigner & A.S. Goldberger (Eds.), *Latent variables in socio-economic models* (pp. 285-325). Amsterdam: North Holland.

Jöreskog, K.G., & Sörbom, D. (1981). *Lisrel. Analysis of linear structural relationships by the method of maximum likelihood. User's guide. Verson V.* Uppsala, University of Uppsala.

Jöreskog, K.G., Sörbom, D. (1983). *Supplement to the Lisrel V manual.* Uppsala, University of Uppsala.

Licht, P. (1982). *Differentiatie binnen klasseverband voor natuurkunde.* Amsterdam: Rodopi.

Mooij, T. (1980a). Conflictgedrag tijdens samenwerking tussen groepen. *Nederlands Tijdschrift voor de Psychologie, 35, 5,* 299-314.

Mooij, T. (1980b). Multi-level onderzoek van samenwerking in het part-time onderwijs. *Mens en Maatschappij, 55, 2,* 148-169.

Mooij, T. (1984). Multiniveau-aspecten in de verklaring van leerling-(de)motivatie. In P. van den Eeden & J. Hauer (Eds.), *Analyse van multiniveaudata: theorie en toepassing* (pp. 103-123). 's-Gravenhage: Stichting voor Onderzoek van het Onderwijs.

Mooij, T. (submitted). Leskenmerken en taakgedrag van leerlingen. *Tijdschrift voor Onderwijsresearch.*

Oudenhoven, J.P.L.M. (1983). *Onderwijsmogelijkheid en evaluatieve feedback.* Apeldoorn: Van Walraven.

Rheinberg, F. (1980). *Leistungsbewertung und Lernmotivaton.* Göttingen: Verlag für Psychologie.

Smulders, R.H.M. (1979). *C.B.S.-onderzoek: 'Schoolloopbaan en herkomst van leerlingen bij het voortgezet onderwijs'.* Paper Onderwijsresearchdagen 1979. Voorburg, Centraal Bureau voor de Statistiek.

Tesser, P.Th.M. (1984). De overgang van basisonderwijs naar voortgezet onderwijs in 1977. *Mens en Maatschappij, 59, 4,* 363-387.

Westerlaak, J.M. van, Kropman, J.A. & Collaris, J.W.M. (1975a). *Beroepenklapper.* Nijmegen, Instituut voor Toegepaste Sociologie.

Westerlaak, J.M. van, Kropman, J.A., & Collaris, J.W.M. (1975b). *Beroepenklapper. Toelichting.* Nijmegen, Instituut voor Toegepaste Sociologie.

White, R.W. (1959). Motivation reconsidered: the concept of competence. *Psychological Review, 66, 5,* 297-333.